KEY CONCEPTS IN TOURISM

Palgrave Key Concepts

Palgrave Key Concepts provide an accessible and comprehensive range of subject glossaries at undergraduate level. They are the ideal companion to a standard textbook, making them invaluable reading to students through-out their course of study, and especially useful as a revision aid.

Key Concepts in Accounting and Finance
Key Concepts in Business Practice
Key Concepts in Drama and Performance
Key Concepts in E-Commerce
Key Concepts in Human Resource Management
Key Concepts in Information and Communication Technology
Key Concepts in International Business
Key Concepts in Language and Linguistics (*second edition*)
Key Concepts in Law
Key Concepts in Management
Key Concepts in Marketing
Key Concepts in Medieval Literature
Key Concepts in Operations Management
Key Concepts in Politics
Key Concepts in Psychology
Key Concepts in Strategic Management
Key Concepts in Tourism

Palgrave Key Concepts: Literature
General Editors: John Peck and Martin Coyle

Key Concepts in Contemporary Literature
Key Concepts in Postcolonial Literature
Key Concepts in Victorian Literature
Literary Terms and Criticism (*third edition*)

Further titles are in preparation

www.palgravekeyconcepts.com

Palgrave Key Concepts
Series Standing Order
ISBN 1–4039–3210–7
(*outside North America only*)

You can receive future titles in this series as they are published by placing a standing order. Please contact your bookseller or, in case of difficulty, write to us at the address below with your name and address, the title of the series and the ISBN quoted above.

Customer Services Department, Macmillan Distribution Ltd, Houndmills, Basingstoke, Hampshire RG21 6XS, England

Key Concepts in Tourism

Loykie Lominé and James Edmunds

First published 2007 by
PALGRAVE MACMILLAN
Houndmills, Basingstoke, Hampshire RG21 6XS and
175 Fifth Avenue, New York, N.Y. 10010
Companies and representatives throughout the world

PALGRAVE MACMILLAN is the global academic imprint of the Palgrave Macmillan division of St. Martin's Press, LLC and of Palgrave Macmillan Ltd. Macmillan® is a registered trademark in the United States, United Kingdom and other countries. Palgrave is a registered trademark in the European Union and other countries.

ISBN-13: 978 1–4039–8502–6
ISBN-10: 1–4039–8502–2

This book is printed on paper suitable for recycling and made from fully managed and sustained forest sources.

A catalogue record for this book is available from the British Library.

A catalog record for this book is available from the Library of Congress.

10 9 8 7 6 5 4 3 2 1
16 15 14 13 12 11 10 09 08 07

Printed and bound in China

Contents

Acknowledgements

We would like to thank the following people for their time and support: Cecilia, Oliver, Stanley, Sarah and Glayne Edmunds, Jean Evans, Damon Pearce, Paul Sheeran and Tom Wnuk.

We are also very grateful to Suzannah Burywood, Karen Griffiths and Valery Rose for their patience and professionalism.

L.L.
J.E.

Introduction

This glossary comprises 365 key concepts that students of travel and tourism management are most likely to encounter within their under-graduate or postgraduate modules and courses. Students from cognate subjects (such as leisure, geography or hospitality) will also find this book useful as it can help them understand the key concepts used in tourism books and articles.

Tourism as an academic discipline has a particular language, a termi-nology that combines concepts from a range of subjects, from econom-ics and management to sociology and anthropology. The underpinning multidisciplinarity and interdisciplinarity make the study of tourism particularly challenging, as one is required to master a wide range of concepts, from 'Accommodation' to 'Zoning' via 'Liminality' and 'Logistics'. To learn the language of tourism research and to understand texts written by tourism scholars, one needs a reliable reference book: such is the function of this glossary.

Key Concepts in Tourism follows the same approach as the other books in the *Palgrave Key Concepts* series:

- Concepts are placed alphabetically for ease of use.
- Entries are fully cross-referenced, as key concepts do not exist in isolation but are linked to one another; in the text, the words in **bold** type are all defined as discrete concepts elsewhere in the book.
- Entries vary in length, according to the complexity of the concept and the need to further explicate and illustrate.
- Suggestions for further reading as well as website references are provided when appropriate.
- A comprehensive index makes it possible to find other terms explained within *Key Concepts in Tourism*.

The authors have produced an integrated reference book that takes into account the whole range of academic disciplines that have contributed to the development of tourism, business disciplines and social sciences alike. The definitions cover all the elements of the tourism system and service providers, from travel agents to visitor attractions via travel and transport.

The generic concepts that are defined in other books of the *Palgrave Key Concepts* series (such as *Key Concepts in Management, Key Concepts in Strategic Management, Key Concepts in Business Practice*) have not been included here, as the remit is to address management in the context of the travel and tourism industry.

Tourism is a global geographical phenomenon; the authors have endeavoured to provide a range of international examples – readers will need to apply the concepts to their own environments and to their local, regional and national tourism circumstances. This is particularly the case with regard to legislation: readers will have to access the legislation of the country in which they are working or studying.

L.L.
J.E.

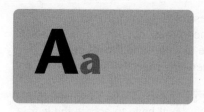

Aa

Accessibility

Accessibility refers to the ease or difficulty of taking advantage of an opportunity. In tourism management, the concept of accessibility may refer:

- to *buildings*, especially accommodation and attractions. Proponents of the 'universal design' approach recommend designs that are accessible to as many people as possible regardless of age, ability or situation, for example the use of wide interior doors, lever handles for opening doors rather than twisting knobs, and use of meaningful icons as well as text labels.
- to *destinations*. Geographical proximity is not the only factor that contributes to the accessibility of a destination: other factors need to be taken into account, such as the travel time, financial costs or fatigue involved. Contrary to a common idea, improvements in **infrastructure** (for example road access) are not always beneficial as they can turn an overnight destination into a day-trip destination, to the detriment of small, local accommodation.
- to *tourism in general*. Accessibility is then linked to the concepts of **tourism for all** and **social tourism**, and to the controversial notion that tourism is a right and that everybody ought to have the opportunity to travel, irrespective of their social or physical circumstances.

Sheller, Mimi and Urry, John (eds), *Tourism Mobilities: Places to Stay, Places in Stay* (London: Routledge, 2004).

Accommodation

The accommodation sector forms a major part of the tourism **industry** and is required by all travellers apart from **excursionists**. It is arguably the most capital-intensive and labour-intensive area of tourism, which is why most hotels are built by property developers and managed by hotel companies such as the Hilton Group. The accommodation product can be defined along the following criteria:

- its location (based on how accessible it is to customers);
- the facilities offered (not only bedrooms, but other amenities such as bars, restaurants, conference facilities and fitness centres);
- the services offered to customers (as reflected in its grading and classification rating);
- the image of the hotel (linked to wider issues of ownership and marketing);
- pricing policy (which derives from the previous criteria).

There are many different types of accommodation; authors and professional associations have proposed several taxonomies, using different criteria. Simply put, the sector is usually broken down into the following units:

- hotels, motels, hostels;
- guesthouses, bed and breakfast, farmhouse accommodation;
- self-catering accommodation (apartments, cottages and gites);
- **timeshare**;
- camping and caravan sites;
- medical facility accommodation, health care centres;
- cruise liners and ferries;
- other types of accommodation (such as sleeping carriages on night trains).

The hotel sector of the industry is today dominated by global brands such as the Hilton Group, Marriott and the Holiday Inn Group. Within these main brands a number of sub-brands are used to attract different market segments, for example the Holiday Inn Group operates Holiday Inn Select, Holiday Inn Express and Crowne Plaza. The **quality** of the accommodation product is often based on classification (types of development and service offered) and grading (quality of the product). Most national and commercial schemes concentrate on classification, with quality being seen as an 'add-on'. Similar to the airline sector with the introduction of **low cost carriers**, the hotel industry has started to see the introduction of 'budget hotels' led by the Accor Group with the Formula 1 product; other new entrants to the market include the easyGroup with the easyHotel concept. The in-depth study of the accommodation sector is part of the wider subject of **hospitality** management, which is supported by a well-developed literature and specialised journals.

A

Medlick, Richard and Ingram, Susan, *The Business of Hotels*, 4th edn (Oxford: Butterworth-Heinemann, 2002).

Acculturation

Acculturation refers to the social processes and consequent cultural and psychological changes that occur when people from different cultures come into contact. In tourist settings, locals' acculturation results from their interactions with tourists. This slow phenomenon is one of the main socio-cultural impacts of tourism. Little by little, maybe imperceptibly, local culture will change. Rather than the direct acquisition and assimilation of new cultural features, it may involve the development of a hybrid culture, initially most noticeable in language and clothing. Linked to the **demonstration effect**, this cultural appropriation occasionally operates the other way round, with tourists being influenced by locals' culture, collectively and individually, and possibly behaving differently even after they have gone back home.

Nash, Dennison, *Anthropology of Tourism* (Oxford: Pergamon Press, 1996).

Agenda 21: 'Rio Summit'

Agenda 21 is a key document from the United Nations Conference on Environment & Development that took place in 1992 in Rio de Janeiro (Brazil). It stresses the importance of promoting sustainable development and made several explicit references to tourism, specifically to **ecotourism** and **sustainable tourism**, exhorting governments and businesses 'to promote more comprehensive use and economic contributions of forest areas by incorporating eco-tourism into forest management and planning' and 'to promote the formulation of environmentally sound and culturally sensitive tourism programmes as a strategy for sustainable development of urban and rural settlements'. Only gradually will Agenda 21 be implemented, but tourism managers (especially the ones working in public sector policy-making) need to be aware of that framework. It confirms and reinforces international awareness and concern for sustainability in tourism development, as emphasised by the **World Tourism Organization** in other **international agreements on tourism**.

United Nations Division for Sustainable Development, www.un.org/esa/sustdev/documents/agenda21

Agents of tourism development

The phrase 'agents of tourism development' is occasionally encountered in the **literature** to refer to groups of people who may directly play an active role in **tourism development**:

- agents from the **private sector**, such as local landowners, tourism operators, developers, investors and financing agencies;
- agents from the **public sector** such as local authorities and tourism government agencies;
- agents from the **voluntary sector**, such as pressure groups from the local community.

As these agents may have different priorities and concerns, conflicts may occur between them (typically, local objections towards a new tourism project that may negatively affect the natural environment or the local identity, especially in rural contexts). Mediation may be necessary to help the agents work together so as to ensure not only mutual understanding, but also only cooperation and integrated **planning**. Instead of the word 'agents', many texts use the broader concept of **stakeholders**.

Agrotourism

Also called agritourism and farm tourism, agrotourism is a form of **rural tourism** taking place in or around working farms. Agrotourists are usually city-dwellers who want to enjoy the countryside, possibly as a way to reconnect with forgotten rural roots, or to enable children to discover animals and learn about agriculture. **Accommodation** may be provided in the form of bed and breakfast or camping sites. Activities may include low-impact outdoor sports such as hiking or horse-riding, as well as farm tours or opportunities to assist with farming tasks, depending on the season and type of farms. Agrotourism is particularly developed around the Mediterranean Sea; 'dude ranches' are the adult American version. As it can really complement farmers' income and contribute to local economic development, agrotourism is increasingly being conceptualised as a business model in terms of product **diversification**. In some regions, chambers of agriculture and public sector tourism organisations are actively promoting agrotourism, although farmers may not always have the time, the capital and the necessary skills and knowledge to develop the tourism potential of their business.

Page, Stephen J. and Getz, Don (eds), *Business of Rural Tourism: International Perspectives* (London: Thomson, 1997).

Airline alliances

Airline alliances is a **strategy** initiated as a consequence of the dynamic changes experienced by the airline industry. In the 1990s, airline managers began to realise that by forming groupings and alliances with like-minded **carriers** they could help protect their market position due to increasing pressures of competition and **globalisation**. The current crop of alliance groupings was initiated in 1997 when Lufthansa and United Airlines created the Star Alliance. This was followed a year later by British Airways and American Airlines who formed the Oneworld Alliance. The final alliance grouping, Skyteam, was created in 1999 by Air France and Delta Airlines. Airlines are quick to highlight the advantages such groupings can offer the customer, for example, Skyteam identifies on its website the following ten advantages that alliances bring to passengers including:

1 more miles
2 more lounges
3 guaranteed reservations
4 more flights
5 more fares
6 easy connections
7 enhanced check-in
8 single check-in
9 quality standards
10 reservation network

As the industry continues to consolidate, it is possible that passengers in the future will fly not on the current crop of alliances but with a virtual entity such as 'Star Airlines in association with Lufthansa'.

Although the study of airline alliances in still in its infancy, it is possible to classify them in different categories. In *The Airline Business in the 21st Century* Rigas Doganis proposes eleven types:

1 ad-hoc pool arrangements
2 consortium arrangements
3 project-based joint ventures
4 full-blown joint ventures
5 revenue pooling
6 block space arrangements
7 code sharing
8 equity participation alliances
9 other marketing co-operation alliances
10 franchising
11 international joint ventures

A

Doganis, Rigas, *The Airline Business in the 21st Century* (London: Routledge, 2001).
Kleymann, Birgitt and Seristo, Hannu, *Managing Strategic Airline Alliances* (Aldershot, Hants: Ashgate Publishing, 2004).

Sky Team Airline Alliance, www.skyteam.com

Airline & airport management

Airline & airport management pertains to both the field of academic study and the application of professional practice:

- Academically, airline & airport management consists in the **multi-disciplinary** study of civil aviation, incorporating themes and topics related to this field such as airport planning, airside logistics, airline operations and customer service. Airline & airport management shares many concepts and concerns with other management subjects, especially **tourism management**, hospitality management and **leisure management**. Within the UK the development of courses within airline & airport management is still limited to a few institutions; however courses are offered all over the world. Most of these educational establishments tend nonetheless to concentrate not on the business elements of civil aviation, but on the engineering aspects of flight.
- Professionally, airline & airport management relates to the management of individual organisations in both public and private sectors. The professional practice of airline & airport management also relates to how the sector infringes on global concerns including issues relating to environmental degradation.

Gordon, Alastair, *Naked Airport: A Cultural History of the World's Most Revolutionary Structure* (New York: Metropolitan Books, 2004).

Alienation

In the academic literature on tourism management, the concept of alienation can be encountered with two different meanings:

- As a sociological concept, it refers to the way modern society makes people feel estranged, powerless, purposeless and unhappy in their daily lives. Tourism is then presented as an escape from social alienation, even if only temporarily. Theoreticians have analysed how that alienation explains the quest for **authenticity** that motivates many tourists, consciously or not.
- As a legal concept, it refers to (forced) transfer of ownership when locals are made to sell their land to make way for tourism development projects (it is then akin to the concept of **displacement**) or, more generally, when locals are deprived from their local resources (such as water) because priority is given to tourists.

Sharpley, Richard, *Tourism, Tourists and Society*, 3rd edn (Huntingdon: ELM, 2003).

A

Alternative tourism

Alternative tourism is a reaction against **mass tourism** and its detrimental impacts on destinations. Coming from a range of perspectives (ethical, ideological, political, environmental or anthropological), proponents of alternative tourism advocate a necessary change in tourism practice, including:

- alternative motivations (to encourage travellers not just to indulge in the type of **3S** tourism that has made some resorts overpopulated and soulless);
- alternative destinations (yet being careful not just to redirect flows of mass tourists towards fragile environments);
- alternative behaviour (with a need to educate tourists);
- alternative management (empowering the residents through **community tourism** or contributing to their training and employment);
- alternative providers (supporting the tour operators and accommodation providers who in turn support local communities and do not exploit them);
- alternative philosophy (caring for the environment, for example through recycling of used water).

Alternative tourism is underpinned by the principles of **sustainable development**, as translated in **ecotourism**. It must be noted that in the 1970s and 1980s numerous terms have been used, rather interchangeably, to express the same idea: appropriate tourism, integrated tourism, adapted tourism, controlled tourism, equitable tourism, green tourism and **responsible tourism**, amongst others. There is not necessarily any strong difference in semantics, it just depends on the authors and their perspectives.

Singh, Ter Vir, Theuns, Leo H. and Go, Frank M. (eds), *Towards Appropriate Tourism: The Case of Developing Countries* (London: P. Land, 1989).
Smith, Valene L. and Eadington, William R. (eds), *Tourism Alternatives: Potentials and Pitfalls in the Development of Tourism* (Chichester: John Wiley, 1992).

A

Amenities

The concept of amenities refers to the essential **services** catering for the needs of tourists. There is no exhaustive list of possible amenities; in a destination, amenities may include local transport and local banks; on a luxury cruise ship spas, pools, casinos and restaurants; in enclave resorts tennis courts and other sports facilities as well as entertainment programmes; in a conference centre office services such as photocopying and internet access, video conferencing with large screens and a range of catering options. Amenities are particularly important for two reasons:

- The availability (or non-availability) of some amenities may be a discriminatory factor in tourists' choice of a resort or destination, especially when many places are seemingly similar (see **identikit**). Amenities represent an added element that may be key in terms of product differentiation: a given hotel may be the only one in a resort to offer a particular amenity, for example an infinity pool, and that detail may matter to potential customers.
- Amenities may substantially contribute to the quality of the tourist experience, or to dissatisfaction and subsequent complaints. Tourists as consumers may have increasingly high expectations and later seek redress if promised amenities are not available or operational.

The words 'amenities' and 'facilities' tend to be used interchangeably, 'facilities' being more commonly employed in the tourism **industry**, whilst 'amenities' tends to be more scholarly.

Ransley, Josef and Ingram, Hadyn (eds) *Developing Hospitality Properties and Facilities*, 2nd edn (Oxford: Butterworth-Heinemann, 2004).
Rogers, Anthea H. and Slinn, Judy A., *Tourism: Management of Facilities* (London: Macdonald & Evans, 1993).

Ancillary services

Ancillary means auxiliary, secondary, supplementary; in the tourism **industry**, ancillary services refer to the organisations that support and facilitate the core services of **transportation**, **accommodation** and **entertainment**. Ancillary services may be located at the destination (car rental businesses, cleaning services) or may be involved earlier on in the process (insurance, passport and visa services, currency exchange).

The concept of ancillary services is relative: depending upon the perspective taken, travel agents and tour guides may be regarded as ancillary services or as essential services. The word 'ancillary' does not mean that they are superfluous: their role is important, even though they are often neglected in the academic literature because they are made up of small providers and are not always fully integrated in the **tourism system**.

Anti-tourism

Anti-tourism is not a unified movement or campaign, but an umbrella term for the criticisms articulated against tourists and the tourist industry:

- Tourists themselves are criticised for several reasons, ranging from their occasional crass behaviour (for example with regard to excessive drinking in **3S** tourism resorts) to self-indulgence (see **egotourism**) via a lack of respect for the destinations (including regarding locals as inferiors: see **ethnocentrism**).
- The tourist industry is criticised for exploiting destinations (culturally, economically, environmentally), for failing to take local needs and sustainability into account and sometimes for lacking business ethics.

Such criticisms come from different perspectives, representing different agendas, from conservationists motivated by ecological concerns, to consumer organisations willing to protect travellers against unprofessional practices. Tourism managers need to understand the backgrounds of these criticisms, to objectively assess the extent to which they are justified and to plan for the future. This is particularly difficult because of the conflicting priorities expressed under the banner of anti-tourism.

The term 'anti-tourist' is also occasionally used to describe local residents' attitude of resentment and **xenophobic** annoyance towards tourists (for example with reference to an anti-tourist act), or independent travellers who prefer to go off the beaten track, loathe mass tourism and do not want to be identified as tourists.

Kalder, Daniel, *Lost Cosmonaut: Travels to the Republics that Tourism Forgot* (London: Faber & Faber, 2006).

Attitude

This psychological concept refers to the opinion one holds about somebody or something: it can be a person, a behaviour, an event or, in tourism, a destination (for example the USA), a type of attraction (for example **theme parks**) or a form of holiday (for example **backpacking**). Attitudes are linked to expectations, beliefs and values, for example some people may be reluctant to even consider travelling to some developing countries because they are worried about hygiene and health issues; in other contexts, some travellers may be unwilling to travel to destinations in developed countries, for example from Europe to the USA, because of the hassle pertaining to security check and related issues. Attitudes may be positive, negative, ambivalent or neutral; identifying and assessing attitudes can be done through **quantitative research** or **qualitative research**. The psychology of attitude change is particularly important in tourism management, as marketers and destination managers may need to work to change potential tourists' attitudes towards a place or a form of tourism that needs a new **image**.

Crouch, Geoffrey I. et al. (eds), *Consumer Psychology of Tourism, Hospitality and Leisure* (Wallingford: CABI, 2004).

March, Roger S. G. and Woodside, Arch G., *Tourism Behaviour: Travellers' Decisions and Actions* (Wallingford: CABI, 2005).

Attractions

Attractions form the cornerstone of the tourism industry: they are often regarded as the primary draw of a destination, which is why they play a major role in destinations' marketing campaigns. For example, Orlando in Florida is entirely marketed on its attractions such as Walt Disney World Resort, Seaworld and Gatorland; without these flagships attractions, Orlando would receive a fraction of its current visitor numbers. Attractions can be owned by either the **public sector** or **private sector**, or through **partnerships.** Typically, public sector attractions are more concerned with **conservation** and education, whilst private sector attractions concentrate on profit maximisation. A comprehensive list of attractions in a given destination is sometimes called 'attraction inventory'.

Attractions are usually broken down into the four types, as shown in Table 1.

Table 1   Main types of attractions

Man-made, specific attractions	Built specifically to cater for tourism, such as **theme parks** or casinos.
Man-made, non-specific attractions	Initially built for purposes other than tourism, yet their cultural significance has turned them into tourist attractions. Examples include cathedrals, historical buildings and monuments.
Natural attractions	Examples include designated Areas of Outstanding Natural Beauty (AONB) and national parks. Subcategories are possible, according to the main factors of interest: topography, wildlife, vegetation, etc.
Events	Events may have a limited time or occur on a regular basis. They are usually cultural (from battle re-enactments to sporting events), though some natural events attract tourists (such as bird migrations or volcanic eruptions).

A

Tourist attractions do not only play a key role in tourism: they may also be part of wider socio-economic plans, hence their recognised importance for both national and local governments; for example, **mega-events** such as the **Olympic Games** can contribute to the **regeneration** of rundown urban areas.

Fyall, Alan, Garrod, Brian and Leask, Anna (eds), *Managing Visitor Attractions: New Directions* (Oxford: Butterworth-Heinemann, 2002).

Swarbrooke, John, *The Development and Management of Visitor Attractions*, 2nd edn (Oxford: Butterworth-Heinemann, 2002).

Authenticity

According to Dean McCannell in his seminal book *The Tourist*, tourism is a quest for authenticity. His thesis, widely accepted nowadays, is based on a sociological analysis: contemporary society is dominated by feelings of **alienation**, superficiality and disenchantment, and as a consequence many people go travelling and sightseeing in order to find some authentic experiences. They travel to rural areas (to reconnect with the past, with forgotten roots and **heritage**) or to remote places (where locals' lifestyles have not been 'contaminated' by modernity and Western culture). Tom Selwyn further distinguishes between authenticity as knowledge ('cool authenticity') and authenticity as feeling ('hot authenticity'), but in both cases tourists are on a quest for genuine experiences. They want to avoid the traps of **staged authenticity** and **pseudo-events**, such as the performances put on just for tourists (flamenco dancers in Mallorca, whirling dervishes in Turkey, for example).

Rooted in this deep, quasi-spiritual desire for authenticity, tourism as a socio-cultural phenomenon can then be interpreted as a form of secular **pilgrimage**, but this analogy does not mean that all tourists can be compared to pilgrims, whose motivation is primarily devotional. The concept of authenticity is very important in tourism studies, especially in sociological and anthropological perspectives; many authors have used it, along with the related concepts of **backstage and frontstage**, in their analyses of specific tourist destinations and of tourist **motivations**.

A

McCannell, Dean, *The Tourist: A New Theory of the Leisure Class* (New York: Schocken Books, 1976).

Selwyn, Tom (ed.), *The Tourist Image: Myths and Myth Making in Tourism* (Chichester: John Wiley, 1996).

Wang, Ning, 'Rethinking Authenticity in Tourism Experience', *Annals of Tourism Research*, 26(2) (1999): 349–70.

Backpacking

The word 'backpacking' has two meanings:

- It sometimes refers to a form of **rural tourism** that involves both hiking/trekking and camping, with food supplies and camping equipment carried in a rucksack. Trips may be as short as a weekend, though they can last much longer.
- It sometimes refers to a form of low-cost international travel, usually by young people, typically as part of a gap-year experience; backpacks are used in the interest of mobility and flexibility, though they do not necessarily carry sleeping gear.

In tourism, the word 'backpackers' and its accompanying image are rather associated with the latter sense. It is linked to a youth subculture akin to a romanticised version of **wanderlust**. It is reflected in novels such as Alex Garland's *The Beach* and James Michener's *The Drifters*. As an important socio-cultural phenomenon, it is studied in an increasing number of **journal** articles, from a range of perspectives, including:

- historical: the roots of contemporary backpacking in the hippie trail of the 1960s and 1970s;
- demographic: the profile of backpackers, who tend to be middle-class English-speakers from particular developed countries (such as Germany, the UK and the Netherlands);
- geographic: the choice of favoured destinations such as Australia for Europeans and the emergence of 'circuits' and fashions (such as Eastern Europe) and even 'backpackers' ghettos' (such as the Khaosan Road area of downtown Bangkok);
- anthropological: the development of 'rites of passage' activities (such as Australian backpackers working in pubs in London) and a whole mythology;
- philosophical: the construction of an approach to travelling focused on a desire to be both independent and yet to interact with others (both locals and tourists);

- cultural: the development of a cheap travelling lifestyle with its symbols such as cheap hostels and *The Lonely Planet* series of guidebooks.

Garland, Alex, *The Beach* (London: Penguin, 1996).
Michener, James A., *The Drifters* (New York: Random House, 1971).
Townsend, Chris, *The Backpacker's Handbook*, 3rd edn (London: McGraw-Hill, 2004).

Backstage and frontstage

The theatrical concepts of backstage and frontstage were introduced in the social sciences by Canadian sociologist Erving Goffman (1922–82) to compare life analytically to a theatre: backstage is where the actors prepare, frontstage is where they perform. In his landmark book *The Tourist* (1976), MacCannell applied that metaphor to the spaces occupied by local residents in tourist destinations: backstage is where locals live and are themselves, frontstage is where they interact with tourists. Frontstage is the public sphere that may include commercial encounters (shops, restaurants, museums) as well as **staged authenticity**; backstage is where the authentic local way of life is preserved, usually beyond access for tourists, with a few exceptions such as **visiting friends and relatives (VFRs)**. Backstage is where many tourists would like to go, hence their participation in **festivals** or community events, where **communitas** may give them the feeling (rightly or wrongly) that they have crossed the anthropological barrier between **hosts and guests**. Numerous articles have been written on the topic, typically with case studies of how frontstage and backstage operate or are separated. Some of the subsequent analyses may seem remote from tourism management as a practice, although the conceptual metaphors of frontstage and backstage do help understand some tourists' motivation as well as behaviour.

MacCannell, Dean, *The Tourist: A New Theory of the Leisure Class* (New York: Shocken, 1976).

Backward linkages

Backward linkages are the commercial transactions between the tourism sector of a local economy and the non-tourism industries that provide goods and services to tourism, notably:

- agriculture (and associated sectors such as commercial fishing);
- construction (building);
- local transportation;

- manufacturing;
- other services, such as the local **entertainment** industry (local dance groups).

Linked to the **multiplier effect** (the cascading effect of tourist expenditure), the concept of backward linkages shows that tourism can benefit local economies in a number of ways, when tourism is properly integrated in a nexus of local economic transactions. Imports (of food, furniture and all consumables) prevent backward linkages and lessen the economic impact of tourism (see **leakage**). The concept of forward linkages is less common; it refers to the tourism industry as a supplier of services for other sectors, for example in the case of **mega-events** such as the **Olympic Games**. Studying backward linkages as well as forward linkages can be done as part of what is sometimes called 'linkage analysis'.

Balance of payments

The balance of payments is a country's financial account: it is a measure of the movements of monies between that country and other countries as trading partners. It is determined by a country's exports and imports of goods and services, including **international tourism**. Outbound tourism affects the balance of payments in a negative way, whilst inbound tourism affects it in a positive way. The difference between these two is called the 'travel account' of a country, or its 'travel and tourism balance'. In 2004, according to Office of National Statistics, the United Kingdom received 27.8 million visitors who spent £13 billion, yet the number of visits abroad made by UK residents in that same period amounted to 64.2 million spending £30.3 billion, so the UK travel account is negative. According to data from the **World Travel and Tourism Council** for 2004 the same is true of the USA, Germany and Japan, whereas Canada, Spain and Italy have a positive travel and tourism balance. For those latter countries it means that tourism contributes to their economies as a source of income: some of their citizens may well travel abroad and spend money there, but this is counterbalanced by an even larger number of foreign visitors. The phenomenon is even stronger in the case of developing countries, although the danger then is to become too dependent on tourism.

Benchmarking

Benchmarking is a process whereby a business compares its products or services to industry standards, which are known as benchmarks. These benchmarks result from identification of good practice or even **best**

practice in a specific sector. Benchmarking has two aims: first, to measure performance (through comparisons), secondly, to identify areas for strategic improvement. Benchmarking is increasingly common across most sectors, including higher education. In the tourism industry, benchmarking was initially more common in the **private sector**, especially in **hospitality**, with systems of ratings such as stars for most types of **accommodation**. Increasingly, **public sector** organisations (such as visitor **attractions** and **tourist information centres**) are also taking part in benchmarking programmes organised at a regional or national level. A key criticism against benchmarking in the tourism industry is the fact it leads to **standardisation** and contributes to the bland **globalisation** of the **tourist experience**.

Wöber, Karl W., *Benchmarking in Tourism and Hospitality Industries* (Wallingford: CABI, 2002).

Best practice

The concept of best practice goes back to Frederick Taylor's writings about so-called scientific management in the early twentieth century. It refers to the belief that, in any given sector, there is an ideal way of doing things (for example, in **branding** or gathering tourism **statistics**). A cornerstone of **benchmarking**, best practice can be the standard that organisations use to measure their own performance. In tourism, the notion presents two weaknesses: first, in a volatile industry which keeps changing, even the best procedures and methods may need to evolve more rapidly than the established standards; secondly, in a **globalisation** perspective, best practice is not always transferable from one context to another, from one organisation to the next, from one country to another. Examples of good practice, when properly disseminated, are valuable inasmuch as they can lead to other providers improving their methods and approaches, by adapting ideas to their own contexts and circumstances. That an instance of *good* practice deserves the label and accolade of *best* practice may sometimes be arguable, even within large organisations or consortia: precise criteria and comparative systems are necessary to help identify what constitutes *best* practice.

B

Block spacing agreements

The concept of block spacing agreements is very important in understanding how airlines work with one another. They are arrangements by which one carrier contracts a block of seats on another carrier. This is often associated with other code-share agreements (see **code sharing**) and occurs due to airlines needing to secure onward connections for their passengers, or carriers being unable to obtain access to certain routes or airports. Airlines must today make it clear on tickets and **itineraries** as to which airline the passenger will be flying with; however, this was not always the case and often led to passenger confusion and frustration as they found they were flying with a less desirable airline than previously thought. A past example of such an arrangement is that of Continental Airlines contracting seats aboard Virgin Atlantic's London Heathrow to New York services. Due to the congestion and lack of slots available at Heathrow, it was the only way Continental could access the airport.

Branding

Branding is part of **marketing**. Branding is a means by which travel and tourism companies are able to differentiate their offer from that of their competitors. In his book *Marketing for Tourism*, Holloway explains that a brand may be 'a name, sign, symbol or design or combination of these, intended to identify the products of an organisation and distinguish them from those of competitors'. He also suggests that by branding a product, companies are able to add additional perceived value to the product, which may indeed be a key factor influencing potential customers' **decision-making**. Branding is not specific to services, although because of their **intangibility** they may require the perceived safety carried by a famous brand name (such as 'Hilton' or 'McDonald's'; brands are not synonym with elite or premium). By purchasing a branded travel product, customers reduce any perceived risk and can help build **loyalty** for that product. Having branded a product, it also becomes easier for companies to stretch the brand into new product areas. An excellent case study of brand stretching is the Virgin Group which has stretched the original Virgin Atlantic Airways to create Virgin Holidays, Virgin Express, Virgin Nigeria, Virgin Blue, Virgin Pacific, Virgin USA and Virgin Galactic, not to mention the other Virgin products, from Virgin Mobile to Virgin Radio.

Holloway, J. Christopher, *Marketing for Tourism*, 4th edn (Harlow: Pearson Education, 2004).
Kotler, Philip, Haider, Donald H. and Rein, Irving, *Marketing Places* (New York: Free Press, 2002).

Breakeven point

The concept of breakeven point comes from the study of microeconomics. It helps determine when an organisation will start covering all its

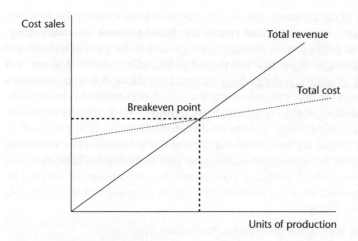

Cost sales

Total revenue

Total cost

Breakeven point

Units of production

Figure 1 Breakeven point

costs (fixed costs plus variable costs) or, put another way, when the venture starts being profitable. Graphically it refers to the position where the total cost of producing a product equals the revenue earned from its sales (see Figure 1). In the tourism industry, for both accommodation providers and transport operators, one of the biggest problems associated with the breakeven point is the high level of fixed costs (owning and maintaining aircraft or hotels). By understanding when the breakeven point is reached and how much capacity is available, managers are able to increase or decrease the price of the product (the flight ticket or the hotel night) to ensure revenue is maintained and ultimately increased. Tourism managers use sophisticated **yield management** algorithms to help judge the best price based on the breakeven point and the capacity available, yet it is important to understand the underlying logic with regard to the two types of costs (fixed costs and variable costs), as well as the notions of loss and profit.

Business plan

A business plan is an essential business document both for start-up businesses (see **entrepreneurship**) and for existing ones. It provides a detailed description with regard to all key business functions and shows how the venture will be successful, both operationally and strategically. Concretely, it is presented as a report, whose length may vary from fifteen to thirty pages plus appendices. As a narrative, it starts with a vision of the business, followed by pages of texts covering key business functions (such as **human resources management** and **marketing**). The last pages usually provide financial data in the form of budgets and cash flows to show that the project is financially viable. It is not only useful to attract and convince potential investors, but also provides a roadmap for new entrepreneurs. It is a live document that needs to be reviewed regularly, comparing **forecasting** to what actually happened, and drawing strategic lessons for the future. There is not a single authoritative format for the design and contents of a business plan. Banks and enterprise agencies (such as Business Link in the UK) all have their own templates, which provide a good blueprint that may then be adapted for the specificities of the business (such as its management structure or its industry sector).

Finch, Brian, *How to Write a Business Plan* (London: Kogan, 2006).

Business Link, www.businesslink.co.uk

Business tourism

Business tourism is the name given to all forms of tourism that are work-related, i.e. when people are not primarily motivated by recreational pursuits but travel because of their work, especially to attend meetings, **incentives**, **conferences** and exhibitions.

The accronym MICE (<u>m</u>eetings, <u>i</u>ncentives, <u>c</u>onferences, <u>e</u>xhibitions) is sometimes used in business tourism to cover these four core market areas. Business tourism can occur domestically or internationally, at **short haul** or **long haul** ranges. According to the **World Tourism Organization**, business tourism accounted for 16 per cent or 120 million international tourist arrivals in 2004. The **World Travel and Tourism Council** estimated business travel spend for 2006 at $672 billion. Business tourism is particularly important for two sectors:

- The airline and airport sector, because business tourism creates most of their revenue from the first- and business-class sections of the aircraft.
- City centre hotels and establishments that have conference facilities attached (because attendants are then a captive audience for catering and other amenities).

With the progress in telecommunication technology (video-conferencing, the Internet) it was initially feared that business tourism would decline, but companies still prefer to send representation, as face-to-face contact is still deemed to be the main selling tool for businesses

(British Airways has led advertising campaigns stressing that particular point).

Rogers, Tony and Davidson, Rob, *Marketing Destinations and Venues for Conferences, Conventions and Business Events: A Convention and Event Perspective* (Oxford: Butterworth-Heinemann, 2006).

Butler Sequence

Also called the resort lifecycle model, the Butler Sequence is named after Richard W. Butler who proposed it in 1980 in an article published in the **journal** *Canadian Geographer*. It helps synthesise and represent the processes that a destination will pass through as it becomes exposed to tourism. It is an application of the **product lifecycle** to destinations, based on the analogy that destinations go through the equivalents of birth, growth, maturation, decline and even death; it uses time and visitor numbers as the two key factors in locating a resort upon a lifecycle continuum. The S-shaped model devised by Butler rapidly gained international recognition and has become a classic of tourism management education. Two factors account for its popularity: firstly, its intuitive simplicity, which allows effortless knowledge transfer, and secondly its straightforward applicability to most destinations found within both the developed and the developing world. The key thesis of the Butler Sequence is that under free market conditions and without undue internal or external factors (no sudden drop in demand, no policy-imposed restriction on tourism development), destinations go through five stages of growth:

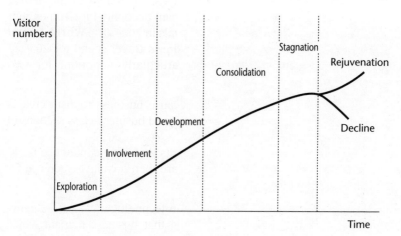

Figure 2 Butler Sequence

- **exploration**
- **involvement**
- **development**
- **consolidation**
- **stagnation** (also called saturation), which may then be followed by **rejuvenation** or **decline**

Empirical research has broadly confirmed the validity of the Butler Sequence (see Figure 2), although some deviations have been identified for certain **case studies** of destinations (for example Niagara Falls or Grand Cayman Island). It is a useful model for tourism planners and tourism managers, although they need to remember that many factors and **pressures** may affect the destination lifecycle, both internal and external, from **policy** actions that may boost or block **demand**, to natural disasters such as cyclones and hurricanes that may halt tourism development.

B

Capacity

The capacity of a container is the maximum amount it can hold; by analogy, the concept of capacity in tourism refers to the total number of units available to be sold by an airline, a hotel, a conference centre or a similar provider. Capacity cannot change but **demand** does fluctuate (for various reasons, including **seasonality**), hence the key problem for managers to balance demand and **supply**. During peak periods, capacity is operated at full stretch (hence the phrase 'at full capacity') and the company is able to make healthy returns. However, during off-peak periods (also called 'troughs') the operator needs to market or price the product accordingly thus stimulating sales. The amount of capacity sold is usually specified as a percentage; in the airline industry it is termed 'load factor', in hospitality the phrase 'occupancy rate' is used.

Carrier

The term 'carrier' refers to the form of transport used to go from the generating region to the destination region, via the transit region. Within aviation, 'carrier' is always used as a synonym of 'airline', especially in legal documents such as the Warsaw Convention of 1929 and the Montreal Convention of 1999. The Warsaw Convention is based on the liability that airlines face in the event of an accident occurring to an individual or their baggage whilst in the care of the carrier; the aim of the Warsaw Convention was to limit the amount of liability that airlines would experience in the event of an accident, including death to their passengers. Due to the limits that were set by the Warsaw Convention, it has been necessary for the aviation industry to update the amount of compensation payable due to such circumstances. These were updated under the Hague Convention of 1955 and the Montreal Convention of 1999, although these conventions only cover international flights. This information is displayed on all airline tickets and highlights the liabilities associated with the carriage of passengers.

Carrying capacity

The concept of carrying capacity comes from the studies of population and ecology. In tourism, it may be defined as the amount of tourist activity that can be accommodated in a site (such as a beach, a village or a whole region) without incurring serious damage. Directly linked to the notion of **impacts of tourism** development, carrying capacity can be divided into socio-cultural carrying capacity, environmental carrying capacity and economic carrying capacity. It is usually expressed as a threshold (for example in terms of maximum number of visitors per day), but calculations are very difficult, and some would even say subjective. Most specialists agree that it can be done only on a case-by-case basis because parameters and tolerance levels vary from site to site, according to numerous factors and variables. Once established, thresholds of carrying capacity may then help articulate **policies** of **sustainable development**, hence their importance for **tourism management** and **planning**. After implementation, control, monitoring and feedback, tolerance levels will still keep changing: carrying capacity is a dynamic concept, so in a way measuring carrying capacity is a never-ending task. Models have been designed, linking development stages, impacts, scale (for example large scale concentrated effects and small-scale dispersed effects) and growth, yet this is an area still developing in terms of research and methodologies.

Mason, Peter, *Tourism Impacts, Planning and Management* (Oxford: Butterworth-Heinemann, 2003).

Case study

Using case studies is a common method of **research**, knowledge generation and knowledge dissemination in tourism management. Many articles in academic **journals** such as the *Annals of Tourism Research* adopt that approach, and so do an increasing number of books, which are called 'monographs'. A case study enables the researcher to focus in depth on one 'case', which in tourism could be a destination, an event, an attraction, a type of tourist behaviour or a specific issue. Before the case study properly speaking, the context (of the case) and the theoretical framework (of the study) must be presented and taken into account: contextualisation and theoretical underpinning are two important aspects of any case study. Case studies may adopt different perspectives: they may be exploratory or illustrative, or they may help develop a model, a theory or a hypothesis. Case studies are not just descriptive but analytical: their academic value comes from the explanation they provide, hence the importance of background reading, preparation and secondary research. Case studies have their limits, though, especially in terms of generalisation and application to other cases, even cognate ones: the danger of the findings is that, ultimately, they are so context-dependent that they cannot really benefit researchers and practitioners working elsewhere. A case study of good practice in **community tourism** in Kenya might not be transferable to apparently similar tourism projects in Tanzania because the local community structures are different.

Yin, Robert K., *Case Study Research: Design and Method*, 3rd edn (London: Sage, 2003).

Catering

Catering is the commercial provision of food and beverage to the public. In dividing the catering industry into sub-sectors for analysis, several taxonomies can be used, employing criteria such as ownership (independent operators vs companies) or system (event catering vs industrial catering). Different national systems will have different ways to categorise restaurants. In the UK, the British Office for National Statistics has a classification (revised every decade on average in order to reflect changing professional practices) called the Standard Industrial Classification (SCI); with regard to catering, the SCI identifies two main categories simply called 'restaurants' (group H 55.3) and 'bars' (group H 55.4), the former including the provision of food (so pubs that have menus are considered within H 55.3). The SCI subcategories for H 55.3 are:

55.30/1   licensed restaurants (including self-service restaurants such as cafeterias and the dining car activities of railway companies);

55.30/2   unlicensed restaurants and cafes (including fast-food outlets such as burger bars);

55.30/3   take-away food shops such as sandwich bars and ice cream parlours;

55.30/4   take-away food mobile stands.

The SCI also has a particular subcategory called 'catering' in a restricted sense (group H 55.52), which includes food provision in airlines, corporate hospitality at conferences and other functions.

Other countries will have cognate systems, though notions of 'licensed' and 'unlicensed' will need to be reinterpreted. The in-depth study of the catering sector is part of the wider subject of **hospitality** management, which is supported by a well-developed literature with books and specialised professional publications.

Davis, Bernard, Lockwood, Andrew and Stone, Sally, *Food and Beverage Management*, 3rd edn (Oxford: Butterworth-Heinemann, 1998).

Dorf, Martin E., *Restaurants that Work: Case Studies of the Best in the Industry* (New York: Whitney Library of Design, 1992).

Catering Update Magazine, www.cateringupdate.co.uk
UK Food Standards Agency, www.foodstandards.gov.uk
UK Office of National Statistics, www.statistics.gov.uk

Caveat emptor

In Latin, the short phrase means 'let the buyer beware'; used in legal texts, it refers to the fact that buyers must have absolute knowledge of the product when they enter into a contract. Sellers are legally obliged not to mislead buyers, but for the rest the onus is on the buyers to make sure that they know and understand exactly what they are going to buy. That legal point is particularly important in property transactions, but also in the travel and tourism industry, for two reasons:

- In a stricter sense, it means that purchasers of any tourism product (be it a flight, a package tour or an entry to a tourist attraction) are responsible for assessing the quality of their purchase before buying – but, as many tourism products are not goods but **services**, it can be very difficult for tourists to do so, especially because of the **intangibility** of the service they buy. Service providers are expected to display **professionalism** and give accurate information enabling customers to make an informed choice, but travellers may not always understand some aspects (for example with regard to policies such as cancellation policies).
- In a broader sense, the principle of caveat emptor is a reminder that problems do occur, with dissatisfied travellers who may have less ground for compensation than they would hope. Caveat emptor means that ignorance of conditions or elements of a travel and tourism product already bought is no defence legally. Some consumers' associations (see **consumerism**) are fighting for more clarity in contracts, and some specialists will argue that tourists are not always well protected against the industry.

Grant, David and Mason, Stephen, *Holiday Law: The Law Relating to Travel and Tourism* (Andover: Sweet & Maxwell, 2003).

Lawtel: Online legal information service, www.lawtel.co.uk

Civic tourism

Civic tourism is an American concept that emerged in the late twentieth century at grass-roots level. The adjective 'civic' refers to the involvement of citizens in **decision-making** about tourism development in their local community. The focus of civic tourism is on quality of life as well as the **conservation** of the built **heritage** and other cultural and natural **resources**. It stems from the recognition that tourism is a double-edged phenomenon: on the one hand, tourism may ruin a sense of place and local people's quality of life, but on the other hand it brings extra income to a place. A fine balance has to be found, and civic tourism is a platform for that. This seems to be the American version of **community tourism**, without any new idea or new argument beyond the obvious and the well-known; in the absence of any conceptual work on the topic (except for one book chapter), it is difficult to assess the exact meaning, originality and value of the concept. An increasing number of small American towns are developing their civic tourism organisations, strategies and councils; many mayors and civil leaders have made speeches on the topic, and it seems to be an important new concept in American tourism. The First National Conference on Civic Tourism took place in Arizona in 2006.

Clark, Gregory, *Rhetorical Landscapes in America: Variations on a Theme from Kenneth Burke* (Columbia: University of South Carolina Press, 2004).

US civic tourism project, www.civictourism.org

Clustering

A business cluster is the name given to the concentration of interconnected businesses in an area, with suppliers, facilities and services enabling them to work together. Silicon Valley in California for computer technology or Toulouse in France for the aerospace industry are two famous examples. In tourism, clusters are sometimes called 'honey pots', with the image of both tourists and tourism providers attracted like bees. Orlando, Florida is an example of tourism clustering, with the **attractions** of Disney World, Universal Studios and Sea World as well as hotels and other **amenities** located in the same geographical area. Tourism businesses benefit from that spatial proximity because they feed off and help market one another, even if they are competing; tourists also benefit from the geographical arrangement as it lessens the need to travel from one venue to another. The American business management guru Michael Porter was one of the first scholars to conceptualise the economic model of clustering (which is why clusters are sometimes called 'Porter's clusters'). He analysed how they have the potential to affect competition in three ways: by increasing the productivity of the companies in the cluster, by driving innovation in and by stimulating new businesses.

Porter, Michael, *The Competitive Advantage of Nations* (Basingstoke: Macmillan, 1998).

Code sharing

Code sharing is an example of cooperation between airlines whereby one **carrier** allows another one to share a route and market it under its own flight number. Bilateral code sharing has grown in importance with the development of **airline alliances**. Code sharing can be broken down into two predominant forms: 'parallel' and 'complementary'.

- *Parallel code sharing* occurs where two airlines operate flights on the same route allowing both to gain advantages of increased frequencies and shared resources. An example of a parallel code share arrangement can be seen between British Airways (BA) and Iberia (IB): BA will, for instance operate a flight to Barcelona which will not only carry its code but also that of Iberia, and vice versa.
- *Complementary code sharing* transpires where two carriers join to increase global reach by tapping into routes operated by one another and where only one carrier operates the route. The advantage of complementary code sharing is that it allows carriers to concentrate on their core network while still allowing them to offer routes that would have otherwise been unprofitable or impossible to undertake. For example, Cathay Pacific is able to offer passengers a seamless service from Glasgow to Hong Kong using just their flight codes – not because Cathay Pacific flies directly from Glasgow to Hong Kong, but because they have an agreement in place with BA whereby passengers will fly initially from Glasgow to Heathrow and then on to Hong Kong. Code sharing also gives carriers the ability to increase the frequency on a route, which is an advantage for passengers as well, although they need to be aware of two drawbacks of code sharing: the need for transfers (sometimes between different terminals in larger airports) and the possible confusion between different policies (for example free vs paid catering).

Commodification

Commodification (or commoditisation) is the process of turning something into a commodity, that is a product, something that can be bought and sold. In tourism, it generally refers to the way a destination's culture becomes commercialised. It can include material objects which originally were not for trade for tourists (for example religious objects) but also **events**, performances, even people and their ways of life. As a factor of **acculturation**, commodification is usually presented as one of the most common negative impacts of tourism development on host societies, when new goods and services become available on the market following (real or perceived) **demand** by tourists. Numerous instances of commodification have been studied by tourism scholars, especially dances (the Polynesian dances of Western Samoa, the limbo dancers of the Caribbean), artistic objects (which start looking different in order to please tourists' tastes), sacred artefacts (which then lose their religious significance and are produced in great numbers and sold cheaply; this is called 'trinketisation'). Sex can also be regarded as a commodity, **sex tourism** being then the commodification of sexual services for tourists.

Appadurai, Arjun (ed.), *The Social Life of Things: Commodities in Cultural Perspective* (Cambridge: Cambridge University Press, 1986).

Cohen, Erik (ed.), 'Tourist Arts', *Annals of Tourism Research*, special issue.

Graburn, Nelson H. H. (ed.), *Ethnic and Tourist Arts: Cultural Expressions from the Fourth World* (Berkeley, CA: University of California Press, 1976).

Communitas

This Latin word, part of the vocabulary of the anthropology of tourism, refers to the spirit of solidarity and camaraderie that defines an ideal community in a shared moment of togetherness. Religious ceremonies are a privileged setting for communitas, but so are other secular events such as concerts or other **festival** celebrations. The concept of communitas can help us understand the dynamics occurring in groups of travellers who experience **liminality**: for a limited time, people who otherwise would not necessarily be together (because of differences of class, age, occupation, etc) share the same tourist experience, for example sitting together on Mount Sinai and watching the sun rise, or getting ready for a sky-dive over the rainforest in North Queensland. This group experience is comparable to a rite of passage and to **pilgrimage**, which is why these notions are often discussed together. Even independent travellers will want to experience communitas at times, so it is a useful concept for tour managers in helping them to understand how tourists need to be provided with opportunities for communitas. Organised group holidays (such as **holiday camps** and summer camps) are collective experiences where communitas plays an important role (bonding, group activities and entertainment).

Community tourism

The phrase 'community tourism' (sometimes 'community-based tourism') refers less to the tourists' motivation to visit an ethnic community (this is rather called **ethnic tourism**), than to the community's central role in managing tourism. Community tourism is a type of tourism that consults, involves and benefits a community; this empowering model is becoming increasingly common in some rural villages in developing countries. It has proved successful in maximising the economic benefits of tourism in the host community, whilst minimising socio-cultural and environmental costs. Concretely, the community keeps control of **tourism development** and collectively participates in **decision-making**; for example visitors stay with local families and engage in low-impact activities such as bush-walking and caving; in some schemes, the overall profits are shared by the community.

Mann, Mark, *The Community Tourism Guide* (London: Earthscan, 2000).

Competition

Competition refers to the act of competing, with the aim of being better than the opposition; it is used in many fields, from ecology to sports to politics. In business and economics, competition usually aims to secure maximum revenue through maximum sales. For consumers, it has several advantages as it may stimulate innovation and drive prices down, as opposed to situations of monopolies (which explains why, in market economies, monopolies are discouraged and regulated). The travel and tourism industry is highly competitive, with companies needing regularly to improve upon the goods and services they offer (see **product development**). The need to compete dynamically and strive constantly to improve is termed hypercompetition. The airline industry is a good illustration of hypercompetition: the drive to gain premium-class passengers sees airlines changing the layout and comfort of their business and first-class products every two to three years. British Airways is in the process of upgrading its 'Club World' concept at the cost of £100 million. The new features and services offered by British Airways will prompt other competing carriers to review and where necessary update their product. This constant cycle of one-upmanship is an example of hypercompetition. A cognate concept is that of contestable market: it refers to a (niche) market where only one firm is presently operating, although competitors can easily join because of low barriers to entry (and exit). However, this situation of apparent monopoly does not result in anti-competitive pricing strategy: should the firm prove very successful financially in its market, competitors will rapidly appear. The many routes flown by **low cost carriers** are an example of contestable markets: even when only one company operates a seemingly minor route (for example Exeter–Bergerac), prices need to remain competitive as competitors could easily lease one more aircraft and contest the market.

Computer Reservation Systems (CRS)

The first Computer Reservation System was developed by International Business Machines in the 1950s for American Airlines. The system was called Semi-Automatic Business Research Environment, abbreviated as SABRE. It was developed for American Airlines to replace antiquated booking procedures. Previous reservation systems would be completely unworkable in today's market: travel agents would need to telephone a call centre on behalf of a client and the booking details then placed on a blackboard for the day of travel. As air travel became more popular and aircraft grew in size, many mistakes were made, especially with aircraft often being overbooked, hence the need for a more reliable system. The utilisation of CRS helped cut out such inefficiencies. The competitive advantage enjoyed by American Airlines did not last long however, with Delta introducing its DATAS system in the 1960s, followed by United launching Apollo and TWA PARS respectively in the early 1970s. CRS were initially created for individual airlines to deal with their own reservation systems. They were therefore somewhat limited in their ability to sell a full complement of travel services. Travel agents and customers had to wait until the latter part of the 1980s for the introduction of **Global Distribution Systems**.

Pender, Lesley, *Travel Trade and Transport: An Introduction* (London: Continuum Books, 2001).

Concept

A concept is an abstract name for a phenomenon. It is important to understand the terminology and use concepts properly, in order to avoid misunderstanding or to show lack or frailty of knowledge. The key concepts used in tourism management are of two types:

- Some are rarely encountered outside the subject, such as **liminality** and **irridex**, hence the possible impression of a jargon and the challenge presented by some scholarly texts that use unfamiliar terms.
- Some are well-known words that have a particular meaning in the context of tourism management, such as **leakage** or **backstage**; the danger here is to fail to realise that these concepts do have a specific sense.

Tourism management has a language, yet it is not necessarily a difficult one, for three reasons:

- First, the subject is still young: only in the 1970s did it become a university subject.

- Secondly, it borrows concepts from other disciplines (for example **diffusion** and **carrying capacity**); this is due to the intrinsic **multidisciplinarity** of tourism management.
- Thirdly, many terms are part of common language and experience (such as **backpacking** and **attitude**), though again it is important to realise that, as academic concepts, these terms have particular meanings and implications.

Dann, Graham, *The Language of Tourism: A Sociolinguistic Perspective* (Wallingford: CABI, 1996).

Conferences

The term 'conference' applies to a large gathering of people who want to share information and ideas pertaining to a common interest (be it professional or recreational). Conferences (usually called 'conventions' in America) may relate to business decisions and the sale of products, for instance a medical conference where both new techniques and drugs can be discussed, or they may relate to personal hobbies, such as a group of science fiction fans getting together to discuss and meet the stars of their favourite show (the phenomenon of 'Star Trek Conventions' is a well-known example). In the United Kingdom, there is a key conference period in September and October when the major political parties gather at a UK seaside location to discuss future policy decisions. Conferences are critical for the success of business within resorts as they tend to offer the following benefits:

- Delegates stay at resorts and therefore make use of the full range of travel and tourism services.
- The use of public transport plays a greater role within conference tourism.
- Conferences tend to be held outside the main holiday period and therefore help to extend the resorts' season.

Conference tourism is at the interface of hospitality management and event management.

Rogers, Tony, *Conferences and Conventions: A Global Industry* (Oxford: Butterworth-Heinemann, 2003).

Conservation

Conservation refers to the protection of resources; in the context of tourism management, it can apply to both natural resources (the most common use of the term) and cultural resources (the phrase 'cultural conservation' is sometimes used in that case).

- Conservation of natural resources is linked to the negative impacts that tourists may have on natural environments, from direct impacts (such as trampling on soil and vegetation) to indirect ones (such as the emissions of hazardous polluants in the upper atmosphere by aircraft). The relationship between **nature-based tourism** and nature conservation is a complex one: tourism may stimulate measures to protect nature (as nature attracts tourists), but tourism presents environmental risks that may grow beyond the **carrying capacity** of a natural area. As a philosophy, **sustainable tourism** aims to ensure that conservation and tourism coexist in a symbiotic way, benefiting from each other.
- Cultural conservation proceeds from the awareness that **tourism development** contributes to **acculturation** and **globalisation**. It refers to the need to understand and manage the cultural changes taking place in tourist destinations, yet without turning them into 'living museums'. Cultural conservationists are motivated by a range of political ideologies which paradoxically have not always been well received by the indigenous populations themselves.

Many authors use the words 'conservation' and 'preservation' interchangeably, but some highlight subtle differences (the term 'preservation' may suggest a more radical approach, eliminating human interference and intervention in a perspective more akin to the Deep Ecology movement).

Butler, Richard W. and Hinch, Thomas (eds), *Tourism and Indigenous Peoples* (London: Thomson, 1996).

Johnston, Alison M., *Is the Scared for Sale? Tourism and Indigenous People* (London: Earthscan, 2005).

Consolidation stage

The consolidation stage of the **Butler Sequence** is the fourth stage of the destination lifecycle, following the **development stage**, where destinations are very popular resorts, such as the Balearic Islands or parts of the Bahamas and Florida. The main characteristics of the consolidation stage are the following:

- The resort has developed recreational districts entirely focused on tourism, without any other type of economic activity; **accommodation**, restaurants and **attractions** are all located in the same area, as a form of local **clustering**.

- Psychocentric tourists are the dominant force, having been shipped to the destination by mass market package **tour operators**.
- Most attractions are not owned by locals; besides, they are predominantly artificial; the cultural attractions which had once attracted the first visitors have either disappeared or have lost their initial meaning.
- The **multiplier effect** is low, **leakages** are very high.
- The resort is beyond its **carrying capacity:** environmental and socio-cultural impacts of tourism are negative, which may create tensions between proponents of further tourism development and pressure groups.

The consolidation stage gradually becomes one of **stagnation** as the destination struggles to change or further develop.

Consultancy

Consultants are specialists who give expert, professional advice; a consultancy is a commercial venture that may offer a variety of services such as applied **research**, market development, visitor **demand** forecast (see **forecasting**), project evaluation, **feasibility studies**, design of strategies or policies, etc. Some consultancies may also offer training and bespoke courses, for example on **entrepreneurship** or on sales techniques. Some tourism consultancies specialise in sectors (such as **heritage tourism** or the aviation business) or subjects (such as **marketing**). Their customers include the private sector (tourism developers) and the public sector (tourism authorities, governments), more rarely voluntary sector organisations. Some consultancies tend to operate and be known at a local or regional level, others have an international profile. Consultants are people with substantial knowledge and understanding of their area of expertise, as well as research skills and commercial skills to sell their services.

Cope, Mike, *The Seven Cs of Consulting: The Definitive Guide to the Consulting Process*, 2nd edn (London: Prentice Hall, 2003).

Forter, Timothy, R. V., *How to Succeed as an Independent Consultant* (London: Kogan Page, 2002).

Consumer behaviour

Consumer behaviour is the name given to the study of how people behave as consumers. Building primarily on methods and concepts from the social sciences (especially psychology and sociology), consumer behaviour is usually presented as a part of **marketing**. With regard to tourism, consumer behaviour is particularly concerned with tourists' **motivations** and what influences their choices: choices of destinations, of holiday types, of **accommodation**, etc. A wide range of factors need to be considered: some generic ones (economic factors, cutural factors, etc.) but also industry-related factors (because to understand the demand for tourism products one must also know what is on offer and what potential customers know and think about the available products). Consequently, consumer behaviour in tourism requires a solid knowledge of the tourism industry; it needs to be based both on **empirical research** and on theoretical models in order to map and understand recurrent patterns. **Maslow's hierarchy of needs** is one of the most famous models of consumer behaviour, but others have been proposed by specialists of tourism; in a way, concepts such as the tourist **gaze** and search for **authenticity** are part of consumer behaviour. Consumer behaviour is not limited to the pre-purchase stage; it also examines issues pertaining to tourists' on-site experiences as well as satisfaction and reflections on what they have done, seen and accomplished. Knowledge and understanding of customer behaviour is very important for tourism managers. Because of their experience, many professionals often have established ideas about consumer behaviour (what motivates their customers, why they have come here) but some of these ideas might not necessarily be accurate.

Pearce, Philip L., *Tourist Behaviour: Themes and Conceptual Schemes* (Clevedon: Channel View, 2005).

Pizam, Abraham and Mansfeld, Yoel, *Consumer Behavior in Travel and Tourism* (New York: Haworth Press, 1999).

Swarbrooke, John and Horner, Susan, *Consumer Behaviour in Tourism: An International Perspective* (Oxford: Butterworth-Heinemann, 1999).

Consumerism

The word 'consumerism' has two meanings:

- It may refer to an ideology of happiness through material **consumption**; in that sense, it is usually articulated as a critique of contemporary obsession for material cultural and materialism, alongside ideas of capitalism and neo-liberalism and conspicuous spending. From that perspective, tourism is presented as a purely commercial, status-enhancing activity. That thesis was first presented by the Norwegian-American economist Thorstein Veblen in a path-breaking important book entitled *The Theory of the Leisure Class* (published in 1899, yet still influential in leisure studies).

C

- It may refer to the protection of consumers' rights, as supported by both consumer legislation (such as the 1999 Unfair Terms in Consumer Contracts Regulations in the UK) and consumer advocacy groups (such as the Consumers' Association, founded in the UK by social activist Michael Young). In the case of tourism, travel insurance is one of the sensitive issues with regards to consumers' rights, as well as possible compensation when flights are cancelled, delayed or overbooked.

The phrase 'ethical consumerism' refers to the practice of buying goods that have been produced without harming humans, animals or the natural environment. Applied to tourism, it corresponds to concepts of **fair trade tourism** and **ethical tourism.**

Veblen, Thorstein, *The Theory of the Leisure Class: An Economic Study of Institutions* (New York: Dover Publications, 1994).

Consumers' Association, www.which.co.uk

Consumption

Consumption is the purchase of goods and services. In the tourism industry, it is not always apparent that something is being 'consumed' because tourism is usually experienced as a series of **services** or abstract notions (see **gaze**, **sightseeing**). Tourism providers and tourism managers need to remember that tourists are, first and foremost, consumers, as this has two important corollaries:

- Tourists as consumers have rights. When dissatisfied with their holidays, they may seek redress or compensation, although their grounds may be limited because of the **caveat emptor** principle; dubious marketing claims, questionable business practices or blatant lack of **professionalism** may nonetheless result in litigation and lawsuits.
- Tourists as consumers adopt particular behavioural patterns that can be analysed in order to understand their expectations and to ensure that they are satisfied with their experience. **Consumer behaviour** is the study of tourists' motivation and consumption patterns.

Although in economics the concepts of consumption and production are intrinsically linked, 'production' is rarely used in the literature because it is not an appropriate concept to analyse tourism. Production could be said to be on **supply** side (the combination of all industry providers as producers), although tourists themselves both 'produce' and 'consume' their own tourist experience. This is an example of a situation where borrowing concepts borrowed from other fields (here, **economics**) does not help the study of tourism.

Content analysis

Content analysis is a **research** technique commonly used to examine communications and their contents, both explicit and implicit. It aims to analyse documents closely, for example by paying systematic attention to the recurrence of terms, stylistic forms or semantic fields. In tourism, it can prove useful to analyse the way texts written for tourists (for instance tourist guides or travel brochures) contribute to the creation of the **image of a destination** and to tourists' perceptions or misconceptions. Content analysis goes beyond subjective and impressionistic perceptions: it is an objective attempt at deconstructing and understanding communication, which makes it particularly important in **marketing**. Content analysis is usually presented as a form of qualitative research, thought it may also include quantitative elements, for example about word frequencies or category frequencies (that latter notion includes synonyms). Consequently, it is possible to use simple software programmes such as Microsoft Word or Excel for content analysis, although several commercial packages also exist, such as QSR Nvivo (the new generation of NUD*IST products). They are very helpful for complex research projects but they require training and practice to be used optimally.

Krippendorf, Klaus, *Content Analysis: An Introduction to its Methodology*, 2nd edn (Thousand Oaks, CA: Sage, 2004).

QSR, www.qsrinternational.com

Contingency plan

A contingency is the course of action prepared for periods of uncertainty caused by disasters and major crises. As a document, it is comparable to a descriptive **policy** followed by details of procedures and operations (for example with an action checklist), mentioning responsibilities and communication lines. It should be also be regularly updated. It takes an 'in case of' approach that imagines the worst scenarios and plans accordingly. The travel and tourism industry has sadly become accustomed to disasters which require an immediate response; recent examples of such unpredictable and uncontrollable events include the terrorist attacks of 11 September 2001 in New York and the Indian

C

Ocean tsunami of 26 December 2006. Such events represent periods of chaos and anxiety for the industry, but so do situations of threats even in the absence of any catastrophe (such as the crisis in the UK in August 2006 about fears of an imminent terrorist attack on transatlantic flights). Tourism managers need to have a framework in place in order to move their customers and employees out of danger, or to deal with the consequences of any fatalities or injuries that may occur. These contingency plans may have been previously rehearsed, or they may just follow a logical process in line with emergency services, local and national governments, the media as well as the families of those affected by events. On a smaller scale, a contingency plan can be designed to cope with any unexpected event, for example a summer camp manager could have a contingency plan to deal with the unexpected illness of some key staff. A cognate concept is that of crisis management, which refers to the process of identifying, confronting and resolving all aspects of a crisis.

Journal of Contingencies and Crisis Management

Cook, Thomas

Thomas Cook (1808–92) is commonly regarded as the father of **package tours** and the grandfather of **mass tourism**. His importance is such that the history of tourism is commonly divided between the so-called 'pre-Cook period' and 'post-Cook period'. Several dates are remembered as milestones:

1841 first organised tour (day return from Leicester to Loughborough for 570 temperance campaigners).
1846 first tour of Scotland (with overnight accommodation and sightseeing stops for 500 passengers).
1855 first European tour (to Paris for the World's Fair Exhibition).
1870 opening of first offices abroad.
1874 introduction of the Thomas Cook credit note.

Thomas Cook's genius resided in the way he applied to tourism some key principles and techniques from the industrial revolution, especially with regard to preparing standardised packages, whose model still exists today. Cook paved the way for the industrialisation of the tourism sector, before the favourable socio-economic context of the 1950s turned it into the democratised mass phenomenon known as mass tourism.

Brendon, Piers, *Thomas Cook: 150 Years of Popular Tourism* (London: Secker & Warburg, 1991).

Core/periphery

A core region can be defined as an area that has prospered economically and socially due to its accessible location, diversity of industry and a large number of **amenities** and **attractions**, making it a desirable area to invest in. A peripheral area, on the other hand, may suffer economically and socially from under-investment. At a national level, it often becomes a government's responsibility to subsidise peripheral regions to maintain services (hence flows of capital from core areas to peripheral areas); within the European Union, subsidies for peripheral regions also come from the European Regional Development Fund and the European Social Fund. On a global scale, it is possible to see the world in terms of a core/periphery dichotomy: the core countries are characterized by high levels of development (hence the phrase 'developed countries'); they are sometimes referred to as 'the North', as opposed to 'the South', made up of developing countries. Tourism flows from core countries to the **pleasure periphery** reflect the **dependency theory** and the vulnerability of some peripheral countries which are over-reliant on tourism. The model has its limits though, and the concept of 'semi-periphery' is increasingly used.

Cost benefit analysis

A cost benefit analysis (CBA) is a common technique for project appraisal; in tourism, it is used to critically assess and compare the advantages (benefits) and disadvantages (costs) of taking a special course of action, be in on a large scale (for example taking over a competitor's hotel) on or a small scale (for example introducing group discounts for an attraction's entrance fees).

At a basic level, a CBA consists in identifying costs and benefits, merely naming them, but at a more advanced level it involves estimating these elements, especially through monetary calculations (initial expenses, expected profit) taking several factors into account (such as short term/long term, **opportunity costs**). In tourism development, other elements must be taken into account, such as the possible socio-cultural and environmental impacts, although they are sometimes very difficult to quantify.

CBA can help with **decision-making**, bearing in mind that intangible elements (such as risk and reputation) may also affect the proposed course of action. An impact study (see **impacts of tourism**) often follows a CBA methodology, typically with a table with two columns: 'costs' (the – side) and 'benefits' (the + side).

C

Cross Price Elasticity of Demand (CED)

The cross price elasticity of demand examines the change in quantity of a product required, based on the change in price of another product and the degree of complementarity between items. The change is represented as a percentage and can be either positive or negative, depending on whether the alternative product is a substitute or complements the original product. Therefore, the CED reflects the degree of response in the quantity demanded to changes in the price of a different good.

The standard formula calculates a value to measure the CED:

$$\frac{\text{\% Change in the quantity demand of B}}{\text{\% Change in the price of good A}}$$

For example, if a business passenger has been happily using the British Airways 'Club World' product based on the price charged, but then discovers that Virgin Atlantic has lowered the cost of its own upper-class product, in all probability the passenger will transfer their business to Virgin Atlantic. Therefore, the cross price elasticity of the British Airways seat would be negative as passengers would look at travelling on the cheaper but still high quality Virgin product (which is then called 'a substitute product').

Crowd management

Crowds occur in many tourism settings such as sports stadiums (see **mega-events**) or airports (for example, queues because of delays or security alerts). Crowds need to be managed for safety purposes, hence the development of crowd management into a **multidisciplinary** subject building upon event management, communication, transport planning, the law, safety studies as well as sociology and psychology. Crowd psychology has developed several models to explain collective behaviour (for example contagion theory and convergence theory). Even if crowd control is often outsourced to specialised agencies or to public authorities (police forces), tourism managers may need some basic knowledge and understanding of crowd dynamics and crowd management, for example about the vital importance of information (as in a crisis the lack of information may make people aggressive and frustrated). Poor crowd management may have very serious consequences, not only in terms of people's stress and anxiety, but also injury and even death. As part of their work, tourism managers may have to carry out **risk assessments** where issues pertaining to crowds and crowd management need to be identified.

UK Health and Safety Executive, www.hse.gov.uk

Cruising

The cruise industry is one of the most successful sectors of tourism. Geographically, the main areas for undertaking cruises are the Caribbean and the Mediterranean. Conceptually, cruising means that the three tourism elements of **accommodation**, **transportation** and **entertainment** are combined on a ship. According to Cartwright and Baird (1999) the three main reasons for undertaking a cruise are relaxation, safety and the social status that cruising brings. On its website the Passenger Shipping Association highlights the United States as the world's largest market for cruise holidays. Within Europe, the UK accounts for 33 per cent of the market. As cruise passenger numbers grow, so too have the ships. The world's largest cruise ship or 'megaship', the *Freedom of the Seas*, was launched in 2006 and can accommodate 4,375 passengers. The popularity of cruising has seen consolidation taking place within the industry with the three largest operators Carnival, Royal Caribbean (RCI) and Star (including Norwegian Cruise Lines (NCL)) operating a number of brands. Over the past decade the cruise product has changed considerably with the introduction of programmes by **tour operators** which have more in common with **package holidays** than the luxury and elegance normally associated with cruising. The dynamics of cruising were further modified by the entrance of 'low cost cruising' by the easyCruise company which operates one ship on traditional cruise holidays and another on river cruises. The Passenger Shipping Association has categorised cruising as follows:

- luxury cruising
- family cruising
- singles cruising
- themed cruising
- wedding and special event cruising
- working ships (cargo vessels with accommodation)
- conference and incentive cruises

Cartwright, Roger and Baird, Carolyn, *The Development and Growth of the Cruise Industry* (Oxford: Butterworth-Heinemann).

Passenger Shipping Association, www.the-psa.co.uk

Cultural tourism

Curiosity and education are the main motivation of cultural tourists: they want to learn about other people and their culture, a term that must be interpreted here in a broad sense. Cultural tourism is not just 'high arts' (as preserved and presented in **museums**, or as performed on stage) but it may also include popular folklore, traditional **events**, **festivals**, music, food, handicrafts, daily work, etc. Unfamiliar cultures often need to be explained and interpreted, hence the need for **culture brokers** such as **tour guides**, without whose mediation the educational purpose of cultural tourism cannot always be realised. Cultural tourism may be broken down into subcategories in order to distinguish between different foci such as **ethnic tourism**, **heritage tourism**, **industrial tourism** or other **niches** of **special interest tourism** (such as garden tourism). Cultural tourism does not exclude **hedonism**; many recreational holidays do include cultural elements, either incidentally (for example a visit to the local folk museum one day when it is too windy to be on the beach) or systematically (for example a cruise in the Greek islands with daily lectures before the visits of archaeological sites). Besides, the difference between 'cultural' and 'recreational' is not always clear-cut (for example, attending a bull-fighting *corrida* in Spain can be both).

Culture brokers

Brokers are intermediaries in transactions (for example insurance brokers, mortgage brokers); in the context of tourism, culture brokers are the people who act as mediators between the destination's culture and tourists' culture, or put another way between **hosts and guests** at a cultural level. Tour guides have the role of **interpretation**, but so do other intermediaries, for example local business people organising seminars for potential investors, or writers of travel publications, as well photographers and other artists. The concept of culture brokers emphasises the fact that cultures are not readily understandable by outsiders, even within the same linguistic community. This is important not only with regard to international tourism, but also domestically, as different regions may have different traditions and cultures that need to be explained. **Tour operators** and **public sector** agencies may also operate as culture brokers inasmuch as they may recommend or decide what should be part of tourists' **itinerary**. This makes them quite powerful culturally as they can really influence the tourists' experience and opinion of a particular destination, as well as the subsequent **image** that these tourists take back home and possibly share around. The phrase 'cultural brokerage' is sometimes used too.

MacCannell, Dean, *Empty Meeting Grounds: The Tourist Papers* (London: Routledge, 1992).

Culture shock

The phrase 'culture shock', which has now entered popular language, was coined and conceptualised in the 1950s by Canadian anthropologist Kalvero Oberg (1901–73) to analyse the feelings of people on their first cross-cultural experience. Culture shock is not just about the surprise of encountering unfamiliar and possibly mysterious cultural traditions: it is a deep psychological process marked by several stages. The first phase (a sort of 'honeymoon phase') is characterised by enjoyment of the new (new foods, new habits); this is followed by a negative phase where **ethnocentrism** makes one very anxious, stressed and confused, when the new culture is perceived only in a negative way and homesickness is at its peak. The length of that second phase may be days, weeks or even months. A period of adjustment will eventually enable the individual to get accustomed to the new culture. Depending on their previous experience, their psychological make-up, the degree of cultural difference (for example, new language and problems in communicating even simply) and the length of their stay, tourists may not be able to reach that third phase and may happily leave the destination as they miss home and their routines and habits. In turn, tourists who have adapted well to the new culture may experience a reverse culture shock when they return to their home culture and find it hard to readjust; this can be the case of travellers who have been away for a long time, for example backpackers or field anthropologists. Culture shock is experienced not only by tourists: locals (host communities) may also experience some forms of culture shock, hence the phenomenon of **acculturation** and the **demonstration effect**.

Furnham, Adrian, 'Tourism and Culture Shock', *Annals of Tourism Research*, 11:1 (1984) 41–57.

Customer relationship management (CRM)

Customer relations refer to companies' need to communicate effectively with their customers. The subject of customer relations has been transformed over the past decade to create a new strategy of customer relationship management (CRM). CRM includes a range of methodologies and technologies designed to help manage customer relationships and all transactions with clients. In tourism, CRM applies logically to the dynamic process by which tourism organisations communicate and sell to their customers. The strategies followed by airlines in setting up **frequent flyer programmes** (for example, British Airways' Executive Club and Virgin Atlantic's Flying Club schemes) are examples of CRM. Concretely, the introduction of members to these programmes and the

C

data held on ordinary passengers travelling with the airline have allowed the aviation industry to create vast databases of passengers' trip patterns, socioeconomic data and flight preferences. These databases are used to dispatch product information and special offers, with the anticipation of enticing customers to book flights, or use up mileage points they have accrued with the company. Some authors use the abbreviation CRM for customer relations marketing, but the overall approach is the same.

Peppers, Don and Rogers, Martha, *Managing Customer Relationships: A Strategic Framework* (London: John Wiley, 2004).

Rajola, Pederico, *Customer Relationship Management: Organizational and Technological Perspectives* (Berlin: Springer Verlag, 2003).

Customer service

Customer service is the art of gaining and then looking after clients. The phrases 'customer service' and 'customer care' tend to be used interchangeably, and so do the terms 'client' and 'customer'. Because tourism is a **service** industry, customer care is particularly important; it may occur in a range of settings, for example:

- Knowledge transfer occurs when a customer visits a **travel agent** for advice and recommendations. Customers may be put off by a perceived lack of interest shown in their needs, a perceived lack of **professionalism** from staff or disbelief towards the information they receive. The *Travel Trade Gazette*, the main travel newspaper, features a weekly mystery shopper who aims to expose how travel products are sold through traditional travel agents.
- Within the first and business class sections of a flight, a particularly high level of customer service, personal attention and professional friendliness are expected. Frequent flyers on board flights with the majority of the world's airlines expect to be greeted by their surnames and offered the services that they have expressed a preference for in the past, for example with regard to catering.
- In emergency situations and crises, communication is particularly important (see **crowd management**).

The use of customer service questionnaires has become a vital part of the quality feedback loop and of the quality assurance system of many tourism organisations, asking customers to comment on their experience. These questionnaires are useful, although they do have their limits, as satisfied customers do not always fill them in, which might give a distorted view of customer service.

Blanchard, Ken, *Raving Fans: Revolutionary Approach to Customer Service* (London: Harper Collins, 1998).

Dd

Dark tourism

Dark tourism is about visiting sites associated with death, war, assassination and other tragic events. Examples abound, from Cambodia (the 'killing fields' of Choeung Ek near Phnom Penh) to England (Jack the Ripper tours in London) to Poland (with the Nazi concentration camp Auschwitz near Krakow) and France (the Somme battlefields). The sites of dark tourism are linked not only to history, but also to contemporary events, such as the Pont de l'Alma in Paris (where Diana Princess of Wales died in a car crash in 1997) or Ground Zero in New York (the former site of the World Trade Center twin towers in New York). Although dark tourism is not a new phenomenon (as pilgrims have always visited tombs and sites of religious martyrdom), there has been a recent scholarly interest in researching, analysing and problematising dark tourism. The phrase itself gained popularity after a 1996 special issue of the *International Journal of Heritage Studies* and a pioneering book in 2000 by John Lennon and Malcolm Foley, who stress that tourism managers have an important mission of **interpretation** and education. Dark tourism is sometimes called thanatourism (from Thanatos, the personification of death in Ancient Greek mythology).

Lennon, John and Foley, Malcolm, *Dark Tourism: The Attraction of Death and Disaster* (London: Continuum, 2000).

Decision-making

Decision-making is the cognitive process that leads to the selection of one course of action after considering and comparing alternatives. In tourism management, the concept is used in two ways, referring either to the **demand** side (tourists and potential tourists) or to the **supply** side (the tourist industry).

- With regard to tourists, it is important to understand which factors influence their choices (choice of destination, choice of accommodation, etc.); these factors include not only factual knowledge and correct information, but also **attitudes**, **images**, preconceived ideas, hearsay, prior experience, gender, constraints, age, budget, opportunities, etc. **Consumer behaviour** is the study of these factors. It is very difficult to build a comprehensive model that fully deconstructs and represents the complexity of tourists' decision-making.

- With regard to tourism managers' decisions, on the other hand, it is possible to use and apply some of the decision-making models and tools designed by business management scholars, such as scenario analysis, critical path analysis, decision trees or **cost benefit analysis**. Decision-making is important not only with regard to long-term strategic **planning** and medium-term **policy** development, but also on a daily operational basis. Experienced entrepreneurs and managers are able to make quasi-spontaneous decisions.

Decrop, Alain, *Vacation Decision-Making* (London: CABI, 2006).
Glaesser, Dirk, *Crisis Management in the Tourism Industry* (Oxford: Butterworth-Heinemann, 2006).

Decline stage

The decline stage is one of the two possible ends of the **Butler Sequence**. In the final part of their lifecycle, destinations may indeed decline: visitor numbers start to fall; repeat visitors lose interest or are disappointed by the deteriorating quality of the place, new visitors prefer other destinations that are more engaging, more dynamic, less artificial. The tour operators who previously supported the destination may pull out, which accelerates the drop in visitor number and in **investment**. A typical example was Atlantic City in New Jersey, until the decision in 1976 to allow casino gambling led to the end of the decline and a **rejuvenation** of the place. Decline stages in terms of tourism development do not mean that a place becomes entirely derelict and dilapidated, though: properties may get converted into retirement apartments or health care centres and the resort may still exist viably, though no longer as a dynamic tourism destination.

Delphi method

The Delphi method is a systematic and interactive **research** method used for **forecasting**. It relies on the independent input of a panel of experts and selected **stakeholders**, whose opinions are collected and anonymously synthesised, usually several times, until a consensus is reached. The panel members do not normally meet face to face with the facilitator: data collection is usually done through questionnaires, so it can be a long process. In tourism, Delphi methods can help forecast **demand**, especially when used in a mixed methodology in combination with other techniques such as **statistics**. Delphi methodologies are difficult to set up, except for large-scale projects coordinated by **consultancies** or **national tourist organisations**, but their methodological underpinning is important.

Demand

Together with **supply**, demand is one of the key concepts in **economics**. The demand for a product is the quantity that consumers are both willing and able to purchase. The term 'demand' is confusingly used by specialists to refer to two groups of people:

- Demand in the sense of 'actual demand' (also called 'real demand' or 'effective demand'): refers to the number of tourists in a given location, at a given point of time. This is the figure provided by statistics about numbers of tourists. In that sense, the demand is restricted to existing visitors: it does not take into account other people who, maybe, were in a position of demand yet failed to come, for a variety of reasons.
- Demand in the sense of 'latent demand' (also called 'suppressed demand') is usually broken down into 'potential demand' and 'deferred demand': both are would-be customers but not actual ones, both are likely to travel when circumstances allow it. The difference is as follows:

  1 Potential demand did not materialise for reasons related to the tourists themselves (for example they did not have enough time or holidays entitlement, were ill at the last minute or were prevented from travelling for other personal reasons).
  2 Deferred demand did not materialise for reasons linked to the supply side, that is the tourist industry (for example accommodation shortages, problems with transport or with booking).

Demand in tourism-generating areas is influenced by several factors including economics (for example exchange rate and personal incomes) and socio-politics (for example, holiday entitlements, taxes); demand in tourism-receiving areas is also affected by several factors such as economics (prices) and politics (policies such as visa restrictions).

Sutherland, Jonathan and Canwell, Diane, *Key Concepts in Business Practice* (Basingstoke: Palgrave Macmillan, 2004).

D

Democratisation of tourism

In politics, the concept of democratisation refers to the transition from autocratic regimes to democratic ones where citizens may take part in the political process, especially through voting. Applied to tourism, it is the process whereby more and more people get the opportunity to take part in tourism, as opposed to tourism being the privilege of a social elite. In the early twenty-first century, the vast majority of people in developed societies have that possibility, whether or not they decide to seize it; even in some situations, those who cannot afford to (for example because of lack of discretionary income) can be helped by schemes of **social tourism**. The democratisation of tourism that took place in the twentieth century is probably the most important socio-economic change in the history of tourism. Several factors have made tourism more accessible and affordable, especially:

- increase in **discretionary income**;
- competition in the tourism **industry** (resulting in decrease in prices);
- multiplication of products, especially **package tours**;
- increase in **leisure** time (especially with regard to paid holidays);
- **diversification** of **supply** (more choice of **destinations**, **attractions**, activities);
- progress in **technology** (especially with regard to **transportation**).

Mass tourism is a direct expression of the democratisation of tourism, yet even within a frame of tourism for (almost) everybody in developed societies, it is possible to distinguish a new tourist elite who can afford certain types of very expensive holidays in exclusive resorts or on cruise ships.

Feifer, Maxine, *Tourism in History: From Imperial Rome to the Present* (New York: Stein & Day, 1985).

D

Demonstration effect

In politics and social history, the demonstration effect refers to the way phenomena taking place in one place will often act as a catalyst for others in another place.

In tourism, it refers to the fact that in a tourist destination a number of locals (usually the younger ones at first) will gradually imitate tourists' behaviour, especially with regard to **consumption** patterns (clothing, food, drinks, leisure activities, music tastes). The anthropological premise is the fact that imitating tourists is desirable. Drawbacks include a sudden demand for imported goods, tensions in the host community (especially inter-generational conflicts and gender-based tensions), as well as the gradual dissolution of the host culture (**acculturation**). The demonstration effect is one of the most salient cultural impacts of tourism development. The complexity of the interactions between **hosts and guests** has been researched by numerous scholars; there is an increasing body of literature on the demonstration effect, notably focusing on the factors influencing it, such as the strength of the host culture, its flexibility and its resistance to change. Tourism development had long been blamed for the negative aspects of the demonstration effect, although it is now being recognised that tourism is not the only source of demonstration effect, but one element amongst others: tourism may contribute to the phenomenon, but there is an ethical danger in believing that, without tourism, some societies would not develop and should not be given opportunities to discover other cultures.

Smith, Valene L. (ed.), *Hosts and Guests: The Anthropology of Tourism*, 2nd edn (Philadelphia: University of Pennsylvania Press, 1989).

Dependency theory

Dependency theory first emerged in the 1950s in the field of macroeconomics and international trade. At its core is the thesis that the wealthier nations of the world need a peripheral group of poorer states in order to remain wealthy. This can be easily applied to **international tourism**, with the unbalanced relationship between developed countries of Europe, North America and Australia, and the developing countries of the so-called **pleasure periphery**. Tourist flows are directed from the wealthy countries ('tourist-generating areas') to the poorer ones ('tourist-receiving areas'), following a simple **core/periphery** model. The subsequent economic dependency can be accompanied by elements of social and cultural dependency, hence the view that tourism is actually a form of **neo-colonialism**.

To a lesser extent, dependency theory also applies to **domestic tourism** within countries marked by a comparably asymmetrical relationship between metropolitan areas (as tourism-generating areas) and rural regions (as tourism-receiving areas). In Great Britain, instances of **second home** ownership in Wales and the south-west of England are symptomatic of that dependency.

The simple notion of dependence is linked to the dependency theory; it refers to the fact that some destinations (such as small island states) are very dependent upon tourism income, even over-reliant, which puts

D

them in a situation of double dependence: dependence upon tourism as a sector and dependence upon some specific tourist-generating countries.

Deregulation

The concept of deregulation refers to the freeing up of organisations from restrictions imposed by the government (control, policy, interventions). Following the 1919 Paris Convention, airlines were highly regulated. The need for regulation used to be based both on safety requirements and on the economic need to protect state-owned airlines (**national flag carriers** such as Air France and British Airways). Further protection was offered to airlines via the International Air Transport Association (IATA): with the consent of governments around the world, it operated a 'Tariff System' whereby airlines would meet together twice a year and fix bilateral and multilateral fares between countries. This situation changed, however, in 1978 when the United States Civil Aeronautics Board made the unprecedented decision to leave the Tariff System and to allow airlines to price seats based on principles of liberalisation, following a neo-liberal emphasis on the free market. This was the first step towards 'open skies', allowing airlines to propose to fly to any destination of their choice. The USA was supported in its stance by a number of countries including the UK, but it was not until 1997 that the European Union passed the final of its three 'packages' consequently allowing full competition. The success of 'open skies' in the USA and Europe has prompted other regions of the world to follow suit. Paradoxically, one of the most regulated markets is that of the transatlantic flights between the USA and the UK, where negotiations on an 'open skies' agreement have stalled for over a decade.

D

Destination substitutability

Some destinations may be markedly unique (for example, Venice or Pompeii), but many others, worldwide, are becoming substitutable for two main reasons: increasing competition and convergence of **supply**. In economics, this is called substitution of demand; it refers to cases where one tourist sees two tourism products as substitutes (for example, one week in Ireland and one week in Scotland), even if in terms of contents and pricing they are not exactly the same. The **cross elasticity of demand** is a model that helps quantify the phenomenon. In many cases, the place where tourists have their holidays could be different without much impact on their experience and satisfaction. This is not just the case for **3S** tourism in **identikit** destinations (Lloret de Mar or Palma de Mallorca) but also for most forms of tourism (scuba-diving holidays in Grenada or Curacao), and even for business tourism (a conference in Manchester or Birmingham). This creates a double challenge for destination managers and marketers:

- in terms of differentiation: creating a difference as a competitive advantage, with can be based on products, services or added values;
- in terms of communication: communicating that difference, hence the importance of branding and positioning.

The concept of substitutability does not apply only to whole destinations, but also to some service providers, for example hotels and restaurants, when there is little difference, if any, between competitors, at least as perceived by tourists who may see some hotels and restaurants as substitutable.

Morgan, Nigel, Pritchard, Annette and Price, Roger (eds), *Destination Branding: Creating the Unique Destination Proposition* (Oxford: Butterworth-Heinemann, 2004).

Destinations

Destinations may be defined and classified in various ways. As with typologies of **attractions** and **events**, different authors have proposed different criteria and different lists. Four aspects are usually taken into consideration: cultural features, physical resources, climatic conditions and availability of attractions.

- The *cultural features* of a destination are pertinent not only for those forms of tourism that focus on culture (such as **heritage tourism** and **ethnic tourism**), but also for all travellers (familiar brand names from the tourism industry, ease in communicating and interacting with locals, **culture shock**).
- The *physical resources* of a destination include beaches, mountain areas, countryside sceneries and even volcanoes or waterfalls as visitor attractions, but they also have implications for **accessibility** and **infrastructure** development.
- The *climatic conditions* of a destination are linked to **seasonality** and cyclic fluctuations (**sunlust** destinations attracting North Europeans and North Americans, or the popularity of ski resorts in winter), but they can also affect safety and consequently **demand** (for example, mid-October during the hurricane season in the south-eastern states of the USA).
- The *availability of attractions* can turn towns and regions (that otherwise would have not had much tourist appeal into tourist

D

destinations; **clustering** is an important factor in that respect, with a concentration of attractions, for example in Las Vegas or Orlando.

Boniface, Brian and Cooper, Chris, *Worldwide Destinations: The Geography of Travel and Tourism* (Oxford: Butterworth-Heinemann, 2001).

Determinants of tourism

The concept of determinants of tourism is used by some authors to try to encompass all the factors that affect a person's ability to travel; other scholars prefer other approaches and models, such as the **push factors/pull factors**. Determinants of tourism are usually broken down into two categories: macro determinants and micro determinants:

- *Macro determinants* refer to the overall situation of the generating area, especially with regard to its political set-up and socio-economic situation. In the latter respect, the model used is that societies develop from traditional models, mainly substance-based and agrarian, then go through an industrialisation phase with the emergence of a middle class interested in tourism, eventually to reach a stage of high mass **consumption** and **democratisation of tourism**.
- *Micro determinants* refer to the **demand** for tourism products, taking into account individuals as opposed to their societies as a whole. Those personal determinants may be further divided into two subcategories: **lifestyle** determinants and lifecycle determinants. The former include **discretionary income**, employment as well as holiday entitlement, education, physical ability, race/ethnicity, gender and sexual orientation, personal mobility, etc.; lifecycle determinants include age and group dynamics (see **family lifecycle**).

The approach of determinants of tourism is systematic and valuable, but it is sometimes criticised as it fails to consider some other potential factors such as the availability of tourism products (**supply** side) and psychological factors (travellers' **motivations**).

D

Development stage

The development stage of the **Butler Sequence** is the third stage of the destination lifecycle, following the **exploration** and **involvement** stages. Its main characteristics are as follows:

- Larger numbers of tourists start to arrive on a regular basis (each week, several times a week); they have midcentric or psychocentric needs.

- The local entrepreneurs start to sell the facilities already constructed as well as available land that will be bought for tourism development purposes by outside investors. This results in the rapid development of **infrastructure** and **transportation** but also in the erosion of local control over the local tourism industry.
- Specialised tourist attractions are created.
- Accommodation facilities are increasingly large and belong to international companies, which contributes to a high level of **leakage**.
- Non-locals start buying **second home** properties or **timeshares**.
- The first signs of over-exploitation of the environment can occur at this stage; landscapes change, with the multiplication of tourism buildings contributing to an impression of 'international tourism landscape'.

The transition from the involvement stage to the development stage is not easy to pinpoint, although some events (such as the construction of the first mega-resort or the opening of a casino or large **theme park**) can be interpreted as milestones. The development stage is easy to illustrate in seaside areas on the eastern cost of Australia (Cairns, Byron Bay), Cyprus or Croatia.

Diffusion

In business, diffusion (also called 'spatial diffusion' and 'geographical diffusion') is the process whereby a new idea or a new product is accepted by the market, and demand starts to grow substantially. In the geography of tourism, by analogy, diffusion refers to the way tourism distribution follows identifiable patterns that can help strategically plan and forecast tourism development. Two models can be used: a model of hierarchical diffusion and a model of contagious diffusion.

D

- The model of *hierarchical diffusion* refers to a hierarchy of places, starting with major urban areas (capital cities, metropolises), where tourists are most likely to go first, because of the presence of transport terminals (for example airports) and of primary attractions (for example museums). From this first urban magnet, tourists are likely then to travel to slightly smaller towns (regional capitals) and so forth, until **urban tourism** has turned into **rural tourism**.
- The model of *contagious diffusion* focuses on the importance of spatial proximity (as opposed to size) and the development of recreational areas and activities in the hinterland. When areas just outside the major centres start becoming destinations for excur-

sionists as well as tourists, their social fabric starts to change, for example with a new demand of services for tourists (for example **accommodation**). This can be observed in the hinterland of cities such as Sydney, Ottawa and Bordeaux.

The two models are not antithetical, but they emphasise different aspects of spatial diffusion and their effects; they are useful for civil planners and approaches to regional development at a macro level.

Hall, C. Michael and Page, Stephen J., *The Geography of Tourism and Recreation: Environment, Place and Space,* 2nd edn (London: Routledge, 2002).

Hanna, Stephen P. and Del Casino, Vincent J. Jr, *Mapping Tourism* (Minneapolis, MN: University of Minnesota Press, 2003).

Direct income

Direct income (also called direct revenue) relates to the amount of tourist expenditure spent on products and services on site; it does not take into account what tourists have paid in advance, for example through package tour arrangements, so it is only a part of tourists' overall expenditure. **Accommodation** and **catering** (food and beverage) are the main categories, but tourists may also spend a fair amount on shopping, **entertainment**, **sightseeing**, tours, local transport, etc. Tourism receipts also include a wide range of taxes, for example departure taxes such as the 'air passenger duty' tax in the UK, room taxes or *taxe de séjour* in France calculated as a fixed amount per night, visas, gaming licences, etc. Added to **leakage** (products that need to be imported to the destination), this limits the local direct revenue. Increasing direct revenue is a common objective of destination managers; several strategies are possible, for example increasing the number of visitors, or not increasing the number but attracting higher spenders, or developing facilities to increase spending (for example a casino), or limiting leakage, etc. The overall economic benefits of tourism spending are wider than just direct income, though: a **multiplier effect** rate makes it possible to calculate or at least evaluate the **indirect income** from tourism.

Goeldner, Charles and Ritchie, J. R. Brent, *Tourism Principles, Practices, Philosophies,* 9th edn (New York: John Wiley, 2003).

Discretionary income

A household's discretionary income is calculated by subtracting the cost of fixed expenses (such as rent/mortgage, food and energy bills) from the overall disposable income. This amount can then be spent on

D

what is desired rather than what is essential, such as leisure participation, including travel and tourism. Although some people without discretionary income may take part in tourism thanks to the schemes of **social tourism** which exist in some countries, very often the availability of discretionary income is regarded as the *sine qua non* of tourism; in any case, finance affects demand and the choice of holiday options. Statistics show complex links between economic trends, discretionary income, propensity to travel and tourism expenditure. A very limited discretionary income usually implies a low **travel propensity**, though higher discretionary incomes do not necessarily result in a proportionally higher travel propensity, as other factors need to be taken into account (such as family situation and possible saving plans, or limited holiday entitlements for households described as 'cash rich, time poor').

Disintermediation

Disintermediation is the act of circumventing conventional sales channels to buy directly from the principal or supplier. The process of disintermediation has been adopted by the travel and tourism industry for two reasons:

- Firstly, travel and tourism organisations operate in a very competitive environment. The use of technology to advertise and sell products has allowed them to access greater markets at reduced cost. Savings are made as the expenditure on producing glossy, magazine-style brochures is reduced, commission payments to travel agents have been stopped or capped, and the range of products offered can be updated and changed within seconds rather than having to produce a second, third or even fourth edition of a brochure.
- Secondly, as consumers' confidence in both travelling and using internet technology has increased, the need to access information from limited two-dimensional brochures and travel agents has decreased. Consumers have become aware of the savings and of the greater product options available to them through **dynamic packaging** or just by booking a traditional package holiday over the internet. More importantly, consumers believe that they can save time as well as money by researching and booking travel and tourism products over the web.

The concept of disintermediation is directly linked to **e-tourism**.

D

Displacement

Displacement consists in moving people from their original place of residence in order to make way for tourism development projects. As a form of forced migration, it is one of the most extreme socio-cultural impacts of tourism, when economic objectives are placed not only before community welfare, but even before the human rights of local people. Construction of hotels, of infrastructure or of golf courses necessitates land, and there have been instances where public authorities have dispossessed local people and forced them from their homes. In some cases, it is paradoxically under the banner of **conservation** that governments and private companies have displaced people, in order to develop **ecotourism** areas and national parks. People may even be evicted without compensation or alternative arrangements. The non-governmental organisation Tourism Concern cites examples from numerous countries, including Australia, Argentina, Bali, Bangladesh, Burma, Brazil, China, Egypt, Honduras, India, Jordan, Kenya, Mexico, the Philippines, Namibia, Peru, Senegal, South Africa, Thailand, Tibet and Tanzania.

Ryan, Chris and Aicken, Michelle (eds), *Indigenous Tourism: The Commodification and Management of Culture* (Oxford: Elsevier, 2005).

Tourism Concern, www.tourismconcern.org

Dissonant heritage

Dissonance means lack of agreement; consequently, the phrase 'dissonant heritage' refers to places (such as sites of major historical events) or themes (such as the slave trade history) where heritage could be interpreted in different ways, following conflicting ideological or political perspectives. The phrase gained popularity after the critically acclaimed book by John Tunbridge and Gregory Ashworth, *Dissonant Heritage*, published in 1996. Many sites of **dark tourism** involve some form of dissonant heritage, for example battlefields, commonly presented from the victorious side, as 'history is always written by the victor'. Even some artificially built attractions designed for tourists can be subject to tensions in terms of interpretation: museums or exhibitions about African-American heritage in America or about the Jewish Holocaust are often chosen as case studies to illustrate that type of dissonant heritage. Commenting on dissonant heritage is difficult because it implies that one puts forward some arguments that go against an established orthoxody or a commonly accepted way of presenting past phenomena. The phrase 'contested heritage' is sometimes encountered as a synonym of dissonant heritage; it highlights the fact that there is ground for disagreement and dispute on politically and culturally sensitive topics.

'Slavery, Contested Heritage and Thanatourism', *International Journal of Hospitality & Tourism Administration*, 2(3–4) (2001), special issue.

Tunbridge, John E. and Ashworth, Gregory J., *Dissonant Heritage: The Management of the Past as a Resource in Conflict* (Chichester: Wiley, 1996).

Distance decay effect

This geographical concept refers to the inverse relationship that exists between the volume of traffic between two places and the distance between them. This intuitive notion can be observed all over the world: the greater the distance between two places, the smaller the number of travellers. This is due to both economic factors (such as transportation costs and travel time) and psychological factors (the perception of distance and remoteness may influence potential tourists' choice of destination). These factors are dynamic and subject to change, though, especially with technological progress (faster transportation), pricing strategies (**yield management**) and marketing (changing the **image of a destination**). There are many instances of situations in contemporary tourism where the distance decay effect operates the other way round, for example it may be easier (cheaper and faster) to fly from London to the Algarve for the weekend instead of driving to Cornwall. The distance decay effect is important when planning regional tourism development, in conjunction with analysis of **diffusion** patterns, though other factors need to be taken into account.

Distribution channels

The term 'distribution channel' refers to the way organisations access their potential customers. The three main methods of distribution available to sell travel and tourism products are:

- agent (both independent and multiple agencies);
- direct booking via call centres (less common);
- websites with booking technology (increasingly common).

Tour operators have traditionally used **travel agents** as intermediaries to sell package holidays, ensuring their cooperation through commissions and incentives such as **familiarisation** trips. Symmetrically, the use of travel agents allows customers to gain expert knowledge and to have a dedicated interlocutor for queries, concerns and after-sale service. Tour operators anticipate that their holidays will be offered for sale by supporting travel agents' marketing campaigns and by supplying brochures. Tour operators have tried to control how customers book their holidays by vertically integrating into the travel agency sector, as illustrated by Thomson Holidays' purchase of Lunn Poly in 1974. The lack of control and the cost of offering multi-distribution channels have led tour operators to disengage from traditional booking methods in a process called **disintermediation**, as customers are encouraged to use direct-sale methods to book their holidays.

Diversification

Diversification refers to the movement of a business into a wider range of activities. Possible reasons range from spreading risks to tapping into a new niche market or limiting dependence on a single product range. In tourism, diversification equally applies to destinations or to organisations breaking into new areas to help maintain or increase revenue. Companies may opt for strategies of diversification in order to extend an already successful brand into new product sectors. An example in the tourism industry is British Airways which built upon its excellent reputation as a high-quality airline provider to tackle the tour-operating sector, creating 'British Airways Holidays', which offers high-quality holidays to both **short haul** and **long haul** destinations. Within the same sector, companies can diversify to attract different market segments, for example in accommodation the Accor Group has diversified their products into all key market segments of the hotel industry: 4 star (with Sofitel), 3 star (with Mercure, Ibis and Novotel) and budget (with Formula 1 and Motel 6). Destinations can diversify by opening new **attractions** that appeal to a different group of tourists from those already found at the resort; this is a useful strategy for destinations entering the **decline stage** of their lifecycle (see **Butler Sequence**).

D

Domestic tourism

Domestic tourism refers to tourists travelling within their own country, as opposed to **international tourism**. Contrary to a common misconception, domestic tourism is by far the main part of tourism: in the USA, domestic tourism accounts for 99 per cent of all tourism, in Australia around 94 per cent and in Great Britain around 80 per cent. It is very difficult to assess precisely the exact size of domestic tourism because there is no reliable system to keep track of flows of tourists domestically. Methods employed include household surveys, destination surveys and cross-referencing information from accommodation providers, but this is far less dependable than the statistics about numbers of international tourists. Nevertheless the **World Tourism Organization** estimates that globally domestic tourism accounts for 70 per cent of the total world demand for commercial accommodation; some tourism scholars give even higher numbers, around 80 per cent. Proportionally, domestic tourism generates less capital than inbound tourism, especially because domestic tourists do not always rely on commercial forms of accommodation, but may instead make use of holiday homes, **second homes** or stay with friends or relatives (see **visiting friends and relatives**). The **purposes** and **motivations** behind international tourism and domestic tourism are seemingly the same, but unlike international tourism, domestic tourism does not enrich the country: it does not bring in foreign currency, but rather redistributes capital within the national territory. From a regional perspective, especially for the regions receiving tourists, it has many of the impacts of inbound tourism. It is also more diffused geographically, does not concentrate on honey pots and repeat visitors tend to be more frequent.

Drug tourism

Drug tourism can be defined by focusing on one activity: buying (recreational) drugs that are illegal or unavailable in one's home country. It is helpful to distinguish between journeys where drugs constitute the main purpose of the trip (drug tourism per se), and journeys where drug-buying and/or drug-taking is only incidental; this latter aspect is quite common in some forms of youth tourism, such as backpacking. Commenting on such aspects of drug tourism is difficult because it is a culturally disputed terrain which has its proponents and opponents, and not much research has seemingly been published on the topic. A related issue is drug smuggling by tourists who attempt to bring back illegal substances with them; because of the criminal element, this is a more serious issue akin to other interfaces between tourism and crime (such as child prostitution and trafficking of endangered plans or animals). Amsterdam is a well-known destination for cannabis smokers because of the Dutch government's legislation and policy of tolerance. Cannabis in the Netherlands is most commonly sold in so-called coffeeshops patronised mainly by foreign tourists. South America and South-East Asia are other drug tourism destinations, though often for harder drugs (for example the opium dens in Laos or ayahuasca all over Amazonia) which are linked to a certain imagery of cultural **heritage**. Whilst the mass media occasionally report on such drug tourism journeys,

D

supported by a predatory, shadowy industry, in the absence of formal systematic research it is impossible objectively to analyse and distinguish between myth and reality. In other terms, drug tourism is still a taboo area of tourism, or at least one where more research is necessary, although this may be particularly difficult because of the ethical issues involved.

Dual use

The phrase 'dual use' is frequently used in leisure management about recreation facilities that can be used by two distinct groups of people, for example a swimming pool built in an educational establishment but also meant to be used by the local community. In tourism, the phrase 'dual use' refers to the use of amenities by both tourists and locals. With the notable exception of commercial accommodation, many amenities can indeed be patronised by both tourists and locals, for example restaurants, shopping precincts, performance venues such as theatres, local transportation such as taxis and buses, etc. This shows why, in urban areas, it is not easy to delineate and measure the exact contribution of tourism to the economy. In rural areas, the concept of dual use is often underpinned by the political argument that locals should arguably be encouraged to make use of tourist amenities. Benefits may then include thwarting the ghettoisation of tourists and maximising the income of local tourist businesses. In some resorts in developing countries, dual use is much more complex: firstly, many locals are economically unable to patronise tourist venues; secondly, tourist venues may be of very limited interest to them; thirdly, they may not be welcome at all.

Dynamic packaging

The concept of dynamic packaging relates to the consumer's ability to create a holiday package themselves, combining individual travel and tourism elements, rather than having to buy them as a prepackaged product. In the UK, the model was first developed by e-mediaries such as Expedia and lastminute.com, and has since been emulated by other operators, for example the traditional tour operator Thomson Holidays developed its own sub-brand just.co.uk; the success of the site has led to the introduction of dynamic packaging onto their main portal Thomson-holidays.com. The use of the Internet has contributed strongly to the growth of dynamic packaging. To offer such services, companies need to be linked to a Global Distribution System so that customers can select the flights, hotels, car hire, transfers, insurance, airport car parking and excursions that they want. Dynamic packaging is at the forefront of marketing technology, with virtual tours of hotels and a combination of satellite imagery, aerial photography and **Geographic Information Systems** to appeal visually to online visitors and convince customers to book (see **e-tourism**).

D

Economics

Economics can be concisely defined as the study of the allocation of (scare) resources; it is a social science that uses scientific techniques to understand how people, organisations and societies organise themselves and their resources in order to satisfy their needs and wants. Economics is usually broken down into two branches: macroeconomics (at national and international level) and microeconomics (at individual, organisational or sectorial level). Both are relevant for the study of tourism management:

- With regard to *macroeconomics*, tourism is an important contributor to national economies; **concepts** such as the **multiplier effect, leakage**, **balance of payments** and **foreign exchange** are at the interface of tourism and macroeconomics.
- With regard to *microeconomics*, tourism covers the economic activities of millions of consumers (tourists) and of service providers from the tourism industry; concepts such as **opportunity costs**, **competition** and **cross elasticity of demand** are at the interface of tourism and microeconomics.

Begg, David, Fisher, Stanley and Dornbusch, Rudiger, *Economics*, 8th edn (Maidenhead: McGraw-Hill, 2005).
Tribe, John, *Economics of Leisure and Tourism* (Oxford: Butterworth-Heinemann, 1999).

Ecotourism

Maybe surprisingly, defining ecotourism is difficult because of the proliferation of definitions and the consequent lack of consensus even amongst specialists. In 2001, David Fennell found over 80 different definitions of ecotourism, from both academic and industry sources. The International Ecotourism Society defines ecotourism as 'responsible travel to natural areas that conserves the environment and improves the well-being of local people'. Other definitions share a similar ethos and concern for local communities and the destination's natural environments, but they will stress particular aspects, such as the fact that ecotourism is a form of **alternative tourism** with a focus on ecology, or that it is underpinned by principles of **sustainable development** and a desire for both **conservation** and **interpretation**. In practice, ecotourism may overlap with other forms of tourism, for example bush-walking is a form of **nature-based tourism**, whilst aboriginal tourism in Australia is a form of **ethnic tourism**. Ecotourism is often presented as one of the fastest growing forms of tourism, although it is not easy to compile precise and comparable statistics, again because of the lack of a precise frame of reference. Despite the praise it generates and the obvious benefits for the destinations, ecotourism has also been criticised for several reasons, notably the fact that some of the destinations visited by ecotourists (such as the Amazonian rainforests, the Galapagos Islands or Antarctica) are very fragile and that even careful, well-meaning travellers can damage them. Besides, the remote and exotic locations of ecotourism projects as well as the high costs incured by such small-scale operations, have given ecotourism a negative image as the expensive, politically correct holiday of a self-indulgent elite (see **egotourism**).

Fennell, David A., 'A Content Analysis of Ecotourism Definitions', *Current Issues in Tourism*, 4(5) (2001): 403–21.

Fennell, David A., *Ecotourism: An Introduction* (London: Routledge, 2003).

International Ecotourism Society, www.ecotourism.org

Egotourism

Based on a pun on the word **ecotourism**, the neologism 'egotourism' is an invitation to cast a critical eye on all the tourism practices that fall under the umbrella term of **alternative tourism**. The argument is that these new tourists are probably more motivated by an egocentric, self-indulgent desire to feel they engage in **ethical tourism**, rather than really caring about ecology and **sustainable development**. This point is linked to the socio-demographics of ecotourists as educated, affluent Westerners for whom expensive ecotourist holidays are a legitimised way to discover unique destinations where few other travellers will have been. This mix of elitism and **hedonism** may also be accompanied by some snobbery towards the hoi polloi of **mass tourism**. Besides, the tourist industry itself is not immune to critique as it actually encourages egotourism, not to mention the fact that some businesses are increasingly using ecotourism and similar claims of environmental friendliness as a marketing ploy to attract tourists. Because of their unacademic style, the words 'egotourism' and 'ecotourist' tend to be used more in the mass media than in academic writing; Brian Wheeler is sometimes

E

acknowledged as the person who coined the word 'egotourism'. (Despite its misleading title, Lee Klein's book *Incidents of Egotourism in the Temporary World* is not about travel and tourism.)

Duffy, Rosaleen, *A Trip Too Far: Ecotourism, Politics & Exploitation* (London: Earthscan, 2002).

Wheeller, Brian, 'Egotourism, Sustainable Tourism and the Environment: A Symbiotic, Symbolic or Shambolic Relationship?', in Anthony V. Seaton (ed.), *Tourism: The State of the Art* (Chichester: John Wiley, 1994).

Elasticity of demand

See **Price elasticity of demand.**

Emotional labour

The term was coined by American sociologist Arlie Russell Hochschild in her 1983 book *The Managed Heart* where she analysed the way female flight attendants learn to repress any negative feeling and emotion for the sake of **professionalism**. Emotional labour (or emotional work) is about controlling and managing one's emotions and feelings because of the particular demands of a job. A **service** industry such as tourism puts such particular demands on staff in service encounters, and this concept is useful in terms of **human resource management**. Hochschild's findings about cabin crew can be generalised to other service encounters in the tourism industry where employees are required to control their emotions, especially in the transport sector, for example in tense situations of flight delays or cancellations, problems with overbooking or lost luggage. In the UK, this is dramatically reflected in the BBC's fly-on-the-wall documentary *Airport* or ITV's *Airlines*. Anthropologically, travellers are in a **liminal**, transit zone, without the relative security of either home or their final destination; as a consequence, they are particularly vulnerable and prone to fits of anxiety (air rage).

Hochschild, Arlie Russell, *The Managed Heart: The Commercialisation of Human Feelings* (Berkeley: University of California Press, 1983).

Kusluvan, Salih (ed.), *Managing Employee Attitudes and Behaviors in the Tourism and Hospitality Industry* (Hauppauge, NY: Nova Science, 2003).

E

Empirical research

Strictly speaking, empirical research is based on observation and experience (hence the founding principle that in science all evidence must be empirical); in a broader sense, the term 'empirical research' is used to contrast a more hands-on form of research (based on data collection and data analysis) to pure theorisation (theoretical research) consisting in conceptualisations and abstract judgements. In tourism, most research tends to be empirical; the quality of the research carried out is then assessed through criteria such as validity and reliability (irrespective of the research strategy, qualitative or quantitative). A particular challenge in tourism is the fact that some important concepts are difficult to observe, appreciate and describe, for example the **tourist experience**, which it is one of the conceptual cornerstones of tourism yet is difficult to address empirically.

Clark, C. et al., *Researching and Writing Dissertations in Hospitality and Tourism Management* (London: Thomson, 1997).

Employment

Employment refers to the situation of being employed: it is a contract between two parties, the employer and the employee. According to the **World Travel and Tourism Council (WTTC)** in their 2006 *Travel and Tourism Economic Research* report, the travel and tourism industry worldwide generates 234 million jobs, representing over 8 per cent of global employment. The WTTC estimates that by 2016 the number of people employed in travel and tourism will have reached 279 million; this represents 9 per cent of the workforce globally or one in every 11 jobs. This includes direct employment but also indirect employment, with calculations based on the relative contributions of other sectors (see **backward linkages**). The European Union has calculated that 8 million people are directly employed within the tourism sector in Europe, and it is anticipated that employment opportunities will grow by a further 2 million within the next decade; some scholars argue that such statistics are inflated, yet the relative importance of tourism as an employer cannot be underestimated.

Employment in the sector suffers from specific problems:

- Jobs tend to be low paid, compared with other sectors
- In certain instances, they tend to be low-skilled, with few opportunities for progression and career development.
- Employment tends to be seasonal or part-time in nature.
- In certain areas, technological progress requires fewer staff to be employed.

E

Enclave tourism

In political geography, an enclave is a piece of land which is totally surrounded by a foreign territory, like West Berlin before the 1990

German reunification. By analogy, enclave tourism refers to holidays in self-contained **resorts**, usually located in tropical, coastal areas, offering activities such as scuba-diving and **amenities** such as swimming pools and tennis courses. Sandals Resorts and Club Med are typical examples.

Enclave tourism is characterised by:

- High level of **leakage**, as the resorts usually belong to multinational firms and most goods are imported.
- Very limited interactions between **hosts and guests**, with the exception of low-paid resort staff.
- Limited benefits for the local community outside the all-inclusive resort, because tourists hardly leave the complex, which prevents an informal tourism sector to develop.
- Local resentment against a form of segregation considered as **neo-colonialism**.

Enclave tourism creates a 'golden ghetto' for tourists; this is an illustration of **dependency theory** and **vertical integration**.

Entertainment

Entertainment is about liberation from boredom, from **alienation** and other mental constraints. Psychologically it is regarded as a normal and healthy part of life. It is not specific to tourism, although when they are away from their home environment (where they have familiar sources of entertainment and relaxation) most tourists will seek some forms of entertainment; this is not the just case of recreational tourists, but also of business tourists, hence the social programmes that often complement conferences and conventions. Sources of entertainment include artificial **attractions** (such as **theme parks**), **events** (such as **festivals**), performances (such as street theatre) or visits (for example to a cinema to see an old classic). In some cases, entertainment can be the explicit purpose of a trip (for example a family weekend at Disneyland Resort Paris) or it may just be incidental, spontaneous and unplanned (for example joining a 'ghost tour' of a city just two hours after seeing the poster advertising it). The entertainment industry is often regarded as part of the leisure industry, and the academic study of entertainment is rather part of leisure than tourism. Entertainment is subjective: what is entertainment for one person (visiting a casino, a cabaret or a zoo) may mean boredom for another person. When entertainment is meant to also be educational, the neologism 'edutainment' (education + entertainment) is sometimes used; this is the case in an increasing number of modern museums, for example the Museum of the Moving Image (London, now closed) or the Cité des Sciences et de l'Industrie (Paris).

Hughes, Howard, *Arts, Entertainment and Tourism* (Oxford: Butterworth Heinemann, 2000).
Saire, Shay and King, Cynthia, *Entertainment and Society* (London: Sage, 2003).

Entrepreneurship

The terms 'entrepreneurship' and 'enterprise' are often used inter-changeably in tourism, although some authors might define them slightly differently. It is generally accepted that entrepreneurship and enterprise have two complementary meanings:

- They can refer to the process of formulating and setting up a business; this involves identifying a business opportunity, developing the initial idea into a **business plan**, and starting up the venture properly speaking. **Franchising** is an example of entrepreneurship, and so are all the small-scale, independent local businesses that make up the bulk of the tourism **industry**.
- They can refer to the skills and mindset necessary to be a successful entrepreneur, including persistence, resilience, resourcefulness, optimism, ambition, strategic vision and creativity. **Case studies** of famous tourism entrepreneurs (such as Richard Branson, the founder of Virgin, and Stelios Haji-Ioannou, the founder of easyJet) help understand what makes a good entrepreneur in the tourism industry, though it is important to remember that these millionaires are not representatives of entrepreneurship as a whole.

Governments and development agencies are usually very keen to encourage and support entrepreneurship because new businesses are the motor of local economies, creating new jobs and resulting in taxes and commercial transactions, particularly in the tourism sector.

Morrison, Alison, Rimmington, Mike and Williams, Claire, *Entrepreneurship in the Hospitality, Tourism and Leisure Industries* (Oxford: Butterworth-Heinemann, 1998).
Zimmerer, Thomas W. and Scarborough, Norman M., *Essentials of Entrepreneurship and Small Business Management*, 4th edn (London: Prentice Hall, 2006).

E

Environmental Impact Assessment (EIA)

An Environmental Impact Assessment (EIA) investigates the anticipated environmental costs and benefits associated with the building of a particular tourist development. Its methodology follows that of a **cost benefit analysis**, focusing on environmental issues. The investigation needs to be detailed, taking into account both pre- and post-developmental concerns. Undertaking such investigations makes it easier for planners to approve or object to planning applications. The European Union has made it mandatory for all large-scale tourism projects to be covered by EIA. The production of EIA reports is a useful technique in helping to reduce the occurrence of environmental damage, but specialists recognise that EIA also has its limits, notably:

- There has been limited take-up of EIA schemes globally.
- It lacks a holistic approach for the area in question as projects are judged individually.
- EIA is compulsory only for large-scale developments within a region or destination (such as the development of London Heathrow Terminal Five) but not for small-scale development (such as a hotel extension), although the latter cases too could benefit from a systematic impact study.
- EIA evaluations look only at new development projects and therefore tend to ignore damage already caused by existing development.

Glasson, John et al., *Introduction to Environmental Impact Assessment*, 3rd edn (London: Taylor & Francis, 2005).

Page, Stephen J. and Connell, Joanne, *Tourism: A Modern Synthesis*, 2nd edn (London: Thomson, 2006).

Ethical tourism

Strictly speaking, ethics is the branch of philosophy concerned with what is right and what is wrong. By extension, the word also refers to codes of behaviour, deontology and value judgements. The concept of ethical tourism is based on principles of **sustainable development**, justice and respect, with the implication that both tourists and tourism businesses should act ethically towards local communities and towards one another. In that respect, it is sometimes used as a synonym of **alternative tourism** and **sustainable tourism**. In 2001, the **World Tourism Organization** published an important document entitled *Global Code of Ethics for Tourism*, which it defines as 'a comprehensive set of principles whose purpose is to guide stakeholders in tourism development: central and local **governments**, local communities, the tourism industry and its professionals, as well as visitors, both international and domestic'. The code itself is not very long (see appendix); it is composed of nine articles setting **policy** guidelines for destinations, governments, tour operators, developers, travel agents, workers and travellers themselves. The tenth article is about implementation, which

E

of course is the most difficult: whilst most people will readily agree that tourism should be ethical, it is not always easy to ensure that it is in practice.

Fennell, David A., *Tourism Ethics* (Clevedon: Channel View, 2006).

Pattullo, Polly, *The Ethical Travel Guide: Your Passport to Exciting Alternative Holidays* (London: Earthscan, 2006).

United Nations World Tourism Organization, *Global Code of Ethics for Tourism* (2001).

Ethnic tourism

Ethnic tourism is a type of **cultural tourism** where the prime **motivation** is the desire to interact with people from a different ethnic group, typically in less economically developed countries. European or American tourists travelling to northern Thailand to meet hill tribes people are a good example of ethnic tourism. Ethnic tourists can be compared to the early field anthropologists who, animated by cultural curiosity, went to stay for months with remote communities in order to study them (for example the Polish Bronisław Malinowski in the Trobriand Islands, and the American Margaret Mead in Samoa). By its invasive nature, ethnic tourism presents some dangers such as **commodification** and **acculturation**, but when properly managed it can prove beneficial to the host community. This is the case when it takes place through respectful schemes of **community tourism** with explicit concerns for sustainability, ethics and **responsible tourism**. At its best, ethnic tourism is not just a setting-up of interactions between **hosts and guests** but an opportunity for cross-cultural communication and ethnic relations; local **tour guides** (who then operate as **culture brokers**) play a particularly important role in this respect. Because it implies a high degree of cultural difference between tourists and locals, the main destinations of ethnic tourism from the West are on the Pacific Rim and in Africa.

Picard, Michel and Wood, Robert E. (eds), *Tourism, Ethnicity, and the State in Asian and Pacific Societies* (Honolulu: University of Hawaii Press, 1997).

E

Ethnocentrism

The word was coined and conceptualised by American sociologist William Graham Sumner (1840–1910). The belief in the cultural superiority of one's own ethnic group ('my culture is at the centre of everything') is accompanied by a disparagement of all other cultures, and even hostility towards them. In the context of tourism, this is a useful concept that helps us understand the reactions of some tourists who

experience **culture shock**, are not able to accept socio-cultural differences (for instance, with regard to hygiene or customs) and find refuge
in negative **stereotypes** and generalisations. Experienced travellers, on
the other hand, tend to be more open-minded and more aware of
cultural relativism. **Travel writing** sometimes indulges in ethnocentrism, consciously or not: consciously when the author indulges in
ethnocentrism because they know that it will make readers smile;
unconsciously when the author does not realise that they look down
upon outgroups because of cultural differences. Ethnocentrism can be
analysed as part of the wider theme of cross-cultural communication; an
important model in that respect is the developmental model of intercultural sensitivity (now commonly abbreviated as DMIS) proposed by the
American scholar Milton Bennett in the 1980s to compare, map and
explain the varied reactions of people to cultural differences.

> Bennett, Milton J. (ed.), *Basic Concepts of Intercultural Communication: Selected Readings*
> (Yarmouth, ME: Intercultural Press, 1998).

E-tourism

The term 'e-tourism' is a way of describing the advance of electronic
front and back office systems. According to Dimitrios Buhalis, one of the
specialist of e-tourism, e-tourism refers to the digitisation of the
processes found within the value chains of the tourism, travel and hospitality industries. The reason behind this transformation is an organisation's need to make its operations more efficient and effective and thus
allow easier communications with its customers. The development of e-
tourism has been championed by **low cost airlines** with Ryanair for
example achieving over 98 per cent of its bookings via the Internet,
which substantially helps reduce commission and administration costs
associated with selling its seats. It is not just low cost airlines that have
seen the Internet as a major cost saver, as other carriers such as British
Airways are also promoting the benefits of booking online with a target
of 100 per cent of sales through such means.

The Internet has also created a new set of travel companies often
referred to as e-mediaries. Examples of e-mediaries include
Expedia.co.uk and Opodo.co.uk and Travelocity.co.uk. These travel
companies are able to use the power of **Global Distribution Systems**
which are often linked to their ultimate owners (for example Travelocity
is owned by SABRE) to find customers the cheapest deals. Tour operators have also started to recognise the benefits of e-tourism, as
evidenced by the growth of **dynamic packaging**, enabling e-customers
to tailor their own holidays.

E-tourism has further advantages for both organisations and customers:

- Customers gain the ability to check-in online, which allows seats to be chosen, frequent flyer details to be entered and meal requests to be made.
- Airlines have integrated their booking and reservation systems to achieve greater **logistics** efficiencies when loading aircraft, resulting in quicker turnarounds.

Buhalis, Dimitrios, *eTourism: Information Technology for Strategic Tourism Management* (Harlow: Prentice Hall, 2003).

Eurozone

Strictly speaking, the Eurozone (also called Eurosystem or Euroland) refers to the twelve European Union member countries that acquiesced to monetary union and the implementation of a single currency called the euro. The euro was introduced on 2 January 2002 in the following twelve countries: Austria, Belgium, Finland, France, Germany, Greece, Ireland, Italy, Luxembourg, Netherlands, Portugal and Spain. For tourists, the eurozone makes travelling much easier, as there is no need to change currencies or worry about **exchange rate** fluctuations (outside the Eurozone, the euro still fluctuates against other currencies). It also makes comparisons much easier with regard to tourism products. The small European states of Monaco, Andorra, San Marino and Vatican City also use the euro, although they are not officially members of the EU. Some other countries outside the EU such as Montenegro have also adopted the Euro. The United Kingdom, Denmark and Sweden have so far declined to join. The ten new members who entered the EU in May 2004 have been given various timelines to implement monetary union, for example Slovenia aims to join the Eurozone in 2007 and Cyprus in 2008. The Eurozone partly overlaps with the **Schengen** zone.

European Union portal, www.eu.int

Events

Events are **attractions** that occur at a certain point in time; they can be classified in many ways, according to several criteria such as:

- *time*: regular (for example the yearly Edinburgh International Festival) or irregular (for example a royal wedding);

- *theme*: sports (for example the FIFA World Cup), heritage (for example a commemoration), arts (for example an outdoor concert);
- *size*: from small-scale (for example a local festival) to **mega-events** (for example the **Olympic Games**);
- *geography*: one venue only (for example the Changing of the Guard at Buckingham Palace) or several (for example the Tour de France);
- *artificiality*: from natural events (for example the yearly coral spawn that attracts divers) to artificial ones (for example a fireworks extravaganza at Walt Disney World Magic Kingdom).

Events attract tourists, which is why they often play a central role in tourism marketing; like tourism as a whole, though, they have a range of impacts (economic, socio-cultural and environmental) which is why they need to be properly planned and managed. They also raise particular issues because of concentration of people, especially with regard to health and safety (see **crowd management** and **risk assessment**). From an academic viewpoint, events are usually studied as part of **leisure management**, although event management is becoming a **multidisciplinary** subject in its own right.

Bowdin, Glenn et al., *Events Management* (Oxford: Butterworth-Heinemann, 2001).
Shone, Anton and Parry, Bryn, *Successful Event Management*, 2nd edn (London: Thomson, 2004).

Exchange rate

The exchange rate (also called foreign-exchange rate or FX rate) is the amount of one currency required to purchase another currency. It is dependent on the strength of the currencies being transacted and consequently on wider international economic dynamics. Exchange rates affect the travel and tourism industry in two ways:

- Firstly, the price of travel-related products will be affected by the oil price. Oil as a commodity is priced in dollar barrels. Therefore, how the dollar compares to the producer's home currency affects the price of services offered. To counter oil price fluctuations, airlines and tour operators can 'hedge' that is, buy currencies when it is favourable to do so or add a surcharge to the cost of the holiday to counter currency fluctuations.
- The second effect that exchange rates have upon the travel and tourism industry is reflected in the affordability of a destination for tourists. Resorts within a country that have a strong currency will find it difficult to tempt tourists compared to areas that are perceived as being 'cheap'; this is a current problem for the United

E

Kingdom, as the British pound is very strong. This has a positive impact on outbound tourism, though, as outbound tourists are comparatively better-off when they travel abroad.

Within the European Union, the **Eurozone** gives travellers the ability to move between countries with one currency, thereby removing the need to worry about free floating exchange rates.

Currency and foreign exchange, www.xe.com

Excursionist

As a **tourist** is technically defined as a person away from their usual place of residence for *more than* 24 hours, an excursionist, consequently, is technically defined as a person away from their usual home for *less than* 24 hours. 'Day-tripper' is a common synonym. When they cross borders, excursionists become international excursionists; Britons on a duty-free cross-channel day trip to Calais are a very good example. The **World Tourism Organization** defines an international excursionist as follows: 'A visitor residing in a country who travels the same day to a country other than that in which he/she has his/her usual environment for less than 24 hours without spending the night in the country visited and whose main purpose of visit is other than the exercise of an activity remunerated from within the country visited.'

Excursionists' contribution to tourism may be quite limited and some destinations deplore the fact that visitors do not stay overnight, as this would substantially increase tourism revenue through accommodation and taxes. In the UK, this is the case of cities such as Winchester and Oxford which are within easy access of London, attracting day-trippers based in London. In other rural regions, excursionism represents a non-negligible input to the economy; this is particularly the case in hinterlands and back countries which are easily accessible by car from main cities. The study of **diffusion** and **rural tourism** helps explain how some places become destinations for excursionists and, later, tourists.

Tribe, John et al., *Environmental Management for Rural Tourism and Recreation* (London: Thomson, 2000).

Exoticism

The adjective 'exotic' qualifies the plants, animals, landscapes and even the cultures far outside the speaker's frame of reference. A mango is an exotic fruit for a Swedish woman, but not for an Indian one. In Europe and North America, exoticism conjures up images of faraway destinations, possibly unusual scenery and unfamiliar fauna and flora. Tourism marketers have learnt to exploit the appeal of that imagery, as **semiotics** and **content analysis** of travel brochures can readily prove. Exoticism is also a key motivation for **ethnic tourism**, with the desire to experience marked cultural differences. By definition, exoticism is **ethnocentric**.

A cognate concept, important in cultural studies, is 'orientalism'. The term became more popular after the publication in 1978 of the controversial book *Orientalism: Western Conceptions of the Orient* by the Palestinian-American intellectual Edward Said. In this influential book, regarded as a founding text of academic postcolonial studies, Said deconstructs and denounces how 'the West' (especially France, England and America) had constructed an exotic image of 'the East' (the Orient, more precisely the Middle East). From a tourism perspective, it is a helpful concept to appreciate and also challenge the representations of tourist destinations in the Arab world and beyond, with the recognition that advertising often relies on unhelpful and discriminatory stereotypes.

Said, Edward W., *Orientalism: Western Conceptions of the Orient* (London: Penguin, 1978).

Exploration stage

The exploration stage of the **Butler Sequence** is at the very start of the destination lifecycle when tourism is a new phenomenon in a place. The main characteristics of the exploration stage are:

- The first tourists are few in number; they can be described as allocentric and they stay for rather extended periods of time (several weeks).
- There is no attraction designed specifically for tourists: the first visitors ('explorers') are interested in local culture (an early form of **ethnic tourism**) and local fauna and flora (an early form of **nature-based tourism**).
- Commercial accommodation is limited or non-existent; the local population is employed in other sectors (such as agriculture) but will be directly involved in providing all the hospitality services (homestay accommodation).
- Infrastructure and transport are limited to the needs of the host population, so access may be difficult.
- Negative impacts of tourism are very limited; the **multiplier effect** is high.

Exploration is sometimes described as 'pre-tourism'. Places still at that stage can be found in the Amazon basin, in some parts of the Australian interior and of rural China, as well as northern Canada and Siberia, that is environments rather hostile or difficult to reach.

Extreme tourism

Extreme tourism is a type of active **sports tourism**; the phrase is increasingly used to refer to holidays which involve travelling to dangerous places (such as caves and deserts) and/or participating in extreme sports (such as ice-diving and abseiling).

Unlike **staged authenticity** in artifical, heavily controlled environments, extreme tourism is real, which raises many issues for organisers in terms of health and safety. Dangers may be minimised and due precautions taken, but there are always elements of risk, and accidents do occur (for example a skydiver's parachute that fails to open). The presence of danger (or at least perceived danger) is a key motivator for extreme tourists, who range from amateurs, engaging in forms of extreme tourism for an occasional adrenaline rush, to professionals who travel to a destination specifically to partake in extreme sports. As a form of **special interest tourism**, extreme tourism (also called 'shock tourism') can be further broken down into subcategories and **niche** markets according to the environment (for example **jungle tourism**) or to the activities (for example parasailing). As there is an increasing number of commercial operators and clubs involved in extreme tourism, tourism researchers have started to examine the motivations, impacts and development of extreme tourism.

Extreme Tourist magazine, www.extremetourist.com

E

Ff

Fair trade tourism

Although the fair trade movement is primarily about the production and distribution of agricultural commodities, the concept has also been associated to tourism in developing countries. It then refers to tourism products that benefit the local communities, instead of exploiting their cultural and natural resources (hence the analogy to ethical **consumerism**). On that basis, fair trade tourism is directly associated to concepts of **sustainable tourism** and **alternative tourism**; the phrase 'equitable tourism' can sometimes be encountered too. Several organisations and pressure groups campaign about fair trade tourism, for example with the International Fair Trade in Tourism Network set up in 1999 by Tourism Concern (see also advocacy). **Pro-poor tourism** and **community tourism** are strategies based on a fair trade ethos. To be implemented, principles of fair trade tourism need the support of everybody, both tourists themselves and tourism providers. The movement is still in its infancy; the first international and interactive exhibition of fair trade in tourism took place in Brussels in 2006.

Tourism Concern, www.tourismconcern.org.uk

Familiarisation trips

Familiarisation trips (sometimes called familiarisation tours, and commonly referred to in the industry as 'FAMs') are incentives offered by tourism operators to some of their suppliers and agents in order for them to discover a particular product (**destination** or **attraction**) and to encourage them to recommend it to tourists. Familiarisation trips are usually free because they are seen as an investment. For example, a destination may organise a familiarisation trip for travel journalists and travel agents, in order to showcase particular facilities, or a new local attraction may offer free tickets to local hotel receptionists. Based on principles of loyalty and gratitude, the logic is that the beneficiaries of the familiarisation trips will later recommend the tour or attraction. The travel agents may be chosen as a reward for sales they have already achieved for that particular tour operator. Such incentives are very common in some parts of the tourism industry; they are seen as a counterpart for the sometimes low salaries; they also create a sense of community amongst workers from different sectors. Familiarisation trips are an essential **marketing** tool very typical of the tourism industry.

Family lifecycle

The family lifecycle represents the demographical position an individual has reached within a traditional representation of families. Travel and tourism marketers place much importance upon this model, as it has considerable affects upon the types of products that an individual or family are prepared to purchase. For example, a young couple who are both in paid employment but without a child (also referred to as 'DINKY' – Dual Income No Kids Yet) have more potential to use long haul, luxury products as their family circumstances and income enable them to move freely. Family units with young children represent a very different market segment as they may well prefer the protection offered by tour operators to allow everyone the opportunity of a break with the use of kids' clubs and nanny provision. The progression of the family unit into adolescence and then children leaving home (with the parents as 'empty nesters') can be seen as a further opportunity for marketers to promote different types of products, moving towards **senior tourism**. The family lifecycle is a useful model for **marketing segmentation**, although its underpinning **heteronormativity** and traditional view of family units may not be fully in line with contemporary changes in society.

Feasibility study

A feasibility study is an in-depth preliminary study meant to help decide whether a proposed project should go forward or not. Examples in tourism may include a feasibility study for the extension of an airport, for a new hotel or for the redevelopment of an existing attraction. Although financial considerations are most important, especially with regard to budgeting, feasibility studies also need to take other factors into account, such as time (scheduling), technical aspects (this is also called 'technical feasibility'), human factors (socio-cultural impacts) and physical factors (environmental impacts). Comparable in some ways to a **business plan**, a feasibility study will include a demand/market analysis, a competition analysis as well as a **cost benefit analysis**. Feasibility studies should be unbiased and not assume that the project will proceed; this is why they are often done by independent **consul-**

F

tancies that do not have any vested interest in the proposal. Feasibility studies have to be paid for, but it is regardied as a minor expense in the interest of avoiding possible problems later on, should the venture prove unsuccessful. A feasibility study is no promise of business success, but it helps reduce risk and uncertainty, especially for prospective investors and planning authorities.

Festival

Historically rooted in the sacred and the religious, festivals are public celebrations that contribute to community pride and sense of identity and are hence more than just amusement and **entertainment**: their anthropological value lies in an ethos of **communitas**. This explains why many tourists are keen to attend local festivals as genuine cultural experiences, in order to participate in an event which is culturally mean- ingful for the locals, while shows their traditions and identity. When these festivals become commodified and marketed as tourist **attrac- tions**, they lose their original value and cultural meaning, though; authenticity and identity politics lose their edge and entertainment becomes the main purpose. Examples of community festivals that have become tourist attractions include the Sydney Gay and Lesbian Mardi Gras (Australia) and the Munich Oktoberfest (Germany); some other festivals are created primarily for tourists and visitors, such as the Baalbeck International Festival (Lebanon) or the Festival des Vieilles Charrues (France).

Allen, Johnny et al., *Festival and Special Event Management* (Brisbane: John Wiley, 1999).
Yeoman, Ian et al., *Festival and Events Management: An International Arts and Culture Perspective* (Oxford: Elsevier, 2004).

Flights (charter)

F

Charter airlines contract out their services to third parties, usually tour operators. As a consequence, the timetable they follow and the routes they serve are dictated by the needs of the tour operator. Most charter airlines offer a one-class service, although certain charter carriers such as Thomsonfly and First Choice Airways have developed a premium service at a supplement to the passenger. Although charter carriers tend to concentrate on **short haul** routes, a number of the larger carriers that are vertically integrated do offer flights to exotic long haul destinations such as the Far East (Thailand in particular), the Caribbean and Africa (especially Mombasa in Kenya). The types of contract offered by charter airlines include:

- time series charters
- part charters
- ad hoc charters.

Flights (scheduled)

Scheduled airline services can be characterised by:

- *A fixed timetable*: flights will operate even if empty as the return journey may have a full complement of passengers.
- *A rigid route structure*: the routes are all published in advance to enable passengers and travel agents to book.
- *The product offered*: unlike most charter flights, scheduled airlines tend to offer a variety of products to cater for different market segments. Most **long haul** carriers offer three classes of service, namely First, Business and Economy (some carriers such as Virgin and British Airways have introduced a fourth product termed Premium Economy which fits between the Economy and Business Class service). For certain long haul carriers, the distinction between first and business class has become blurred: Continental Airlines, for example, has introduced a BusinessFirst product giving the benefits to travellers of both products. The class of travel will affect the seat pitch, entertainment and meals available, as well as ground services.
- *Booking procedure*: due to increased competition between traditional scheduled carriers and the low-cost carriers, companies like British Airways are turning more to the Internet as a means for passengers to book their flights. British Airways is currently working towards selling 100 per cent of its seats via its own website (see **e-tourism**).

Focus group

Focus groups offer qualitative researchers a valuable alternative to working with separate informants and respondents: instead of carrying out semi-structured or unstructured interviews on a one-to-one basis, focus groups give researchers the chance to meet a small group of people (ideally six to ten) and interview them as a group. Group interactions, with participants in discussion, enable the researcher to gain better insight into the topic at stake, for example a group of young mothers talking about the facilities they would ideally like to see in a child-friendly airport, or a group of summer camp staff discussing the

F

development of new types of activities for a research project. Participants are invited because of their relevant experience, knowledge or possible contribution, although they are not expected to be experts as with research employing **Delphi methods**. In **marketing**, focus groups can help gather feedback on an existing product or a new one in more depth than through a survey. The researchers' role is to facilitate rather than systematically lead the discussion, which is why they need to be properly trained. Data collection may be done in complementary ways, for example by note-taking and tape-recording the discussion. Data analysis may be particularly difficult because of the richness and complexity of the material (informants sometimes talking at the same time or contradicting each other).

Krueger, Richard A. and Casey, Mary Anne, *Focus Groups: A Practical Guide for Applied Research*, 3rd edn (London: Sage, 2000).

Forecasting

Forecasting is about predicting in order to adopt a necessary course of action. In tourism management, forecasting is about accurately anticipating how tourism will evolve, especially with regard to **trends** in **demand**. Forecasting is essential for both public authorities (to help **planning** and **policy**-making) and commercial operators (to inform strategies to prepare and respond to changes). Although forecasting tourism trends is not an exact science, unsophisticated forecasts (individual guesswork and teamwork) are increasingly being replaced by methods that are more complex and more reliable:

- **quantitative** methods, either based on pure statistical modelling or on econometrics;
- **qualitative** methods, for example using **Delphi** techniques (especially for long-term trends).

Projection by extrapolation (pursuing past trends into the future) is a common approach, although weights and variables may need to be added. However sound and reliable forecasting may be, it can never be taken for granted because of the major impacts of unpredictable events such as terrorist attacks (for example the 9/11 attacks in America in 2001) or natural disasters (for example the Indian Ocean Tsunami in 2004).

Fretchling, Douglas, *Practical Tourism Forecasting* (London: Butterworth-Heinemann, 1996).
Song, Haiyan and Witt, Stephen F., *Tourism Demand Modelling and Forecasting: Modern Econometric Approaches* (Oxford: Elsevier Sciences, 2000).

Formal vs. informal sector

The concepts of formal sector and informal sector come from labour **economics**, where the informal sector encompasses all the activities that take place outside the control of the state, as opposed to the formal sector which is subject to official regulation and remuneration. In developed countries, most businesses are in the formal sector, as opposed to clandestine or underground activities. In tourism, especially in developing countries, the informal sector can play an important role by providing many locals with a source of revenue. It can include unregulated guest houses and unlicensed tour guides, market stalls, prostitution, street vending, souvenir hawkers, pedicab drivers, etc. Local authorities usually try to discourage such activities for several reasons: they do not bring in any tax revenue; there is no quality assurance system to protect tourists as consumers; they may annoy tourists who take home a negative image of the destination ('too many touts') and discourage other potential visitors. That latter argument is sometimes mistaken because, paradoxically, some tourists may well expect and anticipate beggars and children as part of the experience of a participate destination, instead of a sanitised version.

Franchising

A franchise is a commercial arrangement by which one company (the franchiser) agrees to another company (the franchisee) using its name, logo and brand in return for a royalty payment or percentage of income generated. Franchisees are expected to pay an initial set-up cost to cover issues of training and to gain practical advice; they are also bound by a contract which will affect the quality of the product supplied and the purchasing of raw materials. Depending on the contract, they may also have to pay a regular amount besides the royalty percentage. Franchising has become popular within the hospitality sector as a way of extending brands; many fast-food brands (for example Subway) operate with systems of franchise. For the franchisee, the advantage of franchising is the ability to sell a well-known brand that people are familiar with due to advertising (trademark) and previous experience (loyalty). Franchising is often presented as a way to set up a business (see **entrepreneurship**) with limited risks as the product or system has proved successful elsewhere.

F

Sugars, Bradley J., *Successful Franchising: Expert Advice on Buying, Selling and Creating Winning Franchises* (Maidenhead: McGraw-Hill, 2006).

Freedoms of the air

This concept was developed from the 1944 Chicago Convention. The original idea was to create a multilateral air service agreement. However, with the convention taking place as the Second World War was still being fought in the Pacific, most countries present were not prepared to allow sovereignty of their air space to be reduced. Therefore instead of a multilateral air service agreement being reached, a series of Bilateral Air Service Agreements was initiated, which took into account the following rights (or privileges), called 'freedoms of the air':

- *First freedom*: the right to fly over a country without landing.
- *Second freedom*: the right to stop in a country for refuelling or maintenance on the way to another country, without transferring passengers or cargo.
- *Third freedom*: the right to carry passengers or cargo from one's own country to another.
- *Fourth freedom*: the right to carry passengers or cargo from another country to one's own.
- *Fifth freedom*: the right to carry passengers from one's own country to a second country, and from that country on to a third country.

These five freedoms have been further enhanced through the **deregulation** of the industry, and the introduction of 'open skies' agreements has led to the articulation of the following additional freedoms:

- *Sixth freedom*: The right to carry passengers or cargo from a second country to a third country by stopping in one's own country.
- *Seventh freedom*: The right to carry passengers or cargo between two foreign countries without continuing service to one's own country.
- *Eighth freedom*: The right to carry passengers or cargo within a foreign country with continuing service to or from one's own country.
- *Ninth freedom*: The right to carry passengers or cargo within a foreign country without continuing service to or from one's own country.

The eighth and ninth freedoms are also known as 'cabotage rights'.

International Civil Aviation Authority, www.icao.int

Frequent flyer programmes (FFPs)

Frequent flyer programmes (FFPs) are a marketing concept designed to gain and retain passengers. They represent a key **loyalty** strategy for airlines. FFPs were originally created as a competitive response to US **deregulation** in 1978. The American Airlines launch in 1981 of their AAdvantage scheme is commonly presented as the template for modern FFPs. They were originally based on **premium markets** where passengers gained miles or points for each eligible flight booked. The innovation within schemes has led to their expansion to include full fare economy tickets. On attaining a specified level of credits, passengers may exchange them for free flights and, more recently, ancillary rewards such as car hire. (Nowadays some Visa or Mastercard issuers even offer FFP points on partner airlines – so it is possible to accrue miles without ever having flown.) FFPs offer passengers further incentives by allowing them to use airline lounges, priority check-in areas and free upgrades.

The best-known FFPs, ideal for case studies, are AAdvantage (American Airlines), Flying Dutchman (KLM), Mileage Plus (United Airlines), Miles and More (Lufthansa) and Virgin Flying Club (Virgin Atlantic). Airlines have recognised the benefits that such schemes can create, the single most important benefit being the opportunity to secure a marketing database for follow-up promotions and incentives, thus gaining competitive advantage over its rivals. FFPs can be broken down into three categories:

- programmes operated solely by an airline where passengers gain benefits from the one carrier;
- schemes offered by an airline which allow customers to gain benefits with themselves or partner organisations;
- programmes which link FFPs with **airline alliances** (Star, Oneworld or Skyteam being examples) – such schemes allow passengers to build points across all alliance partners, thereby enabling them to accrue benefits at a faster rate.

Buhalis, Dimitris and Laws, Eric (eds), *Tourism Distribution Channels: Practices, Issues and Transformations* (London: Continuum Publishing, 2001).

F

Frontstage

See Backstage and frontstage.

Gay and lesbian tourism

Gays and lesbians have obviously always travelled, but only over the last decades has gay and lesbian tourism become more visible and identifiable as a niche market. Several reasons account for that: a socio-political climate more inclusive and less homophobic, at least in certain Western countries; the recognition of the financial value of gay tourism; the increasing visibility of an openly gay and gay-friendly tourist industry (as emblematised by the travel guide *Spartacus International Gay Guide*).

Gay and lesbian tourism has drawn an increasing number of researchers since the mid-1990s, and illustrates well the interdisciplinarity of tourism as an academic field. Gay and lesbian tourism can indeed be studied from a number of perspectives, such as geography (favourite gay destinations, such as Sitges, Mykonos and Montreal; their appeal and development), economics (the high economic impacts of the so-called gay pound/dollar), health (issues such as the spread of HIV/AIDS), events management (large-scale emblematic events such as the Sydney Mardi Gras or the Gay Games), sociology (the creation of a global gay culture through gay tourism) and psychology (the liberalising experience of many gay and lesbian tourists who can openly live their sexuality whilst on vacation away from home).

Clift, Stephen, Luongo, Michael and Callister, Carry (eds), *Gay Tourism: Culture, Identity, and Sex* (London: Continuum, 2002).
Waitt, Gordon and Markwell, Kevin, *Gay Tourism* (New York: Haworth Hospitality Press, 2006).

Spartacus International Gay Guide, www.spartacus.de/gayguide

'Gaze'

The concept of 'gaze' became popular in scholarly cultural analysis in the 1960s, notably in books by French intellectuals such as Michel Foucault and Jacques Lacan. In 1990, a groundbreaking book by British sociologist John Urry, *The Tourist Gaze*, applied the concept of gaze to tourism, especially to tourists and their visual consumption of venues, objects and also people. Examining the recent history of tourism development in Great Britain, Urry focused on the way tourist experiences have a fundamentally visual character (this emphasis is even stronger in the second edition of the book, with an extra chapter on the topic). This conceptualisation has paved the way for many researchers who have exploited the notion of tourist gaze, such as semiotic studies of what tourists see and experience (palimpsest landscapes, **events** or scenes of **staged authenticity**) or theoretical analyses of the way tourist sites/sights are individually and collectively constructed, interpreted and experienced. From an industry viewpoint, the concept of gaze is a useful reminder that tourism is first and foremost a form of visual consumption: the desire to have 'a room with a view' is not just a whim but a key element of the tourist experience.

Urry, John, *The Tourist Gaze* (London: Sage, 1990).

Gender

In tourism, the words 'gender' and 'sex' tend to be used interchangeably, although sociologically they have different meanings (sex referring to the biological difference male/female, whilst gender is rather a social construct referring to roles and identity best expressed in terms of masculine/feminine). From an academic viewpoint, gender in tourism management has been studied by focusing on a range of issues, especially:

- the **tourist experience** of female travellers (either alone or in groups);
- the genderisation of some parts of the tourism **industry** (for example, cabin crew or hotel cleaners);
- the changes in gender roles in developing countries because of new employment opportunities in tourism;
- **market segmentation**: differences in **consumption** between genders (for example, souvenir-purchase behaviour of women tourists);
- the representations of gender in the professional tourism **literature**.

'Gender in Tourism', *Annals of Tourism Research*, 22(2) (1995), special issue.
Kinnaird, Vivian and Hall, Derek (eds), *Tourism: A Gender Analysis* (Chichester: Wiley, 1994).

Geographic Information Systems (GIS)

Geographic Information Systems (GIS) are relational databases capable of manipulating both spatial data (in the form of digital maps) and

G

attribute data (comprising datasets that provide precise information). The spatial data is largely derived from existing or historical map coordinates stored in computer files, whilst the attribute data files are made up of detailed records of any feature or item found on these maps with the items being geo-referenced at their coordinates. The significant value of GIS technology is its ability to provide desktop mapping through the graphical display and manipulation of data, in order to identify **patterns** or relationships based on a particular criterion. In a tourism management context, GIS may be used by **tour operators** or for **planning** purposes; for example a GIS file might show all roads represented by lines, which hotels and attractions represented as distinct symbols, with can help assess proximities for itineraries or priorities in terms of **sustainable development**. It is commonly recognised that tourism is not using all the potential provided by GIS technology, especially the refined modelling and simulation tools it offers.

> Tomlinson, Roger, *Thinking about GIS: Geographic Information System Planning for Managers* (London: Transatlantic Publishers, 2005).

Global Distribution Systems (GDS)

Global Distribution Systems (GDS) marked the advancement of the previous generation of Computer Reservations Systems (CRS). CRS were limited in their usage as they could only display information pertaining to one airline. As consumer needs became more sophisticated, airlines and travel agents realised there was a need for a more holistic booking system which would allow not just one airline's data to be displayed, but all airlines operating on a chosen route. GDS allows travel agents to gain instant access to all airline times and booking information, as well as additional information and booking facilities for a range of other travel-related products including hotels, car hire, theatres and sightseeing.

The first systems to incorporate such information appeared in the latter part of the 1970s (Sabre, Apollo and PARS). In 1987 two systems were established by various European airlines, namely Galileo (including British Airways) and Amadeus (whose backers included Air France and Lufthansa). In 1990 TWA and Delta joined forces with a number of other carriers to create Worldspan (which incorporated PARS and DATAS).

The 1990s saw two factors affecting the role of GDS. Firstly, by the mid-1990s airlines had started offering passengers the chance to book directly via their own websites and thus reduce commission costs payable to GDS. Secondly, the ownership of the GDS moved away from the airline sector and is at present controlled by multinational travel companies. The future of GDS is further under threat as airlines have started to establish links with Global New Entrants (GNE). These operate along the same lines as GDS, but at a fraction of the cost, based on their lower operating costs and the use of the very latest technology.

Doganis, Rigas, *The Airline Business in the 21st Century* (London: Routledge, 2001).
Hanlon, Pat, *Global Airlines: Competition in a Transnational Industry*, 3rd edn (Oxford: Butterworth-Heinemann, 2006).

Global inequality in tourism

This concept refers to the imbalance of **international tourism** flows on a global scale. In 1950, 92 per cent of international tourism was in MDCs (more developed countries); in 2000, it was just above 70 per cent. International tourism is still predominantly located in the developed world, but that market share is decreasing as LDCs (less developed countries) have emerged as destinations for several reasons, especially:

- the emergence of a **pleasure periphery** (hardly affected by **seasonality**);
- the economic growth of some LDCs (which provide new markets for other LDCs destinations: it is the image of the Kenyan tourist in Tanzania);
- the development of new tourism products in LDCs, attracting more tourists from both MDCs and LDCs.

Although many LDC governments had initially sought tourism as a tool of economic development in a proactive way, from the mid-1970s onwards one could observe some changes of attitude, mainly because some of the expected promise was not fulfilled.

Boniface, Brian and Cooper, Chris, *Worldwide Destinations: The Geography of Travel and Tourism*, 4th edn (Oxford: Butterworth-Heinemann, 2004).
Boniface, Brian, and Cooper, Chris, *Worldwide Destination Casebook: The Geography of Travel and Tourism* (Oxford: Butterworth-Heinemann, 2005).

G

Globalisation

The term 'globalisation' refers to a range of changes that have been taking place worldwide over the last two decades. Although it is not possible to pinpoint a particular date, globalisation is often said to have started in the 1980s. These changes are of several kinds, especially economic changes and socio-cultural changes. Globalisation has been described in several ways: from a financial angle, globalisation is about the growing economic interdependence of countries, but a simple image, particularly relevant for tourism, is that of a shrinking of time and space. Globalisation means that national markets are being replaced by international investment and sales. This phenomenon has in some respects been driven by the service industry as brands have looked to expand out of their traditional home territories. For example, Holiday Inn is now represented in over 100 countries. The globalisation of certain travel and tourism products has, however, been limited due to government regulations. As an example, the Virgin Group has for a long time wanted to set up an American offshoot but due to ownership rules (US airlines need to be majority-controlled by US citizens) this has become possible only with Richard Branson taking a minor stake in Virgin USA.

The conceptual relationship of globalisation and tourism is double-sided:

- On the one hand, globalisation contributes to tourism, as it is increasingly easier for international tourists to travel, to find brands they recognise and to communicate in English (the language of globalisation).
- On the other hand, tourism contributes to globalisation, as the flows of millions of tourists make the world a smaller place, a 'global village', with the development of a global, mainly Americanised, tourism culture.

MacLeod, Donald V. L., *Tourism, Globalisation and Cultural Change: An Island Community Perspective* (Clevedon: Channel View, 2004).
Wahab, Salah and Cooper, Chris (eds), *Tourism in the Age of Globalisation* (London: Routledge, 2001).

Government

Governments are not just instruments of power or control: through policies and strategies, they can facilitate the development of certain sectors of the economy, including tourism. Within most developed and developing countries, the importance and potential benefits of tourism has led local and national governments to play an active role in the management and financing of tourism projects, as well as the regulation of the services offered by tourism providers. Analytically, it is useful to distinguish between the role of national government and that of local government. (Regional governments tend to have a more limited role, except through regional **tourist boards**.)

- *National governments*: at national level, their responsibilities include the formulation of plans and policy pertaining to the development of tourism within the national context. The financing of tourism projects may indirectly be one of the responsibilities of governments, especially through **infrastructure** (airport, roads) whose cost is very high, and their benefits go far beyond tourism. Historically, the United Kingdom has been led by governments who believe that tourism as an industry is better understood and therefore better managed by the private sector; the national governments have consequently supported a liberal, free market approach to drive development. This explains why major development projects (such as the building of Terminal Five at London Heathrow and the new Wembley Stadium) are constructed using private finance, with the government's role being mainly that of leading the planning process. The government at national level not only strategically affects the tourism sector, but also polices it in order to protect tourists as consumers. In the United Kingdom, the Office of Fair Trading is the government agency responsible for ensuring that companies act in the best interest of the consumer and do not collude against or deceive them.

- *Local governments* (also called local authorities): the role of locally elected governments often mirrors that of national governments, on a smaller scale, in that they are involved in the planning and production of strategies for local tourism projects. The main efforts of local governments are, however, best seen through their promotion of tourism within their area, including the construction and staffing of tourist information centres and their promotion of special events and council-controlled attractions within their area.

Elliott, James, *Tourism: Politics and Public Sector Management* (London: Routledge, 1997).
Jeffries, David, *Governments and Tourism* (Oxford: Butterworth Heinemann, 2001).

UK Office of Fair Trading, www.oft.gov.uk

Grand Tour

G

The term 'Grand Tour' (which is the origin of the two contemporary words 'tourist' and 'tourism') describes the travels undertaken by most young men from the upper classes of the United Kingdom, from the seventeenth to the nineteenth centuries. These literate young men (who did not need to earn a living and were from the aristocracy and, increasingly, from the upper bourgeoisie) travelled to continental Europe (especially France, Greece and Italy) for educational and cultural purposes. Their aim was to become 'educated and civilised' by exposure to European art, manners and society. Anthropologically, these journeys, constituting a 'rite of passage', typically lasted two or three years. The wealthier 'Grand Tourists' were accompanied by a retinue of private tutors, guides and servants. The first destination was usually Paris, followed by Italian cities such as Milan, Florence, Rome, Venice and Naples. The itinerary sometimes included Greece, as well as the Alps and the German-speaking states on the way back. Towner (1996) suggests that around 20,000 members of the British leisure classes were abroad at any one time in the eighteenth century. Besides the educational agenda and the sightseeing opportunities, the Grand Tour was also important for networking, socialising and partying amongst affluent young men (very few women took part), before going back to settle down in England.

The Grand Tour has had two types of impact:

- Socio-cultural impacts for the United Kingdom: cosmopolitanism and enlightenment, as these travellers from the elite and the ruling classes brought continental ideas and values back with them, as well as newly acquired qualities such as self-reliance and self-confidence.
- Economic impacts for the destinations: the beginning of a tourism industry, with the emergence of specialised services such as souvenir trade and guiding.

Together with early travel to spas such as Vichy in France and to coastal resorts such as Brighton and Scarborough in England, the Grand Tour represents the beginnings of tourism as we know it today, and is the precursor of **cultural tourism** with **wanderlust** motivations.

Towner, John, *An Historical Geography of Recreation and Tourism in the Western World, 1540–1940* (Chichester: John Wiley, 1996).

G

Hh

Hard tourism

In the phrase 'hard tourism', the adjective 'hard' refers both to the hard **infrastructure** needed to develop a resort or destination, and to the heavy impacts of **tourism development** on the environment. Hard tourism is associated with **mass tourism**, with psychocentric tourists and with images of high-rise hotels offering the same **identikit tourist experience**. The opposite is soft tourism (a translation of the German concept 'sanfter Tourismus'), referring to forms of tourism that have a low impact on the environment, and consequently overlapping the concepts of **alternative tourism**, **responsible tourism** and **sustainable tourism**. Hard tourism and soft tourism constitute the two opposite poles of a Manichean approach to tourism development; it is important to appreciate that the reality is not always black and white and that a continuum is often a better approach, appreciating nuances and stages.

Health tourism

Historically, travelling for health-related reasons was one of the main **motivations** for travellers whose journeys were fraught with dangers. In Ancient Greece, the sanctuaries and healing temples of Asclepius (the demi-god of medicine and healing) drew thousands of people who stayed overnight in purpose-built dormitories. Four centuries later, the Romans discovered and popularised the healing powers of mineral spring spas across their Empire (the aptly named town of Bath in England is a perfect illustration: it developed substantially during the Roman occupation, with the building of numerous grand temples and bathing complexes). Those health tourists were also motivated by religious beliefs though, and it is not possible to fully dissociate the health dimension from the religious ones; in many respects, this early health tourism was a form of **pilgrimage**. Spa tourism (with the use of hot water for therapeutic purposes) has continued through the centuries: in England, it has contributed to the development of places such as Buxton, Harrogate and Tunbridge Wells, and in continental Europe to hundreds of spa towns such as Vichy (France) and Karlstad (Czech Republic). More recently, new forms of health tourism have developed: travelling abroad in order to obtain medical, dental or surgical care. The main motivations are reduced costs of heath care, no waiting time and convalescence in a pleasant environment. The few widely reported cases of Britons going to France for a hip replacement or Americans crossing the border to Mexico for cosmetic surgery are only the tip of the iceberg; medical tourism is a rapidly growing industry in some countries which explicitly promote it, for example Brazil, Hungary or South Africa. Evidence of market **demand** is proved by the availability of American books and tour guides listing and assessing opportunities for medical surgery abroad.

Hedonism

From the Greek word *hedone* (pleasure), hedonism is a philosophical doctrine that considers the pursuit of pleasure as the most important thing in life. Tourism and hedonism are intrinsically linked. All tourists anticipate pleasure, yet each tourist will seek pleasure in a different way: it can be the pleasure of lying down on a beach doing nothing, the pleasure of going white-water rafting or the pleasure of hiking for days in the Andes carrying a heavy rucksack. Psychologically, one may note that pleasure may result directly from the **liminal** space in which tourists find themselves: part of their gratification may well come from activities that would be forbidden or sanctioned at home (for example with regard to drug-taking, indulging in food or alcohol, or sex with strangers). Hedonism is also used as a euphemistic marketing phrase for holidays in naturist resorts and promises of sensual encounters. In a negative sense, the term is used to refer to behavioural excesses or to the view of the tourist as a child who wants only instant physical gratification.

Heritage

Heritage may be simply defined as the legacy from previous generations. In tourism studies, one usually distinguishes between cultural heritage (for example monuments and buildings of historical importance) and natural heritage (for example sites of outstanding beauty). The 1972 **UNESCO** World Heritage Convention provides a simple yet useful definitional framework:

Cultural heritage is composed of:

- Monuments: architectural works, works of monumental sculpture and painting, elements or structures of an archaeological nature, inscriptions, cave dwellings and combinations of features, which are of outstanding universal value from the point of view of history, art or science.

- Groups of buildings: groups of separate or connected buildings which, because of their architecture, their homogeneity or their place in the landscape, are of outstanding universal value from the point of view of history, art or science.
- Sites: works of man or the combined works of nature and man, and areas including archaeological sites which are of outstanding universal value from the historical, aesthetic, ethnological or anthropological point of view.

Natural heritage is composed of:

- Natural features consisting of physical and biological formations or groups of such formations, which are of outstanding universal value from the aesthetic or scientific point of view.
- Geological and physiographical formations and precisely delineated areas which constitute the habitat of threatened species of animals and plants of outstanding universal value from the point of view of science or conservation.
- Natural sites or precisely delineated natural areas of outstanding universal value from the point of view of science, conservation or natural beauty.

These simple definitions are a basis for the UNESCO Heritage sites (in 2006, the list included 644 cultural, 162 natural and 24 mixed properties). Because of their use by the United Nations agency, they have a semi-authoritative status, although heritage scholars may provide more precise, alternative definitions.

UNESCO, *Convention Concerning the Protection of the World Cultural and Natural Heritage* (Paris: UNESCO Publishing, 1972).

UNESCO World Heritage Centre, whc.unesco.org

Heritage tourism

Heritage tourism (sometimes called historical tourism) may be defined as a form of **cultural tourism** with a particular focus on cultural **heritage**. It fulfils travellers' interest in history and historical attractions such as monuments and sites of important past events, as well as in traditions and their various expressions through the arts or popular lifestyles. Responding to **nostalgia** as a **motivation** for many tourists, heritage tourism has become more popular over the last decades, which has led to some criticism of exploitation and over-commercialisation. Heritage tourism may have a very personal significance for travellers who are seeking their family roots, for example in the case of second- or third-generation migrants keen to discover the original culture of their parents and ancestors. **Interpretation** plays an important role in heritage tourism; this may be sensitive political territory, especially in the case of what has been called **dissonant heritage**. As heritage tourism, heritage studies and the heritage industry have become more important, so has the literature on the topic, in **journals** (such as the *International Journal of Heritage Studies*) as well as many books and websites.

> Kirshenblatt-Gimblett, Barbara, *Destination Culture: Tourism, Museums and Heritage* (Berkeley: University of California Press, 1998).
>
> Orbasli, Aylin, *Tourists in Historic Towns: Urban Conservation and Heritage* (New York: Spon, 2000).

Heteronormativity

Heteronormativity refers to the way heterosexuality is usually presented and represented as the social norm, ignoring the existence of other forms of sexualities, and consequently excluding parts of the population. In tourism, it is true that non-mainstream forms of sexualities have long been overlooked, with travel brochures customarily depicting hetero-sexual couples, and hotels offering two single beds to same-sex couples or even turning them away. In the United Kingdom, the 2006 Equality Act now makes it illegal for service providers to discriminate against gay and lesbian people, so the institutionalised homophobia of some parts of the tourism industry will gradually be forced to change. The develop-ment of an openly gay and gay-friendly tourism industry (travel agents, tour operators, hotels, etc.) has contributed to the visibility of gay and lesbian tourism and can be interpreted as a reaction against heteronor-mativity. Cognate concepts are heterosexism (as a form of racism against non-heterosexual people) and heterocentrism (the assumption that everyone is heterosexual).

Holiday

Although etymologically the word 'holiday' has a religious origin (a holy day being a day of worship or religious observance), the modern concept is best understood in a secular way, when contrasted to (paid) work. Holiday has several related meanings: a public holiday (bank holiday, legal holiday) is endorsed by the state, whilst 'to go on holiday' often

H

implies travelling. If for many people (paid) holidays enable tourism, the two concepts need to remain conceptually differentiated: pensioners can be tourists (and **senior tourism** has little pattern of **seasonality**), as can the unemployed, or people on a sabbatical, gap-year or career break. Many forms of tourism (such as **mass tourism**, **3S** tours, **package tours**, winter sports tourism, short-breaks on long weekends) are closely associated with holidays, which stresses their importance for the tourism industry, especially for the purposes of long-term **planning** and **yield management**.

Baby, George, *Holidays: Holiday Attachment and Customer Loyalty in Tourism* (Delhi: Abhijeet Publications, 2005).

Holiday camp

Holiday camps have strongly marked the history of British tourism. In their heyday (the decades just before and after the Second World War) they offered a form of highly structured residential holiday experience in self-contained resorts for groups, including whole families. A first generation of camps existed at the very start of the twentieth century, yet the success of the formula substantially grew after the set-up of a second generation of camps from the mid-1930s onwards. The name of the entrepreneur Sir William ('Billy') Butlin (1899–1980) is closely associated with those camps because the Butlins Holidays Camps have come to emblematise holiday camps. Particularly emphasising collective **entertainment**, camps were popular (especially amongst working-class families) until the 1960s when **mass tourism** and its overseas packages proved too much competition. Having reached the peak of their life-cycle, holiday camps have gradually reinvented themselves, taking into account contemporary customers' needs and expectations, for example they now offer a higher and wider range of accommodation standards with more modern amenities, from landscaped gardens to room service via cocktail bars. In the summer of 2006, Butlins also launched a time-share apartment scheme, which illustrates their new strategy of loyalty and adoption of modern business management practices. The 1980s sitcom *Hi-De-Hi* (based on the hapless going-ons at a Maplins Holiday Camp whose Yellowcoats staff were obviously inspired by the Butlins Redcoats) has made holiday camps well known even to non-campers, although it has depicted an already outdated image.

Related to holiday camps are holiday villages such as Center Parcs, with their mix of outdoor and indoor activities. The first Center Parc in the UK opened in 1987 at Sherwood Forest. Holiday camps are a particularly British phenomenon, although other countries have equivalents

H

especially for children and young people: 'colonies de vacances' in France and summer camps in America.

Ward, Colin and Hardy, Dennis, *Goodnight Campers! The History of the British Holiday Camp* (London: Mansell, 1986).

Horizontal integration

Horizontal integration is the process of joining together companies at the same stage/level of the production process. In tourism, an example of horizontal integration is the purchase in 2003 of P&O Cruises by Carnival Cruise Line. Horizontal integration offers organisations the advantage of growing rapidly, compared to growth experienced organically. The combined size of the companies will result in increased market presence, and therefore a greater share of the total market. Put another way, horizontal integration is about reducing competition, which is why it raises issues, as most governments and supranational bodies like the EU have competition regulations and restrictions through policies as well as legislation (such as Article 81 and 82 of the EU Competition Law). Competition authorities may wish to consider if the merger/acquisition is in the best interest of the public as well as how it may affect the survival of other firms in the sector. Horizontal integration also creates synergies in the form of greater economies of scale, with the combined group having greater buying and negotiation power. By horizontally integrating, companies are also able to buy experience, for example, First Choice Holidays' acquisition of Trek America allowed it to enter the youth travel market, a market that it had not much knowledge of beforehand. Horizontal integration can be done through **mergers and acquisitions**.

Hospitality

The concept of hospitality refers to the provision of food and beverage, licensed drinking as well as accommodation services in all types of destinations as well as resorts, casinos and clubs. It is usually broken down into two branches: **accommodation** and **catering**. Both are important contributors to local economies, especially with regard to employment, and both are key elements of tourism, even if accommodation requires more **investment**. Whether or not they work in the hospitality sector, tourism managers need some understanding of the key contemporary issues affecting the hospitality sector, such as concentration in the hotel sector and segmentation in the restaurant sector. The development of **theme parks** has led to interesting developments in the hospitality industry, as many theme parks have their own themed hotels.

Hayes, David K. and Ninemeier, Hack D., *Hotel Operations Management*, 2nd edn (London: Prentice-Hall, 2003).

Mill, Robert Christie, *Restaurant Management: Customers, Operations, and Employees* (London: Prentice-Hall, 2001).

Hosts and guests

The title of a pioneering book published in 1977, 'hosts and guests' has become a common phrase in tourism studies to refer to the interactions taking place between tourists and locals. The words 'host' and 'guest' do not have their usual meaning in that phrase as in daily parlance: hosts receive and entertain in their own home, whilst guests are explicitly invited and receive free hospitality. In tourism settings, the relationship between the so-called hosts and guests is particularly complex for three reasons:

- Firstly, it is a commercial relationship, even when **professionalism** makes service provision and delivery seem most friendly.
- Secondly, it can involve hostility or misunderstanding from both parts: when tourists, because of their **ethnocentrism**, fail to understand locals' culture and tradition, or when locals get irritated by tourists' behaviour.
- Thirdly, 'guests' are not necessarily invited, despite their desire to get into the **backstage**, and 'hosts' do not necessarily want to welcome visitors in their community.

Many scholars work on research projects about the interactions between hosts and guests in order to better understand their dynamics and also to articulate strategies to optimise them.

Smith, Valene L., *Hosts and Guests: The Anthropology of Tourism* (Philadelphia: University of Pennsylvania Press, 1977).

Hub and spoke system

Utilised by airlines primarily in the United States, the hub and spoke system is an efficient way of linking countless city pairs together. The model comes from the analogy with a bicycle wheel with its many spokes jutting outward from a central hub. Hub airports tend to work in wave patterns: aircrafts arrive from smaller regional airports into the hub airport; passengers and their luggage are then transferred on to larger aircrafts to fly them to another large airport, which in turn may also operate as a hub. From there, passengers can either finish their journey or may transfer yet again to another flight to complete their trip. There tend to be two main waves per day, associated with the peak periods of early morning and evening.

The main hub airports in the United States are usually controlled by one dominant airline, for example Atlanta by Delta Airlines or Dallas Fort Worth which has most of its operations based around the work of American Airlines. Without using the concept itself, it is actually the same system that underpins many of the world's largest intercontinental hubs, for example London Heathrow where British Airways passengers can transfer between flights, following a network of regional, **short haul** and **long haul** flights. Passengers themselves benefit from it, although many would sometimes prefer direct flights. Aircraft manufacturers and airlines are aware of that concern, which has prompted Boeing to design the Boeing 787 Dreamliner, allows airlines to fly routes which in the past would have been profitable only if flown through a hub. The B787, as a hub bypasser, can be contrasted to the new Airbus A380: once commercialised, the A380-800, the largest passenger airliner in the world, will further contribute to turning some major international airports into hubs, so it can be conceptualised as the hub aircraft *par excellence*.

Human resources management (HRM)

The phrase 'human resources' refers to the staff employed in an organisation. Put simply, human resources management (HRM) is the business function associated with hiring, firing and training staff. In the tourism industry, larger businesses (such as international chains) will have managers or departments specifically responsible for HRM (which used to be called 'personnel'), but in the majority of cases (such as an independent travel agency or a youth hostel) HRM will be the responsibility of a person who also has other roles. HRM is not just a business practice though: it is also a **multidisciplinary** field of study that builds upon psychology (especially its specialised fields of industrial psychology and organisational psychology), sociology (especially industrial sociology) as well as the law. Legal issues are very important with regard to managing staff, and managers need to be aware of their rights and duties (such as the welfare-related 'duty of care' in UK **legislation**). All generic concepts and issues of HRM apply to the tourism industry; current HRM debates (for example about the rhetorics of empowerment or the exploitation of staff in some areas) are also relevant for the tourism industry.

Baum, Tony, *Human Resource Issues in International Tourism* (Oxford: Butterworth-Heinemann, 1993).

D'Annunzio-Green, Norma, Maxwell, Gillian A. and Watson, Sandra (eds), *Human Resource Management in International Hospitality and Tourism: An International Perspective*, 3rd edn (Cassell: London, 2005).

Identikit

Identikits are used by the police to build up the picture of a person by combining a given number of facial features. By analogy, identikit holidays are packaged holidays (typically in **3S** destinations) that travellers can partly customise within certain parameters set by the **tour operator** (for example half board or full board). The phrases 'identikit destinations' and 'identikit hotels' may also be encountered in both academic and journalistic texts, usually used in a derogatory way. Conceptually, identikit is the opposite of an individualised, independent experience, which leads to a dialectical discussion of the role of the individual and the group in tourism: on the one hand, tourism is a subjective, personalised event; on the other hand, it presupposes the provision of standardised products and services.

Berger, Arthur Asa, *Deconstructing Travel: Cultural Perspectives on Tourism* (Walnut Creek, CA: Altamira, 2004).

Image of a destination

The image of a destination refers to the mental attitudes, perception and beliefs that people hold about it. It is a simplified yet powerful version of what they assume the reality to be like. Rarely are images only descriptive: they tend to be evaluative, carrying either a positive or a negative judgement that will directly influence the **decision-making** process when choosing a destination. These ideas might be justified or not, as numerous factors contribute to the image of a destination, including hear-say, preconceived ideas and misconceptions, impressions formed through experience of cognate places, and lack of factual knowledge. The concept of image is very important for tourism marketers in order to properly target potential customers, or to plan and implement campaigns aimed at modifying the image of a destination (for example resorts going through a **rejuvenation stage**). This marketing exercise may involve **branding** or rebranding the destination, for example as part of a wider strategy to minimise demand fluctuations due to **seasonality**.

Impacts of tourism

The very frequently used phrase 'impacts of tourism' refers to the consequence of tourism on destinations. The study of the impacts of tourism is
probably the most developed subfield of tourism management as an academic discipline, with thousands of examples and critical analyses in books
and **journals**, usually in the form of **case studies**. The impacts of tourism
may be positive or negative; they fall in three categories: economic
impacts, socio-cultural impacts and environmental impacts. Overall, the
economic impact tends to be positive (hence the view of tourism as a tool
of economic development) whilst the socio-cultural and environmental
impacts tend to be negative. Tourism impacts are often summarised in a
table reminiscent of a **cost benefit analysis** (see Table 2).

The difficulties associated with the study of the impacts of tourism
include:

- difficulty of measuring the impacts precisely, even the economic
  impacts, although some new tools such as **Tourism Satellite
  Accounts** can help;
- difficulty of comparing and prioritising impacts (for example, are
  some negative impacts worse than others?);
- difficulty in not overstating nor oversimplifying impacts;
- difficulties of using research findings for practical purposes such as
  tourism development policies.

Table 2   Examples of impacts of tourism

	Examples of positive impacts (benefits)	Examples of negative impacts (costs)
Economic impacts	Job creation and employment	Dependence on tourism revenue as a source of income
Socio-cultural impacts	Promotion of cross-cultural understanding	**Commodification** **Displacement**
Environmental impacts	Incentive to preserve the environment	Destruction of fauna and flora as a result of tourists' activities

Incentive tourism

Incentive tourism is based on the notion of an individual being motivated to achieve a particular goal because, as a reward, they will receive

a free holiday. The type of holidays offered through incentive schemes tend to be short but luxurious in nature. Although often viewed as a very American way of motivating staff, incentive schemes are becoming more popular in Europe. A classic incentive package could be a short break to a European city where the employee is allowed to take their partner or in certain cases their family (a trip to Disneyland Resort Paris is a typical example). The use of such city breaks is a popular method for companies to reward their staff, for instance with trips to Paris or Brussels for the weekend with Eurostar. **Familiarisation trips** are also an example of incentive tourism. Rewards may not be offered only to individual staff members: certain companies or departments take groups of staff away, for instance to develop team building or to work as a group on a business project in a different environment: the rationale is that the social atmosphere (**communitas**) may be particularly conducive to creative thinking, idea generation and group work.

Society of Incentive & Travel Executives, www.site-intl.org

Indirect income

Also called indirect revenue, the concept of indirect income aims to assess the overall contribution of tourism expenditure to an economy (locally, regionally or nationally). It builds upon the **direct income** but also takes into account knock-on impacts, hence the use of a **multiplier effect** rate. Specialists sometimes distinguish between 'indirect impacts' (monies spent by tourism businesses to get the supplies and resources they need) and 'induced impacts' (circulation through tourism staff spending their earnings); all these flows of money are indirectly linked to tourism, a key argument for advocates of tourism development. Destinations need to be careful as to how reliant they become on tourism though; its seasonal nature results in low levels of expenditure at certain times of the year, and the problem of economic downturns in generating regions as well as destinations going out of fashion all affect the income entering an economy.

Weaver, David and Lawton, Laura, *Tourism Management*, 3rd edn (Brisbane: John Wiley, 2005).

Industrial tourism

A form of **special interest tourism**, industrial tourism (sometimes called factory tourism) is about visits to industrial sites such as food-processing factories, wineries, diaries, mining operations, power stations and even nuclear plants, ports operations, timber mills or large-scale building sites. Education and cultural curiosity are key motivations. Industrial tourism may be either incidental or part of a specialised tour: there might be some overlap with **business tourism**, for example in the case of fact-finding missions for a group of professionals whose **itinerary** is principally designed around such visits. Unlike **heritage tourism** which is turned towards the past (for example visiting old canals or disused mine buildings), industrial tourism is interested in sites that are currently busy and operating. For health and safety reasons as well as **interpretation** purposes, visitors are usually escorted by a **tour guide**. Purpose-built centres and viewing galleries are part of the facilities sometimes provided for tourists. Although participants normally pay a small fee, the main benefits for the company are not financial, but rather in terms of **public relations**, publicity and customer relations. Conceptually, it is interesting to observe how the same site (for example a factory or a power station) may then have different meanings for different **stakeholders**, including tourists. This is an illustration of the symbolic power of tourism to turn any place into a possible attraction.

Industry

The term 'tourist industry' emerged in the 1960s, and tourism is now commonly presented as a **service**-based industry. In a stricter sense, it refers to the commercial operators involved in the **supply** side of tourism, the key sectors being:

- **tour operators**
- **travel agencies**
- **attractions**
- **accommodation**
- **catering**
- **transportation**
- other **amenities** and **ancillary services**.

In a broader sense, the tourist industry also includes tourism-related organisations from the **public sector** (such as tourist information centres) and the **voluntary sector** (such as the National Trust in the UK). The phrase 'tourist industry' has been challenged by some authors, who prefer the plural 'tourist industries' or qualify the fact that tourism is only partially industrialised and object to the term 'industry' because of its negative connotations.

Cooper, Chris et al., *Tourism: Principles and Practice*, 3rd edn (London: Prentice Hall, 2005).
Holloway, J. Christopher and Taylor, Neil, *The Business of Tourism*, 7th edn (London: Prentice Hall, 2005).

Infrastructure

Infrastructure is an umbrella term that covers all the structural elements constituting the framework on which different activities can take place: it includes transport platforms (such as roads, railways lines, airports) as well as utility systems (such as water and electricity provision, sewage systems) and telecommunication networks. Infrastructure can be of **dual use**, but in some instances (for example, ski resorts) it is developed primarily for tourists' use. There must be some infrastructure in place for tourism to develop; because of the high costs incurred, infrastructure construction is usually financed by the **public sector** (with very few exceptions such as private ports or airports on resort islands). In developing countries, the cost of infrastructure is sometimes met by loans from the United Nations Development Programme or from the World Bank. The European Union, as part of its overall tourism strategy, is also able to help finance some infrastructural developments. Security systems and related facilities (such as customs/immigration and police at destinations) are sometimes regarded as part of the concept of infrastructure. Two particular issues related to infrastructure are infrastructure maintenance (should the tourism industry, as an essential user, contribute to maintenance costs?) and environmental friendliness (as building infrastructure inevitably affects the natural environment).

Inseparability

One of the four characteristics of **services** (along with **intangibility**, **perishability** and **variability**), inseparability refers to the fact that a service cannot be separated from its provider. Put another way, production and consumption occur at the same time and at the same place: a continental breakfast in a Parisian hotel is 'produced' and 'consumed' at the same time, unlike a frozen pizza. From a tourism business perspective, inseparability has several consequences:

- It makes **quality** control more difficult, as there may not always be an opportunity to implement quality control mechanisms.
- It reinforces the importance of the **professionalism** of the staff involved in service delivery, as their work strongly contributes to the consumer's experience and satisfaction.
- It reinforces the challenges of fluctuation in **demand**, as tourism services cannot be stored for a later use.

Tourism managers and marketers need strategies to pre-empt the possible shortcomings due to inseparability, for example through training and staff development policies.

Intangibility

From a **marketing** viewpoint, intangibility refers to the fact that tourism, as a **service**, cannot be seen and tested before purchase and consumption (intangibility is occasionally called 'invisibility'). When choosing a holiday and comparing alternatives, tourists have to make their decision on the basis of limited evidence, such as subjective documents (promotional material like brochures, travel guides or websites), word-of-mouth (recommendation by travel agents or previous visitors) or their own judgement (possibly formed through experience). The intrinsic intangibility of tourism can be partly reduced in several ways, for example:

- through tangible representations such as photographs meant to make the promise visible and to whet the tourist **gaze**;
- through **benchmarking**, with the subsequent expectation of certain standards;
- through brand image and the development of **loyalty** and trust towards a certain tourism provider.

The concept of intangibility may also be applied to the **tourist experience** as a whole because it has no physical substance: even the tangible elements (a meal in a restaurant, a hotel bedroom, the sand on the beach) have a measure of intangibility because they are experienced rather than possessed.

International agreements on tourism

Over the last 30 years, a substantial number of international agreements on tourism have been written and signed, all referring to **sustainable development** and the role of tourism in that agenda. The main ones are:

1980 Manila Declaration on World Tourism
1985 Tourism Bill of Rights and Tourist Code
1989 Hague Declaration on Tourism
1990 Action Strategy for Sustainable Development
1992 **Agenda 21 (Rio Summit)**
1995 Charter for Sustainable Tourism
1996 Agenda 21 for the Tourism and Travel Industry
1997 Malé Declaration on Sustainable Tourism Development
1997 Manila Declaration on the Social Impact of Tourism
1997 Berlin Declaration
1999 United Nations Commission on Sustainable Development Decision 7/3
1999 Global Code of Ethics for Tourism

2002 European Charter for Sustainable Tourism in Protected Areas
2002 Québec Declaration on Ecotourism
2003 Djerba Declaration on Tourism and Climate Change
2005 Muscat Declaration on Built Environment for Sustainable Tourism

These official documents can all be found online through websites such as the World Tourism Organization or the United Nations Environment Programme. The proliferation of so many declarations about issues pertaining to sustainable development in tourism is a good thing, as it shows the commitments of governments and many agencies from both the private and public sector, though one may wonder what impact the many international agreements have in practice, that is how the policies, promises and guidelines are implemented.

United Nations Environment Programme, www.unep.org
World Tourism Organization, www.world-tourism.org

International tourism

International tourism refers to the flows of tourists across national borders, as opposed to **domestic tourism**. The concept of international tourism is broken down into inbound tourism (from the perspective of tourist-receiving countries) and outbound tourism (from the perspective of tourist-generating countries). International tourism is regarded as an export for the visited country and consequently as an import for the country of origin; this might sound paradoxical, but the perspective taken is that of flows of foreign currency. When international tourists travel from developed countries to developing countries, the latter ones earn foreign currency that heavily contributes to their national income. Their **balance of payments** is affected in a positive way, which is why inbound tourism has been used as a tool of economic development by many developing countries. According to the reliable **World Tourism Organization**, in 2004, the top five receiving countries in terms of international tourist arrivals were:

1 France: 75 million
2 Spain: 52.5 million
3 US: 40.4 million
4 Italy: 39.6 million
5 China: 33 million

International tourism has contributed to **globalisation**, both in terms of international understanding and in terms of economic activity (especially with transnational companies like multinational hotel corporations).

Interpretation

Interpretation aims at establishing communication between people who do not share the same linguistic or cultural frames of reference. In tourism, it goes beyond the mere provision of information but seeks to ensure that visitors really understand and appreciate the significance of what they see, be it in a museum, a wildlife centre or a national park. Interpretation is about communication and explanation, but it has two other more practical objectives: firstly, to enhance the visitor experience; secondly, to assist in the **conservation** of natural or cultural **resources**. Concretely, interpretation is carried out not only through guided tours and educational presentations, but also through all material produced for tourists, such as leaflets and guidebooks; even the design of a place (for example a museum) may in itself be a form of interpretation. Interpretation should arguably always be underpinned by concerns for **sustainable development**.

Interpretation is not an easy activity though, and conceptually it is fraught with difficult questions, such as how entertaining it should be, and who should be responsible for the interpretation of sensitive, contested, **dissonant heritage** or events such as war?

Beck, Larry and Cable, Ted T., *Interpretation for the 21st Century: Fifteen Guiding Principles for Interpreting Nature and Culture*, 2nd edn (Champaign, IL: Sagamore, 2002).

Knudson, Douglas M., Beck, Larry, and Cable, Ted T., *Interpretation of Cultural and Natural Resources*, 2nd edn (State College, PA: Venture Publishing, 2003).

Investment

Investment relates to the placing of finance into tourism products or properties with the aim of achieving either economic goals or social ones. Tourism investment from the **public sector** usually looks at creating the **infrastructure** needed to develop tourism. In developed countries, the involvement of the public sector within tourism can be seen as a way of helping communities diversify away from traditional failing industries, which is why it can have a social dimension. For instance, the Welsh Development Agency and the European Union have given considerable sums of money to help create **attractions** in Wales where there were once thriving coal mines. The use of public sector money to boost tourism infrastructure and enterprises should not however be seen outside the contexts of other regional development priorities such as education and health, as this can lead to further detrimental affects on the local economy (**opportunity costs**). The **private sector** will invest, not for social, but for economic gain. All investment opportunities require the development of a **business plan** to help secure finance for the scheme and create a workable strategy. A related concept is 'return on investment' (ROI), also called 'rate of return' or just 'return', calculated in finance through mathematical models in order to compare the money earned through the investment to the amount of money invested.

Involvement stage

The involvement stage of the **Butler Sequence** is the second stage in the destination lifecycle, following **exploration**; tourism starts to develop; the main characteristics of the involvement stage are:

- Number of visitors begins to steadily increase.
- The first tourist infrastructure and commercial services (for example for accommodation and catering) are created by local entrepreneurs: this is the foundation of a local tourism industry.
- Local authorities show interest in tourism because of its benefits (through **infrastructure** and development opportunities).
- In order to cope with visitors' curiosity, locals start to unconsciously demarcate **backstage and frontstage** areas.
- As visitor numbers increase at a stable rate, allocentric visitors may be joined by highly inquisitive midcentrics.
- Environmental stress due to tourism is still low, yet increasing.

Involvement is a process; once triggered, it just continues to grow unless some restrictions are imposed (like in Bhutan); commonly cited examples of the involvement stage are the Central Asian republics, some parts of rural China as well as not yet industrialised parts of the world where many eco-tourists like to go (for example the Galapagos, parts of Alaska and Central America).

Irridex

The irridex ('irritation index') is a model designed in 1976 by George Doxey. It proposes that, as tourism increases in a destination, locals' attitudes towards tourists evolve through successive stages:

- euphoria (visitors are welcome);
- apathy (relationships become commercialised, visitors are taken for granted);

- irritation (or annoyance) resulting from deterioration of relationships.
- antagonism (as the local **carrying capacity** has been exceeded).
- resignation (as local residents realise that they need to adapt to a new situation; many then may decide to leave and move elsewhere).

Simple if not simplistic, this model has been partly confirmed by empirical research, and some tools (such as tourist–host ratios) have helped define thresholds; it has some flaws though, such as the fact that it considers the resident population as a homogeneous entity.

Itinerary

An itinerary is a schedule/timetable produced in association with a **package tour**. For example, a coach tour is normally broken down into a day-by-day format which tells holidaymakers precisely where they will be on a specific day, with detailed information such as departure times, when they will eat and what sites can be found at destinations. The type of itinerary offered can act as a key **marketing** asset for some operators such as cruise companies: in their adverts and promotional documents, very often cruise companies emphasise not the quality of the ships, but the itinerary itself. Put another way, the itinerary is not just a piece of information, but a selling point aimed at convincing potential customers. Itineraries are also produced for travellers booking flights; it then includes departure time, airport, terminal details, flight number, baggage limits, seat allocation and minimum check-in time, yet without any marketing dimension.

Joint venture

A joint venture occurs where two organisations come together and share the costs of setting up a new venture. The use of joint ventures is common in some sectors of the tourism **industry**, especially airlines and cruise companies (see **airline alliances**, **cruising**). It allows operators to gain experience in areas where they have limited expertise, or to bypass regulations that may otherwise have stopped the development of services/routes. Joint ventures normally have a new name, for example the combination of First Choice Holidays with Royal Caribbean Cruises led to the creation of Island Cruises. The advantages First Choice Holidays brought to the venture were unbeatable marketing and sales knowledge of the UK holiday market, whilst Royal Caribbean Cruises brought an unprecedented knowledge of operating cruise ships. Through Island Cruises as a joint venture, both partners formed a symbiotic relationship: First Choice Holidays gained the chance to compete with other tour operators who had already entered this market, such as Thomson Holidays, whilst Royal Caribbean Cruises gained the opportunity to attract passengers from Mediterranean cruises onto one of their more luxurious ships based in the Caribbean. A joint venture is different from **mergers and acquisitions** as the parent companies remain independent: the joint venture is a new, separate legal entity, jointly controlled.

Vermeulen, Erik, *The Evolution of Legal Business Forms in Europe and the United States: Venture Capital, Joint Venture and Partnership Structures* (New York: Kluwer Law International, 2003).

Journals

Also called periodicals (because most of them appear quarterly), refereed journals are very important in academic **literature** because of the articles they publish. All articles go through a rigorous, anonymous peer review procedure, which ensures quality and maintains objectivity, as the authors do not know the identity of the reviewers, neither do the reviewers know the identity of the authors whose papers they assess and comment upon. Articles are at the cutting edge of **research** because this is where scholars present new conceptual constructs they are developing. Besides articles, academic journals also publish book reviews, shorter research notes, case studies, briefings and discussions. Most journals are accessible online, though not all online publications have the quality and objectivity of academic journals, and caution is needed. The most important journals in tourism management in English include:

- *Annals of Tourism Research*
- *Current Issues in Tourism*
- *International Journal of Tourism Research*
- *Journal of Ecotourism*
- *Journal of Hospitality and Tourism Management*
- *Journal of Sport Tourism*
- *Journal of Sustainable Tourism*
- *Journal of Tourism and Cultural Change*
- *Journal of Tourism Studies* (until 2005)
- *Journal of Travel Research*
- *Journal of Travel and Tourism Marketing*
- *Tourism Analysis*
- *Tourism Economics*
- *Tourism Management*

Several journals also exist in other languages, such as the *Revue de Tourisme*. In 2004, there were around 80 journals which had a substantial academic component dedicated to tourism, as for example journals of leisure management or hospitality management may publish articles about tourism activities. This confirms the fact that tourism is now an established **multidisciplinary** area of study.

Jungle tourism

Jungle tourism is a form of **nature-based tourism** defined by the type of environment in which it takes place. Jungle tours have become popular in tropical areas of South America (such as in the Amazon rainforest) and South-East Asia (such as Malaysia and Thailand). Allocentric tourists are attracted by both the hostile environment and the originality of the **tourist experience** it provides. The socio-cultural and environmental impacts of jungle tourism tend to be low and overall positive; from an economic viewpoint, jungle tourism has two advantages: firstly, it can benefit small-scale, local **ecotourism** projects (guided tours by indigenous inhabitants), and secondly, it provides an economic alternative to rainforest destruction. That latter point is particularly important in some areas (South America) but precise comparisons are difficult to draw, especially with regard to opportunity costs. Jungle tourism is usually presented as a viable form of **sustainable tourism**.

L

Landscape

A landscape results from the combination of both natural attributes (topography, hydrology) and cultural factors (human occupation and use may have transformed the natural scenery). The concept of landscape is important in tourism in two ways:

- With regard to **rural tourism** and **nature-based tourism**, all types of landscapes can be tourist attractions (from rolling culti- vated hills covered with sunflowers to arid high mountains).
- With regard to **urban tourism**, urban landscapes (also called 'cityscapes') and skylines (the relief of skyscrapers, towers and similar high structures) have become emblems of some cities (such as New York); such images are often used in promotional material.

Landscapes keep changing; when natural areas are overly transformed by tourism (for example along the Mediterranean coast of eastern Spain), the phrase 'tourism landscape' is sometimes used. Other neologisms exist, such as 'golfscape' and 'winescape'.

Leakage

Leakage is one of the main economic costs of tourism. It refers to the outflow of tourism income from the local economy. It may occur at different stages when money spent by tourists does not fully benefit the economy of the destination – that is, when it does not optimally contribute to the **multiplier effect**. Several factors contribute to leakage:

- the presence of FDIs, the usual abbreviation of foreign direct invest- ments (typical form of leakage: international hotels belonging to foreign chains who repatriate the profits instead of investing locally);
- payment for holidays made in the generating country (through tour operators and travel agents);

- ownerships of transport to the destination (a national airline will benefit the home country more than a foreign one);
- **vertical integration** (because most of tourist spending on transport, accommodation and tour organisation goes to the same foreign-based company);
- lack of local production of goods in demand by tourists or by locals (leading to expensive imports).

Leakage can be measured in a percentage, for example Opperman and Chon (1997) found leakage rates of around 30 per cent in Singapore. Case studies of other destinations (usually in developing countries and small island states) will have different results but as researchers have proposed different methodologies to try to measure leakage, it is not always easy to compare the severity and impact of leakage in different destinations.

Oppermann, Martin and Chon Kye Sung, *Tourism in Developing Countries* (London: Thomson, 1997).

Legislation

The concept of legislation refers both to the process of making laws and to the laws themselves, once promulgated. The tourism industry, as any commercial sector, is heavily regulated: it is affected by legislation at all levels, from local by-laws to national laws as well as international legislation: with regard to the latter, legislation enacted by the European Union has had a dramatic effect on the industry, particularly the 1992 *Package Travel, Package Holidays and Package Tours Regulations* (with regard to the information given to purchasers of package holidays) and the *Denied Boarding Compensation Regulation 261/2004* (forcing airlines to compensate passengers for delays and overbooking of flights). Contract law is one of the fields which has the most relevance for tourism because of all the transactions involved in tourism, even if travellers do not realise that every time they purchase a ticket or a holiday they enter into a contract with a provider. Several textbooks focus on tourism law; tourism managers cannot be expected to be lawyers, but they need some understanding of the key legislation that affects their industry.

Grant, David and Mason, Stephen, *Holiday Law: The Law Relating to Travel and Tourism* (Andover: Sweet & Maxwell, 2003).

Saggerson, Alan, *Travel: Law and Litigation* (St Albans: XPL Publishing, 2004).

Consumer Regulations Website, www.crw.gov.uk

Leisure

Depending upon the context, leisure has two related meanings: it can refer to free time or to the activities taking place in that free time. In the first sense, leisure is the free time a person enjoys outside work (paid employment as well as non-paid work such as family duties, care or housekeeping) and other essential needs (such as sleep and meals). In the second sense, leisure refers to the activities one may do during that free time; these activities are sometimes grouped under the umbrella term of **recreation**.

The leisure industry is the group of providers of activities and opportunities to structure one's leisure, either at home (television, philately, etc.) or outside (sports, concerts, etc.).

The conceptual relationship of leisure and tourism is a complex one: in some cases, tourism is regarded as part of leisure (travelling being one leisure activity amongst others), in other cases leisure is regarded as part of tourism (recreational activities at a holiday destination).

The terms 'leisure studies' and 'leisure sciences' refer to the academic study of leisure, which can be done from several perspectives, such as sports (kinesiology) to social work (with a focus on community leisure) to history (comparing leisure in different societies) and psychology (the human need for leisure).

Leisure management

The concept of leisure management is presented here using the same approach as the concept of **tourism management**; leisure management (or recreation management) refers to both an academic subject and a professional practice.

- As an *academic subject*, leisure management is concerned with the development of management skills and knowledge, as relevant in the leisure industry which, broadly interpreted, may include the arts, tourism, sport, entertainment, play, therapeutic recreation and outdoor recreation.
- As a *professional practice*, tourism management can have two meanings:
  - At a micro-level, it refers to managing leisure operations, that is having managerial responsibilities in the leisure industry (emblematically in a leisure centre).
  - At a macro-level, it refers to the promotion and development of leisure for the well-being and health of the community (with

L

agendas such as work/life balance, volunteering and interventionism).

Robinson, Leigh, *Managing Public Leisure Services*, (London: Routledge, 2003).
Torkildsen, George, *Leisure and Recreation Management*, 5th edn (London: Routledge, 2005).

Institute of Leisure and Amenities Management, www.ilam.co.uk
Leisure Management, www.leisuremanagement.co.uk

Lifestyle

Lifestyle can be simply defined as the way a person or a group lives; as an umbrella term, it may cover a range of behaviours and attitudes (from family interactions to entertainment choices), yet **consumption** and consumption patterns are often regarded as central. A lifestyle is a combination of many sociological and psychological elements, including social class and social position, peer pressure and conformity, sociocultural background, income (especially **discretionary income**) as well as prior experience and personal preferences. Numerous classifications of lifestyles can be found, from 'rural lifestyle' to 'yuppy lifestyle' (young urban professional), from 'digital lifestyle' to 'green lifestyle'. With regard to tourism, lifestyle influences **decision-making**, which is why tourist **market segmentation** may use lifestyle to distinguish between potential groups of customers. The problem with that criterion is the fact that lifestyle, in an age of marked individualism, often loses its collective meaning; this is reflected in the phrase 'market-of-one'.

Thyne, Maree and Laws, Eric (eds), *Hospitality, Tourism, and Lifestyle Concepts: Implications for Quality Management and Customer Satisfaction* (New York: Haworth Press, 2005).

Liminality

In anthropology, liminality refers to the middle stage in a ritual such as a rite of passage: it involves a transition (the word 'liminality' comes from the Latin *limen*, threshold), a change of identity, a breakdown of individual habits, a collective experience (called **communitas**) as well as a regenerative process. The concept has been applied to tourism to characterise the central aspect of holidays taken away from home: because of the distance from a familiar setting and routines, because of the new environment and the overall experience, tourism can be presented as liminal. On that basis, any form of tourism could arguably be interpreted as a secular **pilgrimage** because tourists, consciously or not, go through certain rituals and are different when they return home.

Literature

In tourism management, two types of literature coexist:

- The *academic* literature, with two main types of publications: books and **journals**. Their main audience is composed of tourism scholars (researchers) as well as students, and to a lesser extent some tourism professionals who may be interested in a particular topic (for example **sustainable development**).
- The *professional* literature, either written for people who work in the **industry** (for example the *Travel Trade Gazette* or *TravelMole*) or for tourists themselves (generic or specialised travel guides).

The former literature focuses on theory, the latter on practice, which may explain why there is very little interaction, if any, between the two. Tourism tutors often criticise students' limited engagement with academic literature, whilst tourism employers sometimes deplore graduates' lack of familiarity with the professional literature.

(For travel literature as a literary genre, see **travel writing**.)

Travel Trade Gazette, www.ttglive.com
TravelMole, www.travelmole.com

Logistics

The concept of logistics comes from the military and refers to the primordial need for armies to get their supplies (food, ammunition) on time. Logistics is now commonly associated with **operations management** and **supply chain management**, with an emphasis on transportation. Simply put, it is about getting resources and people where they are needed, which has two particular meanings in the tourism industry: a restricted meaning in the case of passenger transport, and a wider meaning for the industry in general.

It can refer to passenger logistics, that is to all the operations involved in the safe transportation of passengers and their belongings. In a way, **airline & airport management** is all about logistics, with the need to have perfectly running systems to process people and their hold lugagge separately through precise stages (security, immigration, etc.), not to forget all the systems that must run in parallel (fuelling, getting the cabin crew ready and in place, loading the plane with passenger services such as catering and merchandise, etc.). All these coordinated logistical operations are supported by agreements between contractors and complicated rostering systems. They continue until the aircraft has entered airspace, and at the destination logistics need to be in place again as most traditional carriers will expect their aircraft to be turned around in

L

45 minutes to an hour. (**Low cost carriers**, which expect to get more out of their aircraft and to reduce costly time at airports, usually look for a turnaround time of 30 minutes maximum.)

The concept of logistics also applies to the detailed planning necessary for all the organisations and activities of the tourism industry: the logistics of restaurant operations (getting perishable raw materials on time, preparing dishes without delay), the logistics of brochure production (making sure they are flawless and available on time), the logistics of diving expeditions (having all the proper equipment ready on time), etc. The two foci are time management and efficiency in order to ensure the smooth running of all the operations and, ultimately, consumers' satisfaction.

Long haul

Long haul usually refers to flights that last over five hours, although the concept does not have a unique, authoritative definition, and needs to take into account the geographical context and other points of reference. A possible approach (that of the UK Department of Transport for example) is to define long haul as any trip taken outside Europe; that way, even the Concorde flights from London to New York (just over three hours) are counted as long haul (despite their brevity); likewise, a flight from London to Marrakesh lasts under five hours yet it could arguably still be considered as long haul as opposed to **short haul**. To avoid such potential difficulties, the phrase 'medium haul' is increasingly used: London–Paris is considered short haul, London–Montreal medium haul, London–Sydney long haul.

The market for long-haul flights has recently suffered from a bad press, not only because of global concerns such as terrorist attacks which have affected international tourism since the early 2000s, but also because of the media's growing interest in medical conditions associated with longer flights such as deep vein thrombosis (DVT). Nevertheless the long-haul market has shown strong signs of growth, aided by the introduction of a new generation of 'low-cost long-haul' carriers such as Zoom of Canada and Fly Globespan in the UK.

Low cost carriers

Low cost carriers (LCC), also called 'no frills' carriers, are scheduled airlines that are driven by one management objective: cost reduction. Originating as a consequence of **deregulation** within the US and latterly the European Union, LCCs are characterised by:

- bookings made via the internet (telephone booking is possible but incurs a surcharge);
- use of secondary airports;
- ticketless travel;
- no free food or drink service (hence the 'no frill' nickname);
- fast turnaround times;
- aircraft tend to be the latest models for fuel efficiency;
- the use of contract labour rather than in-house personnel for most customer service operations;
- revenue generated from linkages on website to ancillary services (car hire and hotel bookings).

The American Southwest Airlines remains the biggest and most profitable LCC, having achieved an end-of-year profit in each of its operating years. In Western Europe, the dominant LCCs are Ryanair and easyJet, although the market is very dynamic and changes occur fast.

The term 'low fare airlines' is increasingly used instead of 'low cost carrier', as exemplified by the European Low Fare Airlines Association (ELFAA).

Calder, Simon, *No Frills: The Truth behind the Low-Cost Revolution in the Skies* (London: Virgin Books, 2002).

Creaton, Siobhan, *Ryanair: How a Small Irish Airline Conquered Europe* (London: Aurum Press, 2004).

European Low Fare Airlines Association, www.elfaa.com

Loyalty

Loyalty refers to the perception a customer has of a product they have used and their desire to repeat the experience with the same provider. The travel and tourism industry works hard to create a positive perception of their brands, as this often results in repeat patronage. Based on marketing costs and a generic appreciation of **customer relationship management**, it is often said that it is easier to satisfy a client and get them to return than to create a new customer. Business scholars have devised loyalty models to help managers decide which company resources should be used strategically to increase customer loyalty. Travel and tourism companies, aware of the necessity to ensure repeat patronage, have developed schemes to reward loyalty, for example with **frequent flyer programmes (FFPs)**. The development of FFPs has had a dramatic affect on the airline industry, sometimes making customers loyal to one carrier only. However, passengers have also

L

developed their own strategies to counter such marketing schemes by joining a variety of FFPs that cover the three main **airline alliances** and therefore accrue points at a faster rate than if they remained loyal to the one brand only.

Reichheld, Frederick, *The Loyalty Effect: The Hidden Force behind Growth, Profits and Lasting Value* (Boston, MA: Harvard Business School Press, 1996).

Mm

Marginality

Marginality is the state of being on the periphery of something, on the edge, on the border. In tourism, this concept may have two meanings, depending upon the context:

- It may refer to *geographical location*, for example Greenland is marginal as an international tourist destination; in terms of economics, this type of marginality raises issues about dependence and the relationship between **core and periphery**.
- It may refer to the *anthropological situation* of people who are on the margin between two cultures; this is the case of **culture brokers**, of prostitutes and of locals who model their behaviour on tourists (see **demonstration effect**). American sociologist Everett Stonequist popularised the phrase 'marginal man' (coined a few years earlier by his colleague Robert E. Park) through a book precisely entitled *The Marginal Man*.

Ryan, Chris, Page, Stephen J. and Aicken, Michelle (eds), *Taking Tourism to the Limits: Issues, Concepts and Managerial Perspectives* (Oxford: Elsevier, 2005).
Stonequist, Everett, *The Marginal Man: A Study in Personality and Culture Conflict* (New York: Russel & Russel, 1937).

Marketing

Marketing is the business function associated with the process of researching, developing, promoting and selling products; contrary to popular belief, marketing involves much more than advertising. Marketing requires travel and tourism organisations to research and therefore to understand the needs of their potential consumers. Several techniques are used in the tourism industry, both **qualitative research** (for example inviting potential customers to take part in a focus group) and **quantitative research** (for example through surveys to evaluate interests in potential products), although small enterprises are not always able to really carry out much research and tend to rely on managers' knowledge of customers and their needs and wants. As most tourism products are **services**, marketing them is particularly difficult because of their nature (**intangibility**, **inseparability**, **perishability** and **variability**); as a consequence, tourism marketers need to come up with strong long-term strategies and short-term tactics to maximise their companies' operations. **Yield management** is one pricing method that has proved successful in most parts of the tourist industry, especially airlines, although small operators do not always have the skills and knowledge to adopt the marketing approaches that could be most suitable for them. Marketing as a subject of study has developed substantially over the last decades, with a wide literature, several sub-disciplines (such as product development and e-marketing), as well as its own concepts and models.

Middleton, Victor T. C., *Marketing in Travel and Tourism*, 3rd edn (Oxford: Butterworth-Heinemann, 2001).

Sutherland, Jonathan and Canwell, Diane, *Key Concepts in Marketing* (Basingstoke: Palgrave Macmillan, 2004).

Marketing mix (or 4Ps)

The marketing mix is a tool that helps consider the key factors that may be modified in order to influence customers' purchasing decisions. Four variables (all starting with the letter P) are usually considered: the **p**roduct itself, its **p**rice, its **p**romotion and **p**lacement (also called distribution). In the case of tourism:

- *Product* refers to what customers actually purchase: an experience made up of several services, or rather the promise of an experience. Product development needs to be based on market research so as to ensure there is a demand for the proposed product; issues of **branding**, **quality** and **loyalty** are related to product.
- *Price* refers to the choice between pricing strategies: 'cost plus pricing', 'premium pricing', 'discount pricing' and 'value for money pricing' are possible methods, depending upon the company's strategic objectives (such as market share or revenue maximisation).
- *Promotion* refers to advertising (traditionally: travel brochures as well as media campaigns) but also to other methods such as publicity via **public relations**.
- *Placement* refers to **distribution channels** (traditional travel agents, but increasingly websites, following a sectorial trend towards **disintermediation**).

This simple marketing mix (called the 4Ps model) has been widened in order to integrate other aspects particularly relevant for services:

people, process and physical evidence. The so-called extended marketing mix (commonly referred to as the 7Ps model) includes the four above-mentioned points, as well as:

- *People* refers to staff working in the tourism industry whose **professionalism** is essential to the quality of the service encounter and customers' satisfaction.
- *Process* refers to the methods by which products may be booked, which is particularly important with regard to **e-tourism**: online customers can very easily surf from one site to the next if the first one does not satisfy them.
- *Physical evidence* can refer to the atmosphere of a restaurant, travel agency or airline cabin, or to the tourist destination itself.

The 7Ps provide a good model to consider tourism purchases in a holistic way; tourism marketers need to remember that these seven aspects (product, price, promotion, placement, people, process and physical evidence) can be modified separately or together in order to obtain the most suitable mix.

Kotler, Philip, Bowen, John T. and Makens, James C., *Marketing for Hospitality and Tourism*, 4th edn (London: Prentice Hall, 2005).

Market segmentation

One of the most basic yet essential **marketing** tools, market segmentation is about grouping customers into homogeneous subgroups called market segments. In tourism, it consists in dividing the tourist market into distinctive market segments. Criteria and characteristics commonly used include:

- *geographic* segmentation (at various levels: by country or region, or differentiating between urban and rural);
- *socio-demographic* segmentation (based on **variables** such as **gender**, age, sexual orientation, education, family cycle, occupation, class, income);
- *psychographic* segmentation (for example using **Plog's psychographic typology** or distinguishing between **lifestyles** or **motivations**);
- *behavioural* segmentation (according to tourists' activities, loyalty or interests).

Some markets (such as **senior tourism** and **gay and lesbian tourism**) are based on one criterion only, but more refined segments can be identified through multilevel segmentation (for example sacredjourneys.com

M

provides a specialised product aimed at single women travellers interested in spirituality and life-enriching experience). From a marketing viewpoint, by breaking the market down into different segments, companies stand a better chance of attracting customers to their products and services. For a tour operator the need to target specific markets has grown in importance as consumers have become more sophisticated: as needs have changed, a 'one size fits all' package holiday is no longer realistic.

Maslow's hierarchy of needs

Maslow's hierarchy of needs is a very popular model showing different levels of motives in human behaviour (see Figure 3). It can easily be applied to the tourism industry, with regard to the motivations for many choices and decisions (destination, accommodation, activities, etc.). Maslow broke down human needs into five categories, ranging from what he termed 'lower order' physiological needs such as the need to eat and drink (accommodation, catering). When this lower order of needs has been satisfied, a person looks to achieve the next level of need which is security. This is followed by the need to belong (interactions, relationships), then esteem (self-esteem, social esteem) and self-actualisation (through personal achievements). Desires at each level need to be fulfilled before progression to the higher level. Different people will fulfil their needs in different ways, for example social esteem may come from travelling to challenging destinations (for example **jungle tourism**) or to taking part in expensive vacations (for example luxury **cruising**).

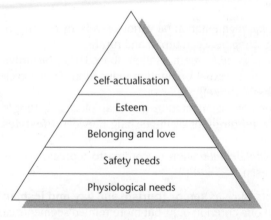

Figure 3 Maslow's hierarchy of needs

Maslow's model is well known and commonly cited, especially because it is intuitive and easy to understand. On its own, it is quite simplistic, which is why it is best utilised in conjunction with other models and theories of **motivations**.

Mass tourism

Mass tourism is one of the most important concepts in the academic field of tourism management. It helps explain the development of tourism in the second part of the twentieth century, as well as the recent changes in the tourism industry and in the philosophical vision of what tourism should and should not do. Mass tourism is a historical phenomenon of outbound **international tourism** that started in developed European countries in the late 1950s. Thanks to growing affluence, longer holidays and cheaper transportation, an unparalleled number of tourists started taking summer holidays abroad, typically in Mediterranean destinations such as the French, Spanish and Italian Rivieras. This seasonal phenomenon was mainly motivated by **3S** tourism, and also to a minor extent by **cultural tourism** and **nature-based tourism**. Awareness of the negative impacts of mass tourism emerged in the 1970s, when mass tourism and tourism in general started being criticised, although one must not forget that it enabled millions of tourists to discover new horizons and contributed strongly to the economic development of many destinations. The initial socio-cultural impacts of mass tourism were not easy to evaluate because tourist flows were not initially directed to developing countries. The availability of less expensive **package tours** to more exotic destinations contributed to the development of international mass tourism to developing countries (especially in the **pleasure periphery**), where some uncontrolled forms of tourism proved detrimental to both the environment and the local culture. As a reaction against mass tourism, new approaches to tourism emerged:

- integrated and controlled **tourism planning** and **tourism management** by tourism authorities (at local, regional or national level);
- new products offering an **alternative tourism** that is more respectful of the destinations and local residents;
- a new understanding of what tourism should do: contribute to **sustainable development** on a global scale.

M

Boissevain, Jeremy (ed.), *Coping with Tourists: European Reaction to Mass Tourism* (Oxford: Berghahn Books, 1996).

Krippendorf, Jost, *The Holiday Makers: Understanding the Impact of Leisure and Travel* (Oxford: Heinemann, 1987).

McDonaldization

In 1990, American sociologist George Ritzer published the first edition of his best selling book *The McDonaldization of Society*. His central thesis is that in the late twentieth century, Western society became rationalised, efficient and predictable to the extreme, as emblematised by the process of McDonald's fast food restaurants. That idea can then be applied to tourism management, where the word McDonaldization refers not only to catering processes, but to an overall approach of both production and **consumption**. It particularly fits the system of **package tours** in interchangeable **3S** destinations and the multiplication of **identikit** short breaks.

The term is also sometimes used in a derived yet different meaning to refer to the Americanisation of the world, as illustrated by the spread of McDonald's outlets from Moscow to Delhi. The word 'coca-colonisation' too can also be encountered, especially with reference to the Westernisation of tourist destinations in less developed countries.

Ritzer, George, *The McDonaldization of Society*, 4th edn (London: Sage, 2004).

Mega-events

In the context of tourism, mega-events is the term used to refer to large-scale events which are usually associated with sports and have an international dimension; on that basis, mega-events include the FIFA World Cup and the **Olympic Games** but not the American Super Bowl. Mega-events have several characteristics:

- They attract hundreds of thousands of visitors, especially international tourists, who contribute heavily to the host country's **balance of payments**.
- They put pressure on accommodation and transport, yet not so much on other attractions, with the exception of the most famous 'must-see' attractions. (Most mega-events visitors are not usually interested in sites of **cultural tourism** or **heritage tourism**, nor do they take part in many sightseeing excursions in the region.)
- Mega-events require extensive preparation, especially with regard to **logistics**, operations, organisation and safety management.
- Mega-events are meant to benefit the area not only in the short term, but also on the long term (although some statistics show that recent Olympic Games have not had the expected long-term boost in terms of tourism growth).

Bowdin, Glenn et al., *Events Management* (Oxford: Butterworth-Heinemann, 2001).

M

Mergers and acquisitions

A merger occurs when two companies agree to combine operations and become one, whereas an acquisition refers to when a company takes full control of another; this involves a cross equity swap to form the new company. Mergers can be based on an equal partnership, hence the phrase 'mergers of equals'; they tend to take place in a friendly way, with executives serene about combining forces, whereas acquisitions are often more hostile, especially with feelings of anxiety amongst staff from the company being purchased. Mergers are relatively common within the tourism industry, with recent activity including the merger of Hilton Hotels Corporation re-merging with the Hilton Group which was part of the betting company Ladbrokes. Acquisitions also occur, especially as part of strategies of **vertical integration** or **horizontal integration**. Other motives for mergers and acquisitions include economies of scale, synergies and diversification.

Reed-Lajoux, Alexandra, *The Art of M & A Integration: A Guide to Merging Resources, Processes and Responsibilities*, 2nd edn (London: McGraw-Hill, 2006).

Motivation

A motivation is the intrinsic reason why a person takes a particular course of action. In tourism, this psychological concept usually refers to tourists and the reasons why they embark on a particular trip. There exists a wide range of motivations (from mere curiosity to search for **authenticity**, to escape from **alienation** or anticipated health benefits) as well as several typologies and terminologies to research and analyse tourists' motivations. Why do people want to travel? The answer is not just of interest to the sociologists and psychologists of tourism, but it is also very important for the tourism industry. Understanding tourists' motivations to engage in specific activities (for example extreme sports) or to go to specific destinations (for example Crete as opposed to Cyprus) may help develop new tourist products, target new customers and create new business opportunities. Motivations are directly linked to the **demand** for tourism, which can be affected by a range of factors, and to **consumer behaviour**, which does not only affect the initial purchase but also the **tourist experience** as well as future decisions.

M

Movie-induced tourism

Also called 'cinema tourism', this concept refers to the fact that blockbuster films shot on location often influence choice of destinations.

Examples include the outdoors (for example Kenya thanks to *Out of Africa*, Thailand thanks to *The Beach*), heritage sites (Petra in Jordan thanks to *Indiana Jones and the Last Crusade*) as well as urban destinations (Paris's Montmartre district thanks to *Amelie*). Successful films that operate as 'virtual brochures' may be more effective than large-scale global advertising campaigns: the New Zealand National Tourism Board reckons that the 400 per cent increase in inbound tourism in the years 2002–4 was largely due to the trilogy *The Lord of the Rings* having been filmed there. Movie-induced tourism is characterised by a sudden, strategically unplanned **demand**, as well as the rapid creation of packages and publicity ('Harry Potter Tours' of England, 'Da Vinci Code Tours' of France and England). Both domestic tourism and international tourism may be affected and the phenomenon is not restricted to Hollywood films: television series and sitcoms may also be a determining factor in some tourists' choice of destination (for example *Sex and the City* has attracted many travellers to New York, *Ballykissangel* to Ireland and *Queer as Folk* to the gay district of Manchester).

Reeves, Tony, *The Worldwide Guide to Movie Locations: The Ultimate Travel Guide to Film Sites around the World* (Sittingbourne: Titan Books, 2006).

Multidisciplinarity

Tourism management is usually presented as a multidisciplinary subject rather than as an academic discipline in its own right (such as geography of economics) because other scholarly disciplines contribute to its study, examining it from their own perspectives, using their own methodologies and focusing on particular aspects.

Three main bodies of academic knowledge contribute to tourism management:

- business management disciplines and related subjects (especially **marketing** and **human resources management**), sometimes referred to as 'business functions';
- social sciences (especially anthropology, geography, history, sociology, **economics**, psychology, political science);
- other fields, including multidisciplinary ones (such as ecology, agricultural studies, urban studies, cultural studies, semiotics and transport studies).

For example, marketing contributes to tourism management through the study of tourist markets and **market segmentation,** anthropology through the study of the interactions between **hosts and guests,** ecology through the study of the impacts of tourism on the natural environment. The lack of integration between these disciplines is a problem inasmuch as it makes tourism and tourism management more difficult in terms of **research**, especially with regard to conceptualisation. The term 'interdisciplinary' is used to describe an ideal situation of synthesis if not fusion between the disciplines. Besides, with the development of other fields of study akin to tourism management (for example heritage management, **leisure management** and event management) one witnesses a blurring of disciplinary boundary, for example an interdisciplinary article about heritage tourism published in the *International Journal of Heritage Studies* may contribute to knowledge dissemination in both tourism and heritage, and maybe also history and social psychology).

Most scholars of tourism management have an academic background in one particular discipline, which influences their work and research, for example Australian Professor Philip Pearce, specialist of consumer behaviour in tourism, has a background in psychology, whilst Professor John Walton, specialist of the social history of tourism, is a historian.

Holden, Andrew, *Tourism Studies and the Social Sciences* (London: Routledge, 2005).

Multiplier effect

In economics, a multiplier effect (also called the spending/income multiplier effect) takes place when spending is circulated through the economy. In tourism, it is a helpful method to conceptualise the beneficial knock-on effect that tourists' spending has on the receiving economy. The multiplier effect explains the difference between the **direct income** and the **indirect income** from tourism at a local, regional or national level. Tourists' initial expenditure does not benefit local businesses only once: it generates indirect revenues (secondary impacts) as these local businesses, in turn, pay their staff who will spend the money locally and so forth. Multiplier analysis is a complex statistical technique that involves several tools (such as a transactions multiplier, an output multiplier, an income multiplier, a government revenue multiplier and so on), models and statistical adjustments; it is not an entirely accurate technique, but it provides valuable frames of reference. There is no agreement amongst scholars about precise values, but the following indicative rates help explain how multiplier effects vary between countries:

United Kingdom overall: 1.75
Egypt: 1.25

M

Barbados: 0.60
Solomon Islands: 0.50

Put another way, £1 spent by a tourist in the UK will result in an extra £0.75 of secondary impacts; the multiplier is much lower in small islands that must import many goods and thereby do not benefit from the local multiplier effect.

Multipurpose tourism

The purpose of a journey is its aim, for example business, visiting friends and relatives, recreation, study, sport or health. When filling in landing cards, immigration forms or visa applications, international tourists are usually asked about the main purpose of their journey; this piece of information helps in the compilation of national tourism **statistics**. Some journeys may have several **purposes** though, for example a business trip abroad followed by a visit to some old friends who now lives in that country, followed by several days of sightseeing: in such a case, which box should be ticked? This highlights one of the limits of international statistics on tourism arrivals, which makes it difficult to measure precisely tourist **balance of payments**. The same is true for statistics on **domestic tourism**: tourism surveys often ignore multipurpose tourism; this illustrates the fact that tourism is a complex phenomenon which is not always easy to research.

Museums

Conceptually, museums are **dual use** tourist **attractions**. They fulfil several missions and functions of collection, preservation, exhibition and **interpretation.** There is a wide range of museums, from world-famous arts museums which are often a 'must-see' for tourists (such as El Prado in Madrid) via specialist museums (on a particular topic, for example Vulcania near Clermont-Ferrand in the Auvergne in France) to small, local eco-museums and interpretative centres (such as the forest museum at the Château Logue, Maniwaki, Quebec, Canada). Because of that diversity, it is difficult to provide a unique, comprehensive taxonomy of museums. Besides size and fame, they could also be divided according to source of funding (public museums vs private collections open to visitors), to the type of items and artefacts they present (fine arts, natural history, etc.), or to their themes and topics (religion, **nostalgia**, etc.).

Museums have evolved substantially over the last decades, especially with regard to their design (renovations to look modern and more appealing to visitors), to the way they want to entertain as well as educate (interactive stations, use of multimedia techniques) and to the way they are managed (with a focus on marketing and fund-raising, especially as public sector subsidies have their limits).

The study of museums is a very broad topic; under the name of museology (museum studies), it has developed into a university subject in its own right. It is supported by a sophisticated literature and enriched by the same **multidisciplinary** approaches as the study of tourism, from more theoretical analyses (anthropology, art history) to practical aspects (museum management and marketing).

Ambrose, Timothy and Paine, Crispin, *Museum Basics*, 2nd edn (London: Routledge, 2005).

Ames, Michael, *Cannibal Tours and Glass Boxes: The Anthropology of Museums* (Vancouver: University of British Columbia Press, 1992).

Kotler, Neil and Kotler, Philip, *Museum Strategy and Marketing: Designing Missions, Building Audiences, Generating Revenue and Resources* (San Francisco, CA: Jossey-Bass, 1998).

'National flag' carrier

A 'national flag' carrier is an airline which is run and managed by the state or government of a country to serve national interests. Up until the latter part of the 1980s, almost all European airlines were national flag carriers, such as Air France, Lufthansa, and British Airways. The aim of these airlines was to support national interests by flying the flag to destinations around the world. Flag carriers were also used as a strategic military back-up, to help fulfil uneconomic routes (as was the case in the Highlands and Islands of Scotland) and to support national airframe and engine manufactures. The problem with national flag carriers was that under state control they tended to be inefficient and made massive losses. Therefore, in 1987 the British government privatised British Airways, having streamlined it, in readiness to fend for itself again commercial competition. All of Europe's major airlines have since been privatised, although some still have stakes retained by the state and a few have also received subsidies from their governments to continue operations. The practice of subsidising airlines is nevertheless barred by the European Union on competition grounds.

National tourist organisation (NTO)

National tourist organisations (NTOs) are **tourist boards** operating at a national level. Their remit and structure vary from country to country, for example France and the UK have distinct NTOs (Maison de la France and Visit Britain respectively) whilst the USA does not have a central tourism office (each state being responsible for its own tourist information); multinational arrangements and partnerships also exist (for example the Scandinavian Tourist Board is a joint initiative by the national tourist boards of Denmark, Norway and Sweden). NTOs are often state-subsidised or QUANGOs (quasi autonomous non-government organisations); they may either fit into a dedicated department or ministry, or fall within the private sector, depending on the importance and priorities attached to tourism development. The main role of NTOs is usually seen in **marketing** terms, especially to promote tourism by disseminating information; this is often done by setting up and staffing national tourist information centres both abroad (in capital cities) and domestically, as well as working with regional tourist organisations. Other roles may include protecting key attractions, grading accommodation facilities as well as facilitating and managing tourism development. NTOs articulate their objectives in different ways; for example, in 2006 Visit Britain defined its remit as follows:

- With regard to the overseas market: 'To promote Britain overseas as a tourist destination, generating additional tourism revenue throughout Britain and throughout the year'.
- With regard to **domestic tourism**: 'To grow the value of the domestic market by encouraging British residents to take additional and/or longer breaks in England'
- With regard to the **public sector:** 'To provide advice to Government and devolved administrations on matters affecting tourism and contribute to wider Government objectives' *and* 'To work in partnership with the devolved administrations and the national and regional tourist boards to build the British tourism industry'.
- With regard to the **private sector:** 'To help the British tourism industry address international and domestic markets more effectively'.
- With regard to their own staff: 'To achieve all goals by making efficient and effective use of resources and by being open, accessible, professional, accountable and responsive'.

Visit Britain NTO, www.visitbritain.org

Nature-based tourism

Nature-based tourism (sometimes just called nature tourism) is about experiencing fauna and flora in their natural environments. It may take a range of forms, from gentle **rural tourism** (in the hinterland of urbanised areas) to adventurous **jungle tourism** (in more hostile settings). The impact of nature-based tourism on the environment will depend on the way the attractions and activities are managed: in some cases, it can contribute to **conservation** and protection of wildlife, but in most other cases, the subsequent disruptions can be detrimental, even when tourists aim to behave in responsible, respectful ways. Tools such as impact analysis and surveys to measure **carrying capacities** can help assess the extent to which a natural area suffers (or not) from visitors. In management, concerns for biodiversity, ecology and sustainability are now prevalent, yet the increasing tourist **demand** can make the equation difficult to balance, for example in national parks as well as regional parks and so-called 'areas of outstanding natural beauty' (AONB) that may have less stringent rules with regard to visitor management (most AONBs in England are inhabited). The **literature** on nature-based tourism includes a high number of case studies, from traditional activities such as safari in game reserves to more fashionable ones such as whale-watching and dolphin-watching. Nature-based tourism is closely linked to the concept of **ecotourism**.

Buckle, Ralf, Pickering, Catherine and Weaver, David B. (eds), *Nature-based Tourism, Environment and Land Management* (Wallingford: CABI, 2003).

Neo-colonialism

Many scholars and analysts argue that the current forms of tourism represent a new form of colonisation, particularly in the case of developing countries located on the **pleasure periphery** of wealthy tourism-generating countries. Economically, the underpinning **dependency theory** confirms the weight of an asymmetrical relationship, accentuated in cases of **leakages** when the financial benefits of tourism are not invested locally but repatriated to the overseas headquarters of foreign-owned tourism operators. Socio-culturally, neo-colonialism (also called neo-colonisation and neo-imperialism) is reminiscent of the exploitation of the locals by wealthy foreigners, who now stay in luxury hotels (into which old plantations buildings have been converted). Tourist destinations appear as new colonies that exist merely for the hedonistic leisure and pleasure activities of visitors from richer countries. This new historical reading of tourism is quite convincing: most of the countries that were decolonised in the twentieth century, especially after the Second World War (India gained its idependence in 1947, Indonesia in 1948, Tunisia in 1956, the Ivory Coast in 1960, etc.), have indeed become tourist destinations, and the ex-colonial powers are often the main source of visitors (French tourists to Tunisia and the Ivory Coast, UK tourists to India). Cultural connections (especially linguistic) explain that tourist relationship, though the image of the wealthy, white European tourist who has replaced the wealthy, white European colonial is a powerful one. If it is true that contemporary tourism has elements akin to colonialism, there are also some counter-arguments, especially in the case of **community tourism** where tourism does contribute to local development.

'New traveller'

The phrases 'new traveller' and 'new tourism' were used in the 1990s to describe a new type of tourist who was more critical, ethically minded and aware of the negative impacts of tourism development. Auliana Poon's 1993 book *Tourism, Technology and Competitive Strategies* contributed to the conceptualisation of so-called 'new tourism'. It corresponds to the double recognition that tourism had to change (in order to remain sustainable) and that it was already changing (with a new form of travelers, hence the name). If those new travellers initially constituted a **niche** market, with the development of **sustainable tourism** (and its many expressions such as **ecotourism** and **community tourism**), new travellers are now more common and the phrase has lost some of its novelty and currency. On the other hand, because of the value judgement underpinning it, the concept of the new traveller continues to raise the question as to what makes a good tourist.

Poon, Auliana, *Tourism, Technology and Competitive Strategies* (Wallingford: CAB, 1993).

Niche tourism

In marketing, a niche market is a small, focused, targetable market, which is arguably so specialised that there is little or no competition offered. To all intents and purposes, a niche market in tourism is a narrowly defined SIT (**special interest tourism**), such as some precise subcategories of literary tourism (for example Jane Austen tours in Hampshire). Many forms of tourism which are increasingly popular (for example **heritage tourism** and **dark tourism**) were once niche markets; as providers multiply and demand increases, these markets move into the mainstream. There is no precise threshold or criterion to assess when a niche markets stops being one; Marina Novelli's book *Niche Tourism: Contemporary Issues, Trends and Cases* includes many case studies of markets which, strictly speaking, do not constitute a marketing niche, except in geographical terms (for example gastronomic tourism, **wildland tourism**). Conceptually, niche tourism builds on notions of fragmentation and **market segmentation**. As they are very specialised, niche tourists can be precisely targeted, which is a marketing advantage; the two counterparts are, firstly, that the demand is initially very small, and, secondly, that competitors may appear if they realise that it is a viable market.

Novelli, Marina (ed.), *Niche Tourism: Contemporary Issues, Trends and Cases* (Oxford: Butterworth-Heinemann, 2005).

N

Nostalgia

Nostalgia is a longing for the past; in tourism, this concept helps us understand the demand for **heritage tourism** and the subsequent number of **events** and **attractions** linked to social history. It is particularly important in the UK; for example, Brighton Tourist Information Centre proposes a 'nostalgia trail' which includes the Sussex Toy and Model Museum in Brighton, 'Rejectamania: The Nostalgia Centre' in Earnley and 'Yesterday's World' in Battle. The relationship between tourism and nostalgia is perfectly summarised by the title of David Lowenthal's book *The Past is a Foreign Country*: nostalgia-based tourism is an invitation to travel into the past, though not a remote historical past. Nostalgia is about memories, so the tourist attractions that use nostalgia as a pull factor need to target tourists precisely by offering them a culture that reminds them of their youth or younger days. Nostalgia has also contributed, albeit to a lesser extent, to the development of **agrotourism** as a motivation for tourists to discover or rediscover their rural roots.

In a few instances, nostalgia has also been associated with diaspora and migration, with tourism being an opportunity to visit sites where one used to live, for example in 2006 the West Bengal Minorities Development and Finance Corporation in India started a cross-border scheme to enable Bangladeshi or Pakistani citizens who left India post-partition (1947) to visit their birthplace in West Bengal. This form of nostalgia tourism is directly linked to social identity, making tourism a powerful existential experience.

Lowenthal, David. *The Past is a Foreign Country* (Cambridge: Cambridge University Press, 1985).

N

Olympic Games

Historically, the original Olympic Games used to take place in the Greek town of Olympia (hence the name) every four years from the eighth to the fourth century BC. At the very end of the nineteenth century, the Frenchman Pierre de Coubertin initiated a revival of them and the first modern Games were organised in 1896 then in Paris in 1900. (In 1924, the first Winter Olympics took place in Chamonix.) From a tourism perspective, the Olympic Games raise conflicting issues:

- On the one hand, the Games themselves mean an intense, incomparable influx of tourists for a few weeks in summer (with maximum occupancy rates in hotels, high revenues due to price increase and complex **logistics** to process so many visitors, for example at airports).
- On the other hand, statistics suggest that, for the host region, the summer Olympic Games do not boost tourism in the long term, but rather translate into a drop in tourism growth in the years surrounding the event, both before and after. This is part of a wider so-called 'Olympic effect' which has been observed for Sydney (2000), Atlanta (1996), Barcelona (1992) and Seoul (1988).

It is difficult to separate the tourism elements from the other impacts of the Olympic Games (for example **regeneration**, status and brand value of the host city). Proponents and opponents cite different figures and impacts studies, and drawing lessons from one Olympiad to the next is epistemologically difficult because of the different context.

> Preuss, Holger, *The Economics of Staging the Olympics: A Comparison of the Games, 1972–2008* (Cheltenham: Edward Elgar, 2006).

Operations management

The concept of 'operations' can apply to all the activities concerned with the acquisition of resources (input), their transformation into finished product, and the supply of that finished product to customers (output). Operations are usually represented in a simple input/output model (see Figure 4).

Figure 4   Linear input/output model

All travel and tourism businesses can be presented in terms of operations, from restaurants to tour operators, although some services may lend themselves less well to interpretation in terms of input/output. Focusing on operations can help understand the core business of an organisation. An extra element of feedback may be added to the basic model (customer feedback or monitoring to quality assurance mechanisms to check that the output corresponds to the initial objectives):

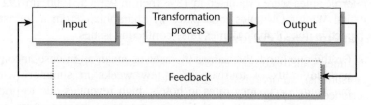

Figure 5   Looped input/output model

Operations management (or operational management) is concerned with the management of resources that directly produce the outputs (goods and services); it is usually presented in contrast to strategic management (which, put simply, is about identifying objectives and developing policies and a strategic plan to reach these objectives). In the tourism industry, the concept of operations management tends to be used for some sectors (hotels, casinos) more than others.

Kilby, Jim and Fox, Jim, *Casino Operations Management* (New York: John Wiley, 1998).
Rutherford, Denney G., *Hotel Management and Operations*, 3rd edn (New York: John Wiley, 2002).

Opportunity costs

An important **economics** concept, opportunity costs can be defined as the profit that would be forgone by not using a particular resource. Put another way, it is the cost of something in terms of an opportunity forgone (and the benefits that could be received from that opportunity). For example, if a village decides to build a new camping site on vacant land that it owns, the opportunity cost is whatever else might have been undertaken with the land and money instead (a new swimming pool or a local cinema). Opportunity costs are very important for **decision-making** in tourism because they need to be taken into account to consider the true cost of any course of action. They are not only assessed in financial terms, but other factors must be considered, for example the human and environmental impacts of developing (or not) a specific project. For example, developing a golf course may seem very expensive, but *not* developing that golf course might eventually cost even more in terms of lost opportunities (as it could then attract a high spending tourist clientele, for example). Opportunity costs are particularly acute in developing countries where tourism competes with other sectors, especially agriculture; money or land allocated to tourism development is, de facto, money or land denied to traditional use and local agriculture.

Organisational culture

Sometimes called 'corporate culture' (especially in the case of large organisations), an organisational culture is about the attitudes, values, experiences, beliefs and values of a particular organisation. The concept of organisational culture has been studied by many scholars who have addressed it from several perspectives, developing different methodologies and models. For example, according to management guru Charles Handy, there are four types of organisational cultures, focusing on: power (based on trust, yet requiring the success of the business to be its main focus); roles (with a strong bureaucracy and limited innovation); tasks (where employees' expertise is key); or people (collective decision-making). Other scholars have proposed other models, the most famous ones being from Edgar Schein, Terence Deal and Allan Kennedy. There is no evidence to suggest that any one approach is more suitable to deconstructing and understanding the organisational culture of businesses in the tourism industry. This is due mainly to the industry being extremely segmented (composed of a very high number of small and medium-sized enterprises). A related concept is that of organisational learning about the way an organisation (as a complex system) learns from its mistakes and experiences.

Easterby-Smith, Mark and Lyles, Marjorie A. (eds), *The Blackwell Handbook of Organizational Learning and Knowledge Management* (Oxford: Blackwell, 2003).
Handy, Charles B., *Understanding Organizations* (London: Penguin 1993).

Package Tour

A package tour is the combination of holiday elements by an intermediary (usually a **tour operator**) to create a product at a set, inclusive price. At least two elements need to be combined to create a package, but usually three basic products come together to create the standard package holiday experience, namely flight, transfer and accommodation. Other products such as car hire, destination excursion and activities can be further combined to form more complex package holidays.

Historically, the first packaged tours were created by Thomas **Cook** and that concept has heavily marked tourism development in the twentieth century, especially after the Second World War when technological progress made air travel faster, easier and cheaper. Package tours are associated with outbound **mass tourism**.

Package tours are typically offered for sale through brochures stocked in travel agencies, although Internet distribution has become an important medium for sales. The future of package holidays has been called into question as consumers have become more confident in organising their own trips. Packages are consequently being replaced by more flexible, dynamically packaged products offered for sale on the Internet.

Laws, Eric, *Managing Packaged Tourism* (London: Thomson, 1997).

Paradox of resentment

Should interactions between **hosts and guests** be encouraged or discouraged? The answer is very difficult for destination managers, as in either case, from a sociological viewpoint, tensions and social problems may occur.

- When tourists and locals are made to mix and interact (called a 'policy of dispersal'), locals may become particularly aware of the differentials in wealth and culture, which may contribute to problems of tourist-directed crime, **demonstration effect** and **acculturation**. This is one of the drawbacks of encouraging **dual use** of tourism facilities.

- When tourists and locals are segregated (called 'policy of isolation', for example in the extreme situation of **enclave tourism**), locals may resent the way their destination being is colonised by visitors whose presence does not benefit the local economy.

The paradox lies in the fact that it is a no-win situation: either policy will have negative effects.

Pareto Principle

Named after the Italian economist Vilfredo Pareto (1848–1923), the Pareto Principle is a rule of thumb stating that, for many phenomena, 80 per cent of consequences stem from 20 per cent of causes (which is why it is also called 'the 80–20 rule' or 'the law of the vital few').

Applications in tourism management may include the facts that:

- 80 per cent of all the bookings received by a hotel are from 20 per cent of the travel agents they work with (whilst the majority of other travel agents provide only a small number of bookings);
- 80 per cent of the tours sold by a tour operator come from the same few products they offer (whilst a high number of tours result only in a very few bookings);
- 80 per cent of the food ordered in a restaurant comes from the same 20 per cent of the many items on the menu.

The Pareto Principle is counter-intuitive because one tends to believe that equal causes have equal consequences. As a principle, it is not precise and scientific, but it can give good ideas to tourism managers and help them consider their customers and suppliers differently. In the above examples, it could be beneficial to focus on the main sources of business, for example in terms of quality assurance to make sure that the more important customers, products and suppliers receive all the attention and satisfaction they deserve, given their contribution to the business.

P

Partnership

In the tourism literature, the word 'partnership' is used in two different ways:

- It may refer to a particular type of business entity ('partnership' is a legal form of business, like 'sole trader' or 'limited company'). The relationship is usually formalised in a partnership agreement drawn up by a solicitor. In tourism, a small **consultancy** or a bed and breakfast may be constituted as a partnership, when a small number of friends or colleagues decide to set up a business jointly (see **entrepreneurship**).

- It may describe the relationship between two (or more) organisations that decide to join forces towards a common aim, for example Tourism Partnership Mid Wales (TPMW) working with partners from both the **public sector** (regional tourist board) and **private sector** (local tourism providers). Such collaborative schemes may be precisely defined (especially when they involve public funding) or they may be more loosely articulated (in the sense of agents of tourism development working in friendly partnership with one another, without necessarily any formal structure). It is in the latter sense that the not-for-profit organisation Responsible Tourism Partnership works in partnership with businesses and destinations.

McKercher, Bob and du Cros, Hilary, *Cultural Tourism: The Partnership between Tourism and Cultural Heritage Management* (New York: Haworth Press, 2002).

Perishability

A good is perishable when it has a limited lifespan; by analogy, the concept of perishability refers to **services**, such as tourism, which cannot be offered for sale beyond a certain date, and cannot be stored for later consumption. The package holiday is a good example of a product that suffers from perishability as, if it is not sold by the date of departure, the product can no longer be stocked or sold and thus a loss is incurred. To help alleviate problems associated with perishability, most tourism providers (such as airlines, hotels and tour operators) have invested heavily in **yield management** systems (the aim is to try to modify and equalise demand). With **inseparability**, **intangibility** and **variability**, perishability is one of the four characteristics of services.

PEST/STEEPLE analysis

PEST and STEEPLE are mnemonics (like the acronym SMART) that provide a quasi-comprehensive framework to help a company systematically identify the factors in the external environment which may influence future strategies. PEST stands for:

P political factors
E economic factors
S socio-cultural factors
T technological factors.

Increasingly the longer STEEPLE is being used to cover other areas as well:

> **S** socio-cultural factors
> **T** technological factors
> **E** economic factors
> **E** educational factors
> **P** political factors
> **L** legal factors
> **E** environmental factors.

These seven groups of factors are relevant in the tourism industry (see Table 3).

Table 3 Examples of factors influencing the external environment in which tourism businesses operate.

Types of factors	Examples
S Socio-cultural	Trends in consumption patterns
	Changing lifestyles and demographics
T Technological	Technological progress: new aircrafts, development of e-tourism
E Economic	Exchange rate (affecting both inbound and outbound tourism)
	Oil price fluctuations
E Educational	Training of workforce employed in tourism
	Professionalism
P Political	Entry and exit requirements, visa regulations
	Government support of tourism (policies, funding)
L Legal	Legislation regulating sectors of the industry
	Legal protection of consumers
E Environmental	Environmental impacts of current tourist attractions, and of proposed developments (environmental impact assessment)

Pilgrimage

Pilgrimage can be defined as any travel undertaken for religious, devotional or spiritual purposes. **Health tourism** is one of the oldest forms of tourism, as the Ancient Egyptians and Mesopotamians travelled to visit holy sites and holy shrines. The phenomenon continued throughout history; a famous illustration is provided by Chaucer's *Canterbury Tales*. Even today millions of pilgrims go every year to Lourdes, Rome or Mecca. Pilgrimages may have declined in importance compared to **recreational tourism** and **business tourism**, but several scholars, coming from an anthropological perspective, have proposed an alternative reading of modern tourism as a form of secular pilgrimage. Several arguments support the comparison (such as the **liminality** intrinsic in the tourist experience or the search for **authenticity**) but, in other respects, hedonistic elements of leisure-centred holidays weaken the analogy.

Eade, John and Sallnow, Michael J. (eds), *Contesting the Sacred* (London, Routledge, 1991).

Planning

Planning consists in organising development processes to benefit **stakeholders** and to reach corporate aims and objectives. Planning may be done over the short term or over the long term. Long-term planning is often referred to as 'strategic' (as it involves the formulation of a **strategy** with strategic objectives, hence the importance of the corporate documents called 'strategic plans'), whilst short-term planning is usually referred to as 'tactical' planning (it is then akin to **operations management**). Tourism planning can be experienced at two levels:

- At a *macro* level, tourism planning involves governments, communities and other stakeholders, with plans for tourism developments for regions, destinations or resorts. This is akin to the meaning of **policy** at a macro level.
- At a *micro* level, tourism planning relates to the way an individual organisation plans future developments, especially **product development** (for example, a tour operation deciding to add a destination to its portfolio or an airline deciding to operate a new route).

In both cases, tools such as **cost benefit analysis** and **forecasting** may be used, as planning involves **decision-making**. The literature on planning overlaps that of policy and strategic management because the concepts are often intertwined, as illustrated by the common use of phrases such as 'strategic planning' and 'policy planning'.

Lake, Neville, *The Strategic Planning Workbook*, 2nd edn (London: Kogan Page, 2006).
Wheelen, Thomas L. and Hunger, J. David, *Concepts in Strategic Management and Business Policy*, 10th edn (London: Prentice Hall, 2005).

P

Pleasure periphery

The phrase 'pleasure periphery' was coined and popularised by a book written in the 1970s by Louis Turner and John Ash which has now become a tourism classic. The word 'pleasure' refers to the hedonistic vacation style of **3S** tourism that attracts tourists to these destinations, whilst the word 'periphery' refers to the marginal geographic locations of the destinations. It was in the 1970s that the existence of a global pleasure periphery became most apparent, along the warmer coastal locations of both developed and developing countries:

- the Mediterranean basin;
- the Caribbean basin;
- the South-East Asian basin (Thailand, Bali);
- the Indian Ocean basin (Mauritius, the Seychelles, the Maldives);
- in the USA a sunbelt that includes Hawaii, Southern California, Texas and Florida;
- in the Pacific the Australian Gold Coast, Fiji.

Many small state islands or dependencies (such as Fiji and the Seychelles) which are part of the pleasure periphery are particularly dependent on tourism (it is their main source of revenue), which makes them very vulnerable to downturns in tourism.

Turner, Louis and Ash, John, *The Golden Hordes: International Tourism and Pleasure Periphery* (London: Constable, 1975).

Plog's Psychographic Typology

In 1974, the American Stanley Plog proposed a model to differentiate between tourists according to a combination of psychological factors including personality, motivation, type and perception. Plog's model of psychographic segmentation has become very popular and is quoted in most tourism textbooks. Its appeal comes mainly from the simplicity of its continuum between two extremes:

- On the one hand, *allocentrics* are confident, enthusiastic, independent, internationally oriented travellers more likely to engage in **ethnic tourism** and **extreme tourism**.
- On the other hand, *psychocentrics* tend to be unsure and insecure; they will rather seek the familiar (in accommodation, catering and activities) and prefer structured, routinised travel.

Between these two extremes are 'mid-centrics', whose personalities are a combination of the two, and according to Plog correspond to two-thirds of the adult population. In more recent publications, Plog has refined and modified his model (for example allocentrics are now called 'venturers' whilst psychocentrics are 'dependables'). Plog's model has been criticised for several reasons, especially the fact that:

- It does not take into account that tourists change over time.
- It is based exclusively on American research and American tourists.
- It is not fully clear how the concepts are operationalised and measured empirically.

Pearce, Philip L., *Tourist Behaviour: Themes and Conceptual Schemes* (Clevedon, Bristol: Channel View, 2005).

Policy

A policy is a plan of action. Policies cannot be considered in isolation: their context is very important because it justifies the contents of the policy. In tourism management, that concept may be encountered in two ways:

- At a micro level, within an organisation, a policy refers to the systems and procedures in place to deal with a particular situation. In that meaning, a hotel will have a cancellation policy, a museum will have an evacuation policy in case of fire or emergency. **Contingency plans** are a form of policy.
- At a macro level, **public sector** authorities will have policies regarding tourism development, that is plans to guide actions and decisions with regard to tourism projects. For example, the Maldives government has a policy of restricting tourism to certain islands of the archipelago, called 'resort islands'. At this level, policies can be regarded as political documents.

The word 'policy' is used in different contexts, for example to refer to social policy, education policy or environmental policies. Sometimes it is confused with **strategy** which, strictly speaking, is another type of document.

Edgell, David L., *Tourism Policy: The Next Millennium* (Champaign, IL: Sports Publishing, 1999).
Hall, Derek (ed.), *Tourism and Transition: Governance, Transformation and Development* (Wallingford: CABI, 2004).

Premium markets

Premium markets (also called luxury markets) are **market segments** characterised by a readiness to purchase the highest quality, which in turn is reflected in the highest prices and an imagery of prestige. Premium markets are important not only in terms of products and marketing, but also in terms of profitability because of the high margins associated with them. The development of premium holidays has helped British Airways return to profitability, as travellers have started to appreciate and buy the perceived benefits offered within the First and Business Class cabins. For passengers unable to upgrade fully to the luxury of First or Business Class, airlines have recently introduced so-called 'premium economy cabins', allowing passengers just a little extra pampering for an increased ticket price. Despite the paradoxical name ('premium' was initially the opposite of 'economy'), this new product is understood by passengers, and the subsequent demand has led several airlines (for example Virgin) to develop the model across the whole of their **long haul** fleets. Other sectors of the tourism industry have started to exploit and demystify the notion of premium markets (initially the field of a few operators such as Kuoni); for example, tour operators such as Thomson (whose package tours were not originally associated with premium markets) have launched new products targeting premium markets.

Pressure groups

A pressure group is composed of like-minded individuals or organisations who, through the power of numbers, aim to influence policy and political decision-making. In the tourism industry, pressure groups exist at all levels, from the global/international (for example Tourism Concern) to the local (for example St Maarten Hospitality & Trade Association) via the professional/sectorial (for example the Association of Professional Tourist Guides in the UK). Some represent the industry (for example the International Air Transport Association (IATA)), and also passengers/customers (for example the Air Transport Users Council (AUC) which fights passengers' grievances with airlines including ticket pricing schemes, lost baggage and misleading advertising). Pressure groups' activities may include lobbying and campaigning, as well as organising events to disseminate information and generate publicity. They do have an influence in the tourism industry. They are usually formally organised as charities or associations (many can then be described as NGOs), but they may also be formed more spontaneously around a particular issue, typically a local tourism project which creates disagreement in the community (see **agents of tourism development** and **stakeholders**). The concept of advocacy is often used as an umbrella term to refer to the work and remit of pressure groups.

Air Transport Users Council, www.caa.co.uk/auc
International Air Transport Association, www.iata.org
St. Maarten Hospitality & Trade Association, www.shta.com
Tourism Concern, www.tourismconcern.org.uk

Pressures

Like any sector of the economy, the tourism industry is affected by internal and external pressures which have an impact on the supply side (product **diversification**, **product lifecycle**), on the demand side (new **trends**, new **niche** markets) and on the overall shape of the industry itself (**mergers and acquisitions**).

A key structural distinction is between internal pressures and external pressures:

- Internal pressures arise within the industry, for example with the emergence of **low-cost carriers** which has caused other airlines to start reducing some of their fares, and has contributed to the democratisation and multiplication of short city breaks within Europe.
- External pressures are beyond the control of the tourist industry but may strongly affect it, for example safety and global security or environmental changes such as global warming; frameworks such as **PEST/STEEPLE analysis** are particularly helpful to map external pressures.

Strategic decision-making presupposes that one takes all these pressures into account, which is very difficult because of the conflicting messages they may give.

Price elasticity of demand

The concept of price elasticity of demand examines the relationship between a change in price and subsequent changes in quantity demand. For most goods, there is an inverse relationship between price and demand: the higher the price, the lower the quantity demands. It is calculated thus:

$$\text{Price elasticity} = \frac{\text{Percentage change in quantity}}{\text{Percentage change in price}}$$

Two situations are possible:

- The demand is price-elastic: this is the case of most tourism products; an increase in price results in a more or less proportional decrease in demand. The discounting of package holidays is a classic example which contributed to the **democratisation of tourism**: when travelling became cheaper, more people could afford to travel, whereas, symmetrically, sharp rises in price (for example, to reflect higher oil prices) may result in lower demand.

The **perishability** of the tourism product explains why operators often reduce their price closer to the point of departure, which has created a late booking market (symbolised by lastminute.com).

- The demand is price-inelastic: this tends to be the case of the business travel market, where an increase or decrease in price of the products (first class flight, business hotels) has little effect on the level of the demand, mainly because the bills are paid by companies, as opposed to the individuals themselves. Some luxury and top premium markets (for jetsetters and high-fliers) too are inelastic.

Private sector

The private sector refers to the businesses and organisations whose primary objective is to create profit for their investors, which is why it is also referred to as the commercial sector (as opposed to the public and voluntary sectors which are both non-commercial). In all its areas, from **transport** to **entertainment** to **accommodation**, the travel and tourism industry relies heavily on the private sector for investment, development and service provision, the only exceptions being **infrastructure** and some aspects of destination promotion (as carried out by **tourist boards** as well as **tourist information centres**). Although the private sector plays a critical role in providing the majority of tourism superstructures, it is very fragmented. Tourism may be associated with brand names such as Holiday Inn, Hilton, Air France and British Airways, which are all large corporations, but the majority of tourism enterprises are small and medium-scale (also called SMEs, 'small and medium-sized enterprises' that have under 250 staff). In the European Union, as many as 99 per cent of tourism enterprises are SMEs. This fragmentation of the industry creates a number of problems including the lack of coherent training policies and career structure for staff, and the difficulty of developing integrated policies at regional level because of the sheer number of small businesses involved.

P

Product development

In business, product development is the process of bringing a new project to the market; it does not only involve the first stages of product formulation (idea generation, concept development), but also advertising and commercialisation/distribution/implementation. In the tourism industry, product development is important not only for tour operators and travel agents (who need something new and different to sell), but also for attractions and destinations. Existing attractions need to develop and update their range of products (this is sometimes called 'product portfolio') in order to attract repeat visitors, that is people who have already visited and need a motive to go again to experience something new. Following the model from Disney Resorts, **theme parks** like Alton Towers keep adding new rides and special events in order to encourage return visits. This represents several challenges, including keeping up to date with competitors, developing economically viable products and displaying innovation so as to maintain a brand name for quality and creativity. Destinations can use new attractions to develop their tourist identity; examples include the Jorvik Centre in York, Montreal's Biosphere and the Guggenheim Museum in Bilbao. Technological innovations play a major role in product development, making it possible to turn ideas into reality and to create a 'wow' effect.

Trott, Paul, *Innovation Management and New Product Development*, 3rd edn (London: Prentice Hall, 2004).

Product lifecycle

The concept of product lifecycle is a basic marketing model illustrating how products in any market go through several stages: introduction (launch), growth (development), maturity (saturation) then decline. It is based on an organic analogy from birth to death (see Figure 6).

With regard to tourism, three factors are particularly important:

- Firstly, knowing where in the lifecycle a particular product is can help tourism managers make appropriate decisions about the various elements of the **marketing mix** (for example, there may be a need to further advertise products still in their growth phase: sales may be low because the product is not well known, even though it has been on offer for a while).

- Secondly, the existence of a decline stage (meaning that some products will soon be obsolete and have to be phased out) reminds managers of the importance of ongoing **product development**: the aim is to make sure their portfolio of products (for example the different packages offered by a tour operator or the different rides in a theme park) always contains new products in the early stages of their lifecycle.

- Thirdly, the product lifecycle model can also be applied to whole destinations: it is then called the **Butler Sequence**, after Richard W. Butler who proposed it in 1980.

P

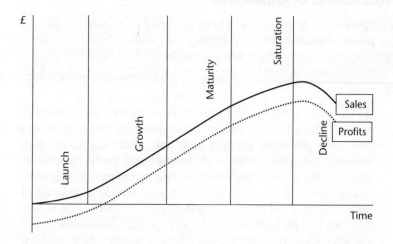

Figure 6 Product life cycle

Professionalism

In any organisation, professionalism refers to the internalised values that will be reflected in the ways staff carry out their work. It is linked to work ethics, behavioural standards as well as competence and proficiency. As tourism is a succession of **service** encounters, staff professionalism is most important in all sectors of the tourist industry. Several factors account for professionalism, such as specialised training, the presence of formal or informal workplace sanctions, the prestige associated with the work carried out and the culture of the organisation itself. Many **research** projects have been carried out in the tourism and hospitality industry about professionalism, producing interesting findings, such as the fact that employees' perceptions and employers' perceptions of professionalism are actually very similar. The concept of 'continued personal development' (sometimes known as 'continuing professional development' (CPD)) is increasingly used and implemented in the tourism industry as raising and maintaining professional standards depends on lifelong learning and the continual development of new skills.

Sheldon, Pauline J., 'Professionalism in Tourism and Hospitality', *Annals of Tourism Research*, 16(4) (1989): 492–503.

P

Professional organisations

A professional organisation is a body designed to maintain or advance the **professionalism** of its members and stakeholders. In tourism, different organisations have different remits (such as regulations, representation or accreditation) which sometimes overlap, for example in the UK:

- ABTA is the Association of British Travel Agents. All its members are part of a particular trade (travel agents and tour operators) so ABTA is a **pressure group** representing that trade, for example ensuring that policy-makers at national and European level are aware of the professional needs of their members. ABTA is also a regulatory body for its members: it has a code of conduct its members must abide by; it monitors their accounts and ensures that they comply with the law (so as to protect consumers).
- The UK CAA (Civil Aviation Authority) is an independent regulatory body, covering areas such as economic regulation, airspace policy, safety regulation and consumer protection. It is not funded by the government (unlike in many other countries), but its costs are met from the charges of the organisations and operations it regulates (for example licensing aerodromes, aircraft or flight crew).
- The ITT (Institute of Travel and Tourism) is a professional membership body; like ABTA it is composed of members, but it does not have any regulatory function. Its main aim is to develop and maintain professional standards. It also plays a role as an accrediting body for higher education institutions, enabling students on accredited courses to enter the industry with a professionally backed qualification after their course is completed.

A few professional organisations operate at an international level, such as the International Air Transport Association (IATA) which has almost 300 members from more than 140 nations.

Association of British Travel Agents (ABTA), www.abta.co.uk
International Air Transport Association (IATA), www.iata.org
Institute of Travel and Tourism, www.itt.co.uk
UK Civil Aviation Authority, www.caa.co.uk

Profitability

Profitability, a simple microeconomics concept, is a measure of how much additional revenue a company generates, based on the costs it has incurred in the production of a good or service. A company's profit is important for future growth, as it is often the measure by which potential investors may judge whether it is worth investing money in a particular business or sector. Where companies fail to make enough revenue to cover the costs of production, the organisation will make a loss. Where losses occur on a frequent basis, the company may be forced into bankruptcy.

Profitability is notoriously difficult to maintain for tour operators and the airline industry. Traditionally, tour operators' profitability has been the second priority after market share and the kudos associated with it: for decades, tour operators have regarded it as more important to be the biggest and to take the highest number of holidaymakers away. The rationale is that profit will follow anyway, as a large market share will either force competitors out of business or put them in a vulnerable position (as potential subjects for acquisitions, for example). Within the airline industry, profits are difficult to achieve on a sustained basis because of external **pressures** (such as increased oil prices) and because the industry is cyclical (typically five or six years of good performance followed by four or five years of poor performance); even in the good years, profitability is quite low (2–3 per cent net profit after interest and tax).

Project management

A project can be defined as a temporary venture undertaken to reach a precise objective. Projects are numerous in tourism management, for example organising a conference, planning and accompanying a tour, or carrying out a **feasibility study**. The project manager is responsible for planning, designing and allocating resources such as time (projects have a beginning and an end), money (projects have finite budgets), people (staff involved in the project), maybe also materials, energy, space, etc. The project manager also has responsibilities with regard to communication as well as quality and quality assurance. Project management is a discipline that necessitates a rigorous approach as well as an awareness of possible risks, hence the need of **contingency plans**. Software programmes such as Microsoft Project Manager are increasingly used for complex projects, while many free applications also exist. Independent travelling can be presented as a form of project management, with the solo traveller being the project manager.

Newton, Richard, *The Project Manager: Mastering the Art of Delivery* (London: Prentice Hall, 2005).

Pro-poor tourism

Pro-poor tourism (PPT) can be defined as tourism that results in increased net benefits for poor people. As explained on the PPT website: 'PPT is not a specific product or niche sector but an approach to tourism development and management. It enhances the linkages between tourism businesses and poor people, so that tourism's contribution to poverty reduction is increased and poor people are able to participate more effectively in product development.' This is directly reminiscent of key aspects of **responsible tourism** and **sustainable tourism**, but with an explicit focus on reducing poverty. Any tourism business anywhere may be involved in PPT, even urban hotels and tour operators. Initially pioneered by Harold Goodwin, Dilys Roe and Caroline Ashley, the concept of PPT is underpinned by ethical principles, effective strategies, as well as many case studies and publications.

Pro-Poor Tourism Partnership, www.propoortourism.org.uk

Protected areas

In all countries, an increasing number of areas are deemed too valuable to be altered by tourism or any other development. Different levels of protection exist, with various terminologies and classifications, for example in the UK there are National Parks, Regional Parks and Areas of Outstanding Natural Beauty (AONB). Usually controlled by public authorities or by ad hoc organisations, protected areas are managed so as to be partly left in their natural state, untouched by humans to a lesser or greater extent. **Zoning** is the methodology commonly used to distinguish between levels of necessary protection and for taking appropriate action.

In National Parks, when visitors are allowed, they must abide by certain rules; in some areas, visitors are not allowed at all. National Parks attract tourists interested in **nature-based tourism** although issues of **conservation** and preservation sometimes conflict with the public desire to enjoy their natural **heritage**. Originally developed in the United States in the nineteenth century (the Yellowstone National Park in Wyoming, Montana and Idaho was the first truly national park, established in 1872), the concept has now spread to many countries; the World Conservation Union (IUCN) has listed over 68,000 protected areas across the world, with or without the label 'national park'.

Association of UK National Parks Authorities, www.nationalparks.gov.uk
UNESCO World Heritage Centre, whc.unesco.org
World Conservation Union, www.iucn.org

Pseudo-events

The term 'pseudo-events' was coined in 1962 by the American historian Daniel Boorstin in his book *The Image*, where he developed a cultural critique of American society, especially with regard to the growing importance of the visual, of simulation and false appearances. Boorstin also applied his critique to tourism, explaining how tourists themselves were often offered only artificial products, that gave the appearance of being real, the exact opposite of the **authenticity** they may have been seeking. Pseudo-events are manufactured sites or events that are created or staged for tourists; this is the case of many tourist attractions, from theme parks to artistic or religious performances that may have lost their original significance (see **staged authenticity**).

Boorstin, Daniel J., *The Image: A Guide to Pseudo-Events in America* (New York: Vintage Books, 1992 reprint).

Dann, Graham, *The Language of Tourism: A Sociolinguistic Perspective* (Wallingford: CABI, 1996).

Public relations (PR)

Public relations (PR) relates to how a company communicates with the outside world. Travel and tourism organisations need to keep good relations not only with the **demand** (their consumers and potential customers), but also with all their **stakeholders** and the wider community, including possibly other investors. The media often play an intermediary role in PR, hence the need to establish and sustain an excellent relationship with them. PR can include a range of activities, such as obtaining publicity for tourism products, for example through **familiarisation trips** (offering a free stay to a TV holiday programme or a journalist from a Sunday newspaper, and expecting them, in return, to feature and recommend it), sending out literature to the media to advertise the launch of a new product (for example a new type of active holiday) or a press release about how well the business is performing. The first method may result in new customers (through information dissemination) and the second may result in a 'feel good' factor for shareholders and an enhanced public image. PR is particularly important after negative stories and crises; typical examples from the tourism industry include reports of outbreaks of food poisoning at resorts (blamed on hoteliers and ultimately tour operators) or strikes that occasionally cripple some sectors of the industry, especially transport, and may have a detrimental effect on tourists (flights delayed or cancelled). PR is also an important tool for pressure groups and professional organisations. In all cases, PR activities need to be integrated into a marketing **strategy**, and ideally into a specific PR strategy.

Baines, Paul, Egan, John and Jefkins, Frank, *Public Relations: Contemporary Issues and Techniques* (Oxford: Butterworth-Heinemann, 2003).
Davis, Anthony, *Mastering Public Relations* (Basingtoke: Palgrave Macmillan, 2004).

Public sector

The public sector includes all the publicly funded agencies created to deliver government policy. The public sector is involved with the tourism industry in a variety of ways including financing development projects, marketing tourism through the creation and funding of **national tourist organisations**, running **attractions** (for example, historic homes and museums), protecting the consumer and monitoring safety **standards** to attractions and accommodation. The public sector is also responsible for the collection of tourism **statistics**. This may be achieved through its national tourist organisation or through another government department. In the United Kingdom the responsibility of collecting tourism statistics falls to the Office of National Statistics which invigilates the International Passenger Survey.

Besides, the influence of the public sector on tourism can be witnessed at several levels, through:

- supra-national organisations, such as the European Union;
- international government organisations (IGOs), based around sector-specific concerns, such as the **World Tourism Organization**;
- national governments, which in some countries include a ministry for tourism (in the UK, tourism is currently housed within the Department for Media, Culture and Sport);
- government-funded agencies: QUANGOs (quasi-autonomous non-government organisations) as well regional **tourist boards**;
- local authorities (which are able to grant planning permission for tourism developments and to promote local attractions and events).

Chris Cooper, Fletcher, Joghn, Fyall, Alan, Gilbert, David and Wanhill, Stephen, *Tourism Principles and Practice*, 3rd edn (Harlow: Prentice Hall, 2005).

Pull factors

The phrase 'pull factors' refers to all the elements and forces that attract tourists to particular destinations; it is based on the dynamic image of people being pulled towards certain places. Many factors combine to make a place attractive to tourists. Marketing plays an important role (for example promotional efforts from **national tourist organisations** or publicity generated from holiday programmes on TV and magazine articles), either reinforcing an established reputation or creating a new **image**, but pull factors are also linked to wider issues outside the control of tourism marketers and managers. David Weaver and Laura Lawton have identified the following seven points:

- geographical proximity to markets (**distance decay effect**);
- **accessibility** to markets (in terms of infrastructure but also governmental policies, as illustrated by the **Schengen Agreement**);
- availability of **attractions** (with **clustering** being an extra factor);
- cultural links (in some cases relative similarities in culture and language are a pull factor, for example for English travellers to North America or Australia);
- availability of **ancillary services** and **amenities**;
- affordability (some forms of tourism such as **backpacking** are particularly price-sensitive);
- peace and stability (also linked to perceived risk of terrorism).

Pull factors can help account for the relative appeal of some destinations over their competitors; it is a useful concept to analyse **destination substitutability** and the **cross elasticity of demand** between destinations that are perceived as similar or as complementary by tourists.

Weaver, David and Lawton, Laura, *Tourism Management*, 3rd edn (Brisbane: John Wiley, 2005).

Purposes of travel

The difference between the concepts of purpose and **motivation** is sometimes misunderstood. Whilst motivations are psychological and not always conscious (for example a search for **authenticity**), the purpose of a journey is its explicit aim, for example business (to attend a convention), sports (to watch or participate in sports), recreation, sightseeing, visiting friends and relatives, etc. For journeys that have more than one purpose (typically a primary purpose and secondary ones), one can apply the concept of **multipurpose travel**. There is not any definite, official, authoritative list of travel purposes: some authors also include health, study, shopping, etc. The word 'motive' is sometimes used instead of 'purpose', which also blurs the semantic difference between purpose and motivation; many tourists would indeed state that their motivation is the same as the purpose of their trip, that is to go on holiday and relax.

P

Push Factors

The phrase 'push factors' refers to all the elements and forces that influence tourism **demand**; it is based on the dynamic image of people being pushed out of their usual place of residence. There is not one established, authoritative, comprehensive list of push factors; tourism management scholars interpret the notion slightly differently from one another, but overall four different types of factors can be systematically identified:

- Push factors affecting individuals personally: the emphasis here is on **motivation**, on psychological factors (the perceived need for a holiday), on **lifestyle** and family lifecycle attributes (see **determinants of tourism**).
- Push factors linked to the overall environment of the tourism-generating country: a range of factors (such as economic development and urbanisation) contribute to increasing the demand for tourism; a **PEST/STEEPLE analysis** is a good method to review these push factors.
- Push factors linked to the tourism **industry**, especially **marketing** techniques that convince potential tourists they ought to go away, enticing them with promises of relaxing breaks or life-changing experiences
- Push factors linked to differences between the tourism-generating place and the destination (for example the weather: the cold and wet winter weather of northern Europe makes many tourists go away for some 'winter sun' destinations).

P

Qualitative research

Qualitative research focuses on how individuals and groups view and understand the world, and construct meaning out of their experiences. In tourism management, qualitative research can help analyse and understand topics that are hard to quantify, such as **tourist experience** and attitudes, the **image of a destination** or of a particular tourism product, the socio-cultural impacts of tourism or the reasons behind tourism **trends**. Pertinent research methods include participant observation, in-depth interviews, **focus groups**, **content analysis** and **Delphi methods**. A high number of books on qualitative research are available, covering not only issues of data collection and data analysis, but also related themes such as ethics and philosophical underpinning (epistemology, ontology). These books are usually written from a social sciences perspective, because qualitative research emerged from the fields of sociology and anthropology before spreading to other academic disciplines such as business management and tourism management. Qualitative and quantitative approaches are sometimes used together to gain a better understanding of the phenomena studied, as qualitative methodologies may provide depth where quantitative ones provide breadth.

Goodson, Lisa, *Qualitative Research in Tourism: Ontologies, Epistemologies and Methodologies* (London: Routledge, 2004).
Silverman, David, *Doing Qualitative Research*, 2nd edn (London: Sage, 2004).

Quality

Although quality is a key concept in business management, it does not have one single, authoritative definition; it has been variously defined as conformance to specifications, fitness for purpose, fitness for use, value resulting in customers' satisfaction level. Recognising this lack of clarity, the American Society for Quality states that quality is 'a subjective term for which each person has his or her own definition'. As tourism is a complex product (a combination of **service** encounters in **liminal** settings resulting in an overall **tourist experience**), notions of quality and quality management are best addressed by distinguishing between several criteria, such as:

- the quality of the tourist service encounters: staff **professionalism**, competence and responsiveness;
- the quality of the physical evidence and tangible products, such as hotel bedroom, aircraft passenger legroom, equipment, food, etc.;
- the quality of the overall experience, bearing in mind that it is also affected by external factors (such as the weather or the tourist's health, mood and personality).

With regard to the first two points, tourism organisations may have policies and systems in place to monitor and improve quality (for example through audits, **benchmarks** or customer feedback questionnaires); external factors are beyond the discrete control of independent operators and make it difficult to ensure that tourists have an overall satisfactory experience (for example in the case of an unhappy guest arriving late at a hotel without their luggage, misplaced by the airline, or a foreign tourist very sick yet unable to communicate with local doctors).

Kandampully, Jay et al. (eds), *Service Quality Management in Hospitality, Tourism, and Leisure* (New York: Haworth Press, 2001).

Sutherland, Jonathan and Canwell, Diane, *Key Concepts in Operations Management* (Basingstoke: Palgrave Macmillan, 2004).

American Society for Quality, www.asq.org

Quantitative research

Quantitative research is based on the measurement and statistical analysis of precise data using **variables** with a limited amount of information collected on a large number of participants. In tourism management, quantitative research enables the compilation of **statistics** and the **forecasting** of **trends**. Secondary data (for example from public tourism authorities) and primary data (typically gathered through surveys and questionnaires) provide information that may then be analysed and manipulated through mathematical models and statistical tools. The computer program SPSS (Statistical Package for the Social Sciences) is widely used for statistical analysis in the social sciences, including tourism management. Academic textbooks on quantitative research distinguish between two stages of the research process: data collection (with issues of sampling and questionnaire design) and data analysis (how to use sotfware such as SPSS or even Microsoft Excel to carry out statistical calculations).

Oakshott, Les, *Essential Quantitative Methods for Business, Management and Finance*, 3rd edn (Basingstoke: Palgrave Macmillan, 2006).

Pallant, Julie, *SPSS Survival Manual* (Milton Keynes: Open University Press, 2004).

Rr

Recreation

Recreation is defined as the activities and interests that are undertaken by an individual during their **leisure** time. Recreation can be broken down into a number of categories such as:

- recreational activities undertaken within the home environment including the activities of watching TV, participating in computer games, playing music or surfing the Internet for fun or to interact with like-minded people through chat rooms;
- outside recreational activities, for example sports (actively or passively: playing or watching a football match) as well as visiting a local public house, walking in the local park or going out to a night club;
- excursions, for instance visits to theme parks or museums within easy travelling distance of the home environment (**excursionists** are defined are people who are not away for more than 24 hours);
- **tourism**, when recreational pursuits take people away from their home environment for more than 24 hours (see **tourist**) – **recreational tourism** is one of the main forms of tourism, next to its counterpart **business tourism**.

Haywood, Les et al., *Understanding Leisure*, 2nd edn (Cheltenham: Nelson Thornes, 1995).

Recreational tourism

As **tourism** usually involves **leisure** activities (for example through **entertainment**), the phrase 'recreational tourism' may sometimes seem redundant, although it can be effectively used to contrast two forms of tourism: 'leisure-oriented tourism' (sometimes just called 'leisure tourism') and 'non-leisure-oriented tourism'. The latter category would include **business tourism**, professional **sports tourism** and **visiting friends and relatives (VFR)**. In the case of multipurpose travel, it is not always easy to differentiate between purposes, but the phrase 'recreational tourism' has the advantage of focusing on leisure and recreation. According to the World Tourism Organization, the recreational leisure tourism market accounts for 52 per cent or 395 million international tourist arrivals in 2004. This figure increases to 76 per cent or 580 million visits if the category of visiting friends and relatives is added (as VFR is arguably a leisure activity). The **World Travel and Tourism Council** has forecast that recreational tourism would be responsible for $2,844 billion of global tourism receipts in 2006, although these statistics are difficult to verify.

MacCannell, Dean and Lippard, Lucy, *The Tourist: A New Theory of the Leisure Class* (Berkeley: University of California Press, 1999).

Ryan, Chris, *Recreational Tourism: Demand and Impacts* (Clevedon, Bristol: Channel View, 2003).

Regeneration

Coming from urban studies and urban planning, the concept of regeneration (also called 'urban regeneration' and 'urban renewal') refers to the process whereby local authorities endeavour to change the dynamics of some rundown urban areas. Famous examples include Paris in the nineteenth century with the work of Baron Haussmann and New York in the twentieth century under the leadership of Robert Moses. Civil planners have now realised that large-scale tourism projects, especially **mega-events**, can also contribute to regeneration, as they provide a catalyst for **infrastructure** improvement. The argument is usually made by all metropoles willing to host the Olympic Games, as their bids explain how the event will help regenerate whole regions around the Olympic Village. This is a good illustration of the economic benefits of tourism-related developments in urban areas.

Preuss, Holger, *The Economics of Staging the Olympics: A Comparison of the Games, 1972–2008* (Cheltenham: Edward Elgar, 2006).

Rejuvenation stage

At the end of the **Butler Sequence**, rejuvenation is an alternative to **decline**. A destination may reinvent itself; a new identity can be created, new products and new attractions may help create new markets. Common examples are Newquay (Cornwall) which has reinvented itself as the surfing capital of the UK, and Atlantic City (New Jersey) from the early 1980s onwards, when casino gambling helped renew and to re-dynamise the place (which is now the second US gambling capital after Las Vegas). Rejuvenation requires the support and collaboration of both the **private sector** and the **public sector**: the private sector for substantial investments, the public sector for planning decisions and an integrated, strategic vision. Substantial **marketing** efforts are necessary, especially in terms of **advertising** and **PR**, in order to create and disseminate a new **image**. Rejuvenation can be proactive instead of waiting for the first signs of decline, as illustrated by Las Vegas now marketing itself as a family destination.

Research

Knowledge of tourism as an industry, as a socio-geographical phenomenon or as an experience comes from research, especially from its two building blocks: analysis and conceptualisation. Tourism students and tourism managers therefore need some understanding of the research process and related methodological issues. There is a large number of books written by academics about research methodologies in general, about research in tourism management and about research in the disciplines that contribute to tourism as a **multidisciplinary** project (such as business management and sociology). Research is a particular type of activity at the interface of tourism management as **theory** and tourism management as practice. Research projects tend to fall into two categories:

- pure research (mainly concerned with conceptual development and exploratory projects);
- applied research (such as market research, forecasting or problem-solving projects directly relevant to the industry).

Finn, Mick, Elliott-White, Martin and Walton, Mike, *Tourism and Leisure Research Methods: Data Collection, Analysis and Interpretation* (London: Longman, 2000).
Veal, Anthony J., *Research Methods for Leisure and Tourism: A Practical Guide*, 3rd edn (London: Financial Times Prentice Hall, 2006).

Resort

A resort is a location which offers tourists a comprehensive array of products including **accommodation**, **attractions**, **transportation**, restaurants, **amenities** for **recreation** and relaxation, and possibly other services such as shops and banking facilities. The word 'resort' is ambiguous as it can refer to either a whole destination (Bournemouth as a seaside resort, Chamonix as a ski resort) or a commercial complex (as epitomised by the Club Med all-inclusive resorts). The latter sense corresponds to a precise tourism product that developed alongside package tours from the 1950s onwards (Club Med was founded in 1950) offering a particular experience for an all-inclusive price covering lodging, food, use of facilities, sports activities, entertainment through games and

R

shows. The concept was reminiscent of **holiday camps** but targeted at a different market: young single professionals instead of families. Having reached the stagnation phase of their lifecycle, all-inclusive resorts are now in the process of reinventing themselves as more upmarket, as illustrated by the 2006 advertising slogan of Club Med: 'Discover the new Club Med, refined, exceptional, a la carte'.

Two other types of resorts were developed in America:

- 'mega-resorts' which usually include casinos, fine dining and shopping (for example in Atlantic City and Las Vegas);
- themed resorts such as the Disney Resorts ('Walt Disney World Resort' is the new name of Disney World).

Murphy, Peter, *The Business of Resort Management* (Oxford: Elsevier, 2007).

Resources

In economics, resources are regarded as the factors of production required for a business. Resources are usually broken down into sub-categories:

- financial resources (money);
- human resources (people, including volunteers if appropriate) as well as the subsequent intellectual capital (including skills and knowledge);
- natural resources (especially land, space);
- physical resources (for example IT equipment, facilities).

Depending upon the organisation, other types of resources may be included, for example energy or cultural resources. In any **business plan** or for any **tourism development** project, resources need to be precisely identified, whether they are already available or will need to be acquired. Resource management is not only about allocating resources, but also about deploying them efficiently: a method often used for that purpose is 'resource levelling', which consists in balancing the use of resources throughout the project.

In **sustainable tourism** projects and the language of **conservation**, the phrase 'resource management' is also used in a stricter sense about control and monitoring of fragile resources such as fauna and flora, for example with reference to wildlife management. The abbreviation NRM (natural resource management) can be encountered in that sense.

Perman, Roger et al., *Natural Resource and Environmental Economics* (London: Prentice Hall, 2003).

Responsible tourism

The phrase 'responsible tourism' is often used as a synonym of **sustainable tourism**; it may actually be easier to understand for people not familiar with abstract concepts of sustainability and **sustainable development**. The concept of 'responsible tourism' has a double focus: responsible tourism in destination and responsible tourism business.

- *Responsible tourism in destination*: this applies to tourists who need to behave in mature, considerate, responsible ways, showing respect towards the destination's culture and natural environment. A basic principle for travellers is to behave as if they were in their home environment.
- *Responsible tourism business*: this applies to the tourist **industry**, especially decision-makers about **tourism development** who also need to demonstrate their understanding of the impacts of tourism, showing responsibility and accountability in their management methods and decisions.

The International Centre for Responsible Tourism provides examples of case studies showing how it relates to other forms and strategies of **alternative tourism**, such as **pro-poor tourism**.

Harrison, Lynn C. and Husbands, Winston (eds), *Practicing Responsible Tourism: International Case Studies in Tourism Planning, Policy and Development* (New York: John Wiley, 1996).

Reid, Donald G., *Tourism, Globalization and Development: Responsible Tourism Planning* (London: Pluto Press, 2003).

International Centre for Responsible Tourism, www.icrtourism.org
Responsible Tourism Partnership, www.responsibletourismpartnership.org

Risk assessment

Risk assessment is about carefully identifying and evaluating the risks to safety present in a site (indoor or outdoor), with regard to both physical and behavioural factors. Risk assessment is about places (design, layout, emergency access) but also about people (which is why some knowledge of **crowd management** may be helpful) and **policies** (evacuation procedures, crisis management, **contingency plans**). There is a semantic difference between 'hazard' and 'risk': strictly speaking, a hazard is anything that may cause accidents and harm (for example detergents and chemicals or electric wires on the floor), whilst a risk is the chance (high or low) that an accident might occur. Risks are also qualified with regard to the seriousness of the possible harm. By law, in the UK all businesses in the tourism industry (irrespective of their size) must carry out

R

a risk assessment (it does not need to involve a specialised health and safety officer). The aims are to pre-empt problems and to protect workers as well as customers and third parties. If particular risks are identified and can be minimised, managers are expected to take action and implement appropriate measures. Risk assessments are particularly important for events, even small-scale ones such as a wedding party taking place in a hotel. In some sectors of the tourism industry (for example outdoor recreation activities, extreme sports) assessment risks are very strict and important.

Tarlow, Peter E., *Event Risk Management and Safety* (New York: John Wiley, 2002).

Rural tourism

Rural tourism makes use of the countryside as a destination. For urban dwellers, the countryside represents tranquillity and **authenticity**, offering opportunities for scenic drives as well as outdoor recreation such as hiking, fishing and horse-riding. The countryside is not a unique environment though: there is a continuum of types of rurality, from the extremely rural (very remote, for example in mountainous regions) to pre-urban areas (often the object of **excursionism**). Differences of **accessibility** but also of provision of tourist **facilities** will account for a range of tourist activities and **experiences**. Rural tourism overlaps with **agrotourism** and **nature-based tourism**, although the latter focuses more on experiencing fauna and flora. Planning and management are important issues, especially with regard to the **impacts** of rural tourism (not only on the environment, but also on the socio-economic fabric of rural communities).

Hall, Derek, Kirkpatrick, Irene and Mitchell, Morag (eds), *Rural Tourism and Sustainable Business* (London: Channel View, 2005).

Roberts, Lesley and Hall, Derek, *Rural Tourism and Recreation: Principles to Practice* (London: CABI, 2001).

Sharpley, Richard and Sharpley, Julia, *Rural Tourism: An Introduction* (London: Routledge, 1997).

R

Ss

Schengen Agreement

Schengen is the name of a small town in Luxembourg where the Schengen Agreement was signed in 1985 by five countries: Belgium, France, Germany, Luxembourg, and the Netherlands. The basic principles are to allow for common immigration policies (including the so-called Schengen visa) as well as a new border system without internal border checkpoints controls within the Schengen area. Other countries have gradually joined and signed the convention (Italy in 1990, Portugal and Spain in 1992 etc.), bringing the total number of signatories to 26, although only fifteen countries have implemented it so far (in 2006): Austria, Belgium, Denmark, Finland, France, Germany, Iceland, Italy, Greece, Luxembourg, the Netherlands, Norway, Portugal, Spain and Sweden. It is worth noting that the United Kingdom and the Republic of Ireland are not part of Schengen. Countries such as Poland and Switzerland have signed but not implemented the convention yet. Foreign tourists from other countries need apply for only one visa (the so-called Schengen visa) and they can then visit any or all of the Schengen countries; for inbound tourism from other continents, this makes tourism within the so-called Schengenland much easier. Tourism operators need to be aware of some minor exceptions, for example not all non-European parts of France are included, neither are Andorra and Monaco.

Schengen visa website, www.eurovisa.info

Seasonality

Seasonality refers to fluctuations in **demand** according to the time of year. In the framework of the one-year cycle, the tourism industry has traditionally had a rhythmic pattern of high season(s), low season(s) and shoulder periods in between, though the patterns depend upon place and operations (especially accommodation). For example in Europe July and August have traditionally been high season in **3S** destinations with occupancy rates at nearly 100 per cent, whilst it was low season for business-oriented city hotels. The predictability of seasonal patterns has enabled the tourism **industry** to turn the threat into an opportunity by devising new ways to minimise the negative impacts of seasonality, for example with some seaside resorts, reinventing themselves as mild winter destinations in Cornwall and the Balearic Islands. Because of their more stable climate all year long, tropical destinations on the pleasure periphery suffer less from seasonality, although some other factors do create rhythmic changes, such as traditional holiday periods (Christmas, Easter) when the demand from families with children rises.

Second home

A second home is a property owned and maintained by someone who lives in a principal residence elsewhere. Properties bought to be rented out permanently ('buy to let' schemes in urban areas as a form of investment) are not normally considered as second homes: the phrase rather refers to properties used for recreational purposes. While the owners may well sometimes let out their holiday home, these places are not normally used all year long. The phenomenon of second-home ownership is by no means recent: two millennia ago, rich Romans had secondary residences in the rural hinterland to escape from the heat of the summer. In the UK, according to the 2005 National Census, 1 per cent of homes are second residences; 500,000 English families have second homes, either in the UK or abroad: in the UK, they are concentrated in some parts of the country such as Devon and Cornwall (where as many as 25 per cent of residences in some local authorities are second homes); while, abroad, Spain (62,000) and France (42,000) are the most popular countries for UK second homes. Second-home ownership raises numeral social issues, for example about local people who cannot afford a home as they are priced out of the housing market (because of tourists who hardly take part in the local community). With regard to tourism, second homes are particularly important because they contribute to a steady flow of tourism (ensuring a constant demand which can help with forecasting, for example for **low cost carriers** operating routes to regions where there are many second homes). in addition second homes reduce the multiplier effect as tourists do not spend money on accommodation.

Semiotics

Semiotics (also called semiology) is the study of signs, including symbols and images. Applied to tourism, semiotics can help analyse and interpret a range of documents, from postcards and guidebooks to personal photographs and television travel programmes. What could appear as a gratuitous and rather theoretical analysis of texts and images is actually a serious and rigorous research process, akin to **content analysis**. It can enable tourism managers to appreciate tourist expectations, or understand the construction of the image of a destination through branding and marketing. Although semiotics tends to be confined to departments of philosophy or linguistics, it may have useful and concrete practical applications for tourism managers.

MacCannell, Dean (ed.) Special issue on 'The Semiotics of Tourism', *Annals of Tourism Research*, 19:1, 1989.

Selwyn, Tom (ed.), *The Tourist Image: Myths and Myth-making in Tourism*, Chichester: Wiley, 1996).

Senior tourism

Sometimes called 'grey tourism', senior tourism is usually defined as travellers aged 55 and above (although other ages are sometimes used as thresholds: 50, 60, 62 or 65). Senior tourism is widely regarded as a new market opportunity for the global tourism industry. Four factors explain the growth of the senior market in Western countries:

- Because of *demographic changes* (an ageing population), the size of the market itself is increasing (which means more demand for suitable holidays).
- Because of *socio-economic changes*, the disposable income of senior citizens will enable them to travel more than previous generations.
- Because of *improvements in heath and heath care*, an increasing number of senior citizens are more physically able to travel.
- Because of the current *democratisation of tourism*, many senior tourists in the next decades will already be well travelled and will have certain expectations and a critical understanding of what travelling implies.

Aware that it is a lucrative developing market, the tourism industry has already started to target senior tourists (the most well-known example in Great Britain being the tour operator Saga). From an academic viewpoint, it is worth noting that there might not be a single senior tourism market, but a range of **niches** and sub-markets with different tastes, demands and needs.

Services

In **marketing** and **economics**, services are defined as the opposite of goods: both are products, but goods are physical and material (like objects) whereas services are intangible (they rather constitute an experience). Although tourism does involve some goods (such as souvenirs and duty-free merchandise), overall it is conceptualised as a service, hence the phrase 'service-based **industry**' used to describe tourism; in the same way, travel agents are 'service providers' and the 'service encounter' refers to the activities involved in the 'service delivery' process. In the academic **literature**, services are widely presented as having four characteristics: **intangibility**, **inseparability**, **perishability** and **variability**. These four concepts help better understand the nature of services as well as the business consequences, especially in terms of **marketing**.

Grönroos, Christian, *Service Management and Marketing: A Customer Relationship Management Approach*, 2nd edn (Chichester: John Wiley, 2001).

Teboul, James, *Service is Front Stage: Positioning Services for Value Advantage* (Basingstoke: Palgrave Macmillan, 2006).

Sex tourism

Sex tourism is tourism partially or fully motivated by the prospect of sexual encounters. The phrase is generally used when the sexual interactions take place between tourists and locals: sex amongst tourists is not usually covered by the concept, although it is a very common feature of the **tourist experience**, especially for many young travellers. Sex tourism often implies prostitution, which implies that sex tourism is legal in the countries where prostitution is also legal. Child sex tourism is a different issue as it is a serious offence in most countries. Many international organisations such as ECPAT campaign for even stricter legislation against the sexual exploitation of children by tourists. Adult sex workers are of both genders, with, for example, white middle-aged women going to the Gambia to meet younger men, or white middle-aged men going to South-East Asia. In all cases, these relationships are fraught with **commodification**, commercial exploitation, power asymmetry and health risks. In terms of sexual orientation, **gay and lesbian tourism** seems less affected by sex tourism. Numerous books, case studies and research papers have been published on the topic of sex tourism; one of their key messages is that one must be careful of simplistic analysis such as 'tourism causes prostitution'.

Bauer, Thomas G. and McKercher, Bob (eds), *Sex and Tourism: Journeys of Romance, Love, and Lust* (New York: Haworth Hospitality Press, 2003).

Clift, Stephen and Carter, Simon (eds), *Tourism and Sex: Culture, Commerce and Coercion* (London: Thomson, 2000).

Ryan, Chris, and Hall, Mike, *Sex Tourism: Marginal People and Liminalities* (London: Routledge, 2001).

ECPAT, www.ecpat.net

Short haul

Short haul usually refers to flights that last under five hours, although the concept does not have a unique, authoritative definition, and it needs to take into account the geographical context and other points of reference; a possible approach is to consider flights taking place within one's home continent, as opposed to **long haul**: Cairns–Sydney, Dublin–Rome and Ottawa–Washington are short haul.

With regard to the history of tourism, the short-haul market has been instrumental in:

- the development of international **mass tourism** from the 1950s onwards (with the popularity of **package tours** and package holidays);
- the commercial success of **low cost carriers** (and consequently the democratisation of air travel),
- the development of short breaks as a popular form of **urban tourism** (called city breaks).

Sightseeing

Sightseeing is one of the usual components of tourism; even **business** tourists and **sunlust** tourists will often look around the place where they are staying (**enclave tourism** being the only exception), if only to see some of the local shops, streets and buildings. The objects of sightseeing range from architecture and monuments to **museums**, events and even people. In the latter instance, there is an ethical danger that locals may end up as victims of **commodification** by tourists in search of local **authenticity**, and yet many tourists often want to photograph or film locals and local scenes to take home as visual souvenirs. The notion of sightseeing reinforces the argument that the tourist **gaze** is a key element of the **tourist experience**, or put another way that tourism is pre-eminently a form of visual consumption.

Adler, Judith, 'The Origins of Sightseeing', *Annals of Tourism Research*, 16(1) (1989): 7–29.
Urry, John, *The Tourist Gaze* (London: Sage, 1990).
Urry, John, *Consuming Places* (London: Routledge, 1995).

S

SMART

SMART is an acronym referring to a set of targets or objectives, especially when they are set in planning documents; there is no consensus for some of the letters:

S   specific (that is, precise)
M   measurable (especially quantifiable)
A   assignable or appropriate or achievable
R   relevant or realistic or resourced
T   timed or timely or time-framed (with deadlines)

SMART is commonly used in marketing, but managers from all sectors may benefit from the simple frame when setting objectives, because it focuses on key objectives (instead of having solely a generic aim). Tables are sometimes used to present the objectives, for example see Table 4.

Table 4   Example of application of SMART concept

S	Recruit and train more volunteers to help with the cathedral visit
M	Minimum ten volunteers
A	Magda Wnuk responsible for that
R	Necessary to help cover in peak season
T	By end of May

At the start of the next planning cycle, one usually goes back to the objectives that were initially set, in order to identify whether or not they have been achieved (and if not, why not).

Social tourism

Social tourism is wide spread in several European countries such as France and Belgium, yet little known and often misunderstood in English-speaking countries where traditionally liberal governments have not financially helped people who cannot afford to travel. To put it in a simplistic and derogatory way, social tourism is 'tourism for the under-privileged': at a purely material level, social tourism is comparable to schemes of housing benefits or unemployment benefit – but it is best conceptualised in terms of its overall aim: the public interest. Social tourism is motivated by the political and psychological belief that the individual's well-being resulting from a holiday and travel will benefit society as a whole, through personal development and social cohesion.

The underpinning philosophical principle is that tourism is a right, and not a privilege: all citizens should consequently be able to enjoy a break away from home. As tourism is expensive, some people (for example adults on limited income) will need some help, which can be provided by public organisations (central government, local authorities), by the voluntary sector (charities, community groups) or even by employers (through associations within large companies). Schemes can take a variety of forms, including direct financial support, the provision of vacation vouchers and the availability of affordable accommodation (holiday villages, camp grounds, specialised lodgings). In France (the uncontested leader in the field of social tourism), associations of social tourism control more than one-fifth of the country's overall accommodation capacity, that is a total of almost one million beds (a quarter of which are in youth hostels).

Validating the globalisation of social tourism and the diversity of its contexts and forms, the 1996 Montreal Declaration is recognised as the "charter" for social tourism. Based in Brussels, the Bureau International du Tourisme Social is the international organisation co-ordinating, representing and researching all aspects of social tourism.

Bureau International du Tourisme Social, www.bits-int.org

Space tourism

After trips to Antarctica and Mount Everest, space is now presented as the new frontier (and the last frontier) of tourism. What was regarded as science fiction fantasy has become reality since the pioneering space journeys of multimillionaires Dennis Tito (in 2001) and Mark Shuttleworth (in 2002). Several companies are investing millions in research and development, for example Virgin Galactic. The numerous challenges include technological issues (propulsion and guidance systems of spacecraft), partnerships between private companies and government research centres, as well as the safety and comfort of the 'leisurenauts' and the associated costs. Visionaries believe that space tourism will become established practice in the twenty-first century, as the next chapter of the history of tourism development.

Spencer, John and Rugg, Karen, *Space Tourism: Do You Want to Go?* (Burlington, ON: Apogee Books, 2004).
Van Pelt, Michel, *Space Tourism: Adventures in Earth Orbit and Beyond* (New York: Copernicus, 2005).

Space Tourism Society, www.spacetourismsociety.org
Virgin Galactic, www.virgingalactic.com

Special interest tourism

The phrase 'special interest tourism' (sometimes abbreviated to SIT) creates a typology of tourists according to their precise motivation, usually linked to a hobby or activity. SIT includes, amongst others, wine tourism, garden tourism, golf tourism, ornithological tourism, cycle tourism, etc. The focus may be recreational, educational, or a combination of both. A taxonomic problem with SIT is that one does not know where to stop in terms of ramification and specialisation, which is why there cannot be an authoritative list of SITs. From an industry perspective, the existence of SITs shows that the tourism market is increasingly fragmented, so for some market segments the one-size-fits-all approach of **mass tourism** and even identikit schemes is becoming less relevant. Special interest tourism means that it is possible to identify and precisely target potential customers, for example garden lovers who can then be reached through advertisements in specialised publications. The increasing number of specialist **travel agents** and **tour operators** is a direct consequence of the division of the tourism market and of the subsequent multiplication of SITs.

Douglas, Norman, Douglas, Ngaire and Derrett, Ros, *Special Interest Tourism* (Chichester: John Wiley, 2001).
Weiler, Betty and Hall, Colin M., *Special Interest Tourism* (London: Bellhaven, 1992).

Sports tourism

The concept of sports tourism encompasses a range of touristic forms and activities. To appreciate the breadth of the concept, it is helpful to distinguish:

- between active sports tourism and passive sports tourism: in the former, tourists participate (for example scuba-diving in Micronesia), in the latter, they travel to attend sports events (for example the Brazilian fans who went to Germany in June 2006 for the FIFA World Cup):
- between sports tourism where sport is the main purpose of the journey (like in the two examples above) or when it is incidental (one afternoon horse-riding in the middle of a farm holiday in Cyprus);
- between sports tourism where the sport is practised professionally (for example the British women's curling team travelling to Vancouver for the 2010 Winter Olympics) and where it is engaged in recreationally (for example a weekend initiation to archery in the French Pyrenees).

From a **marketing** angle, rather than being a large unique market, sports tourism is better considered as a set of specialists markets (which can then qualify as special interest tourism): rugby tourism, diving tourism, etc. An increasing number of specialised operators, especially travel agents, are catering for these tourists. Likewise, the academic literature on sports tourism is becoming more fragmented, with not only books and **journal** articles about sports tourism in general, but also monographs and **case studies** about particular segments.

Hudson, Simon, *Snow Business: A Study of the International Ski Industry* (London: Thomson, 1999).

Ritchie, Brent W. and Adair, Daryl (eds), *Sport Tourism: Interrelationships, Impacts and Issues* (Clevedon: Channel View, 2004).

Staged authenticity

The quest for **authenticity** is often presented as a key motivation for many tourists, even at an unconscious level. Many people will travel to try to experience unspoilt nature (see **wildland tourism**) or other ethnic cultures (see **cultural tourism**), yet in many cases tourists will be offered only **staged authenticity**. Dance shows performed for tourists or religious rituals (detached from their original spiritual dimension) organised for them (for their gaze) are typical examples of staged authenticity. As genuine host culture remains **backstage**, tourists may consume only what is offered to them; the more discerning ones may feel disappointed, frustrated and annoyed when they realise that they are not being given the authentic experience they were after. Staged authenticity is not always negative though; a famous example is the prehistoric cave of Lascaux in the Dordogne in France, where, in order to protect its fragile beautiful paintings, a replica of the cave has been built 200 metres from the original which is now closed to the public. 'Lascaux II' attracts 250,000 visitors a year who know that they are not seeing 'the real thing' yet this is not detrimental to the popularity of the place, nor to the visitors' experience and satisfaction.

McCannell, Dean, *The Tourist: A New Theory of the Leisure Class* (New York: Schocken Books, 1976).

Stagnation stage

In the **Butler Sequence**, the stagnation stage follows the **consolidation stage**. All the features from the consolidation still apply (high spatial concentration of tourists, marked negative environmental and socio-cultural impacts, external ownership of most hotels and attractions), yet three further characteristics may be identified:

- The market is saturated, both in terms of supply and demand.
- The peak level of tourism is reached: hotel development no longer

reflects interest in the destination. This creates over-capacity which in turn leads to price wars and the cheapening of the destination's image.

- Psychocentric tourists are repeat visitors who expect to find the brands and comforts of home without any sense of a local identity.

Examples include some parts of the Spanish Costas, but some authors have also analysed the Laurentians (in Quebec) and Muskoka (in Ontario) as hinterland regions going through the equivalent of a stagnation stage. Stagnation is the opposite of change; the stagnation stage could last for ever, but for destination managers it is rather a time of consideration and decision-making with regard to the future of the place, with the need to devise strategies around a precise vision.

Stakeholders

A stakeholder is a person or a group of people who have a vested interest in a particular business or event. The stakeholders of an existing tourism business (for example a rural hotel) include its staff and managers, its owners and financial backers, as well as its customers and suppliers. The stakeholders of a proposed tourist development (for example creating a golf hotel near the above-mentioned hotel) include:

- people directly connected to the proposal, such as local owners whose land may be needed, investors who would provide the necessary funding as well as local authorities who would need to give their permission;
- people who may be affected by the realisation of the project, such as local golf players (who may be most supportive), the neighbouring village that so far has the only golf in the area or even charities (such as the Campaign for the Protection of Rural England).

Carrying out a stakeholder analysis helps identify and map all the stakeholders involved. This exercise follows a standard methodology, which involves prioritising stakeholders as well as comparing their respective agendas and influences. The aim is to ensure integrated decision-making.

Standardisation

Within an organisation (such as an international hotel chain), standardisation refers to the policy and efforts to ensure that all business units are performing in a similar way. For example, the fact that Hilton Hotels are standardised means that customers know what to expect from any

Hilton Hotel with regard to quality of service, irrespective of the destination. A room at the Hilton Guadalajara will be similar to a room at the Hilton Rabat, and will also correspond to international **benchmarks** across similar hotels. From tourism managers' perspective, standardisation has numerous advantages (expectation management, proven procedures and guidelines), yet it presents an important drawback for tourists: it can make their experience quite bland and homogeneous. Within the **hospitality** industry, catering is a key example, with the development of a global hotel cuisine that sometimes fails to do justice to local gastronomy. In a negative sense, standardisation can be associated with **globalisation**, **McDonaldization** and Americanisation.

Statistics

Strictly speaking, statistics is the mathematical science concerned with the processing, analysis and presentation of data. In tourism management, the word 'statistics' is often used in its simple meaning of 'numerical data' (data resulting from statistical operations that took place earlier on). Published tourism statistics (for example by national organisations such as the Office of National Statistics in the United Kingdom, or by international ones such as the **World Tourism Organization**) help identify patterns and help us understand changes in tourism **trends**. **Tourism Satellite Accounts** are adopted by an increasing number of countries, making international comparisons of tourism statistics more valid and reliable. Some commercial market intelligence companies (such as Mintel) are another good source of tourism statistics, though their reports can be quite expensive. Like all **research** findings, this is potentially very useful for decision-makers (such as destination managers and tourism **policy**-makers) in order to help **planning**. Statistics are a key component of **quantitative research**, although they often offer a mere description of a situation, which then needs to be interpreted.

MINTEL, www.mintel.co.uk
UK Office of National Statistics, www.statistics.gov.uk

Stereotype

A stereotype is a set of characteristics about a type of person; the person stereotyped is not considered as an individual, but as representative of a group. Stereotypes are based on generalisations and simplifications, for example a stereotypical backpacker will be described as a 20-something, urban, educated Caucasian English-speaker on a gap year, travelling on a budget and staying in cheap communal accommodations, yet owning a high-tech MP3 player, a mobile phone and an expensive digital camera. Blogging regularly from Internet cafes around the world, s/he may claim to experience local cultures, though s/he usually congregates with other backpackers and does not discover much beyond the backpacking subculture. In tourism settings, stereotypes are often negative, for example stereotypes that tourists may have about host populations, and vice versa; they correspond to a 'them' and 'us' perspective that combines **ethnocentrism**, prejudice and small-mindedness. The word 'archetype' is sometimes used to refer to neutral stereotypes.

Strategy

A term of military origin, 'strategy' refers to a long-term plan of action designed to achieve particular aims and objectives. The concept of strategy is very important in business management, with a range of models and theories designed by scholars to explain the principles of strategic management. It is helpful to distinguish between strategy formulation and strategy implementation.

- *Strategy formulation*, based on the analysis of the internal and external environments (often using frameworks such as PEST/STEEPLE and SWOT), leads to the drawing up of a strategic plan, articulating both a generic vision and precise objectives as targets (short-, medium- and long-term). This is called strategic planning; for example an independent travel agency will articulate that they aim to have a 25 per cent local market share by the end of the decade.
- *Strategy implementation* is the process of allocating and harnessing resources to reach these objectives, that is to implement the plan at an operational level. In the above example, the travel agency could extend its opening hours and move to a new site on the high street to get more passing trade.

Strategies are not specific to commercial organisations: even small local tourism organisations are likely to have their own strategy, which gives them a sense of purpose and direction.

Evans, Nigel, Campbell, David and Stonehouse, George, *Strategic Management for Travel and Tourism* (Oxford: Butterworth-Heinemann, 2003).
Tribe, John, *Corporate Strategy for Tourism* (London: Thomson, 1996).

Sunlust

The word 'sunlust' was coined in the 1970s to describe the motivation of tourists seeking relaxation in the sun, typically, in a seaside resort, hence the related phrase '**3S** tourism' (sea, sun, sand). It tends to be used in a derogatory way, contrasting that passive and hedonistic form of tourism to more cultural pursuits, more active forms of holidays or forms of tourism that involve discovering the destination. The latter point stresses a key marketing difference between sunlust and its counterpart **wanderlust**: sunlust destinations are not that differentiated from one another, they offer a similar product irrespective of the country (Mauritius, the Seychelles or Caribbean islands), whereas wanderlust destinations offer a specific product and a unique experience. The concept of sunlust intrinsically reflects a north European perspective: it makes sense only from the perspective of travellers, analysts or service providers based in places which are deprived of sun for several months of the year. The concept of sunlust has recently lost some of its appeal due to health-related issues (the fear of skin cancer from over-exposure to the sun).

Superstructure

'Superstructure' is the umbrella term that includes all developments, buildings and facilities which rely on an existing **infrastructure** at a destination. Whereas the infrastructure of a destination is normally funded by the **public sector** (due to the high cost of building airports, motorways and sewage systems), the superstructure is usually the direct responsibility of the **private sector**. The superstructure is mainly made up of edifices and constructions (hotels, restaurants, theme parks, etc.) as well as associated amenities (swimming pool, tennis courts, golf course, etc.). Although not as expensive as the infrastructure which underpins it, the superstructure can also be viewed as being a costly **investment**; this is why many developments such as large hotels are often financed and built by large corporations from outside the hospitality sector; they are then run under management contracts by leading hospitality brands. This allows hospitality companies to extend their brand globally, whilst the investment corporations owning the land and buildings can achieve an income based on the agreement reached with the hotel group.

Supply

The supply of travel and tourism products and services refers to the quantity that companies are prepared to offer to the market at every possible price. Adrian Bull in 1995 gave a simple yet powerful definition of tourism supply as 'what, where, when and how to produce' tourism products. Put another way, the supply is what the tourism **industry** offers. With regard to supply (and the possibility to supply what the demand really wants/needs), the travel and tourism sector suffers greatly from high initial capital costs (such as the purchasing of a cruise ship or aircraft; for example, the price for a new Airbus super jumbo A380 in 2006 stands at £150 million) and from the fixed nature of capacity (for example a hotel in a popular destination may sometimes have a 100 per cent occupancy rate and even be overbooked yet unable to satisfy the demand at peak time). Balancing demand and supply in order to ensure profit maximisation is one of the main challenges of tourism managers. Possible strategies include identifying and targeting new sources of demands (new markets), or developing and advertising off-season opportunities, or changing pricing systems (**yield management**).

Bull, Adrian, *The Economics of Travel and Tourism* (Melbourne: Longman, 1995).

Supply chain management (SCM)

The concept of supply chain is used in **logistics** and **operations management** to help deconstruct and understand the processes involved in production and distribution; the aim is to better manage the supply chain – hence the phrase 'supply chain management' (SCM) – to cut costs, speed the process or improve the final quality of the product. SCM may seem more appropriate for manufacturing, yet some sections of the tourism industry are involved in processes where SCM can help improve performance, for example with regard to tour operations. In the case of a package tour, the supply chain includes as 'raw products' accommodation and transport, plus other services that may added; suppliers are the accommodation providers and transport providers; distributors are travel agents. The need for quality control and efficiency within the supply chain has resulted in many tour operators opting for strategies of **vertical integration** so as to control all aspects of the supply of the product (for example First Choice has its own airline and travel agents, ensuring a continued supply chain). With the development of **globalisation**, outsourcing and more complex international business arrangements, the concept of supply chain management is increasingly studied by management scholars and the literature on the topic is expanding.

Chopra, Sunil and Meindl, Peter, *Supply Chain Management: Strategy, Planning and Operations*, 3rd edn (London: Prentice-Hall, 2006).

Supply Chain Management Institute, www.scm-institute.org

Sustainable development

The most frequently cited definition of sustainable development is the following one: 'Sustainable development is development that meets the needs of the present without compromising the ability of future genera-tions to meet their own needs.' It is from the so-called *Brundtland Report*, a 1987 report from the United Nations (Gro Harlem Brundtland was the Norwegian Chair of the World Commission on Environment and Development which published the report). The need for sustainable development is now widely accepted by governments and most economic sectors; because of its focus on the tension between economic development and environmental problems on a global scale, it has a particular resonance for tourism management. The tourism **industry** has now endorsed the concept, though maybe only in a narrow perspective that fails to address some issues, such as **opportunity costs** when scarce resources are in competition in developing countries. Sustainable development underpins the concept of **sustainable tourism**.

Baker, Susan, *Sustainable Development* (London: Routledge, 2005).
Jamieson, Walter, *Community Destination Management in Developing Economies* (New York: Haworth Press, 2006).
United Nations World Commission on Environment and Development, *Our Common Future (Brundtland Report)* (New York, 1987).

Sustainable tourism

Sustainable tourism is probably the most important idea that has entered tourism management in the last 20 years, both as **theory** and as practice. A high number of definitions can be found in both the acade-mic and professional **literature**. Authors may articulate their views slightly differently, and foci may differ, yet there is a consensus that sustainable tourism is respectful of the destination's social, cultural and natural environments. Sustainable tourism is often discussed as a value-ridden philosophical approach rather than a specific form of tourism; **ecotourism** (with its focus on ecology) and **community tourism** (with its focus on empowering and involving local communities) are then cited as the concrete expressions of the principles of sustainable tourism. Besides, sustainable tourism is usually presented in a prescrip-tive way, stating what tourism should be, what it should and should not do: unlike **mass tourism**, sustainable tourism should not degrade the environment and local cultures and societies, but should take into account the **sustainable development** of destinations. Examples of sustainable tourism practices abound, usually in the form of case studies; they are accompanied by discussions of some of the subsequent

S

challenges and dilemmas, such as the question of how sustainable tourism can be achieved on a global scale.

Aronsson, Lars, *The Development of Sustainable Tourism* (London: Thomson, 2000).

Middleton, Victor T. C. and Hawkins, Rebecca, *Sustainable Tourism: A Marketing Approach* (Oxford: Butterworth Heinemann, 1998).

Swarbrooke, John, *Sustainable Tourism Development* (Wallingford: CABI, 1999).

World Tourism Organization, *Sustainable Development of Tourism: A Compilation of Good Practices* (Madrid: World Tourism Organisation, 2001).

Journal of Sustainable Tourism

SWOT analysis

SWOT analysis is a simple framework that helps systematically map the **s**trengths, **w**eaknesses, **o**pportunities and **t**hreats of an organisation. It is a balanced tool because:

- It covers the present (*SW*) but is also orientated towards the future (*OT*).
- It includes both positive aspects (*SO*) and negative ones (*WT*).
- It takes not only the internal factors into account (*SW*) but also external ones (*OT*).

While the four letters are self-explanatory, the following questions may help us focus on how the concept can be used:

- *Strengths*: What is the organisation particularly good at? What are its advantages over competitors, with regard to staff, structure, services, experience? (Keywords like the 7Ps of the **marketing mix** can also suggest other strengths.)
- *Weaknesses*: What is the organisation not so good at? Which areas could be better with regard to staff, abilities, competence, strategies, policies, methods?
- *Opportunities*: Which external factors are sources of optimism? What changes in the external environment seem beneficial?
- *Threats*: Which external factors are sources of concern? What changes in the external environment seem detrimental?

A SWOT analysis is often presented in the form of a table, with key points identified, although this is only the result of the analysis as a summary.

The acronym USED is then sometimes employed to stress that a SWOT analysis is not an end in itself, but a tool to help take strategic decisions:

How can we	**U**se	each Strength?
How can we	**S**top	each Weakness?
How can we	**E**xploit	each Opportunity?
How can we	**D**efend	against each Threat?

Doing a SWOT analysis is a very common planning activity, be it in the framework of a **business plan** or as part of the preparation of a strategic plan. The difficulty is that one may ignore the importance of some aspects.

Technology

Technological progress is not always considered as part of tourism management, yet it is an essential contributor to tourism development. The two major technological improvements which have marked and shaped contemporary tourism are:

- *Aircraft technology*, as the jet age brought mass travel to the public. As technology improved, the price of air seats fell. The introduction in 1970 of the Boeing 747 (or jumbo jet) made long-distance mass travel a reality. The jumbo has flown through four decades, favoured by the world's airlines as their long-haul workhorse. This supremacy is about to be tested, however, as 2007 sees the first commercial services aboard the Airbus A380, an aircraft that rivals the jumbo in distance but surpasses it in seating capacity by at least 100 seats.
- *Internet technology*, as the Internet age has revolutionalised the distribution process of tourism products, by giving travellers the power and transparency to book individual elements of the travel product themselves, without the requirement of either a **travel agent** or **tour operator**. **E-tourism** is still in its infancy and it is not possible to imagine how it will develop over the next decades.

Technological progress has radically changed the way people travel and the way people think of tourism: not only has technology contributed to the **democratisation of tourism**, but it has also demystified the process of organising tourism. Technology also plays an ongoing role in **product development**.

Theme parks

A theme park (also called 'amusement park') is an artificially created attraction. It is an entirely user-oriented, purpose-built entertainment complex, usually on a large scale, containing numerous sub-attractions such as rides and shows. Whole family groups are the main market targets, with products for all age groups, including young children, teenagers and adults. Whilst most theme parks offer an all-day recreational experience, others also provide on-site accommodation. The Disney-related theme parks (Walt Disney World Resort in Florida, Disneyland Resort Paris, etc.) are the most famous examples, although strictly speaking they are resorts containing several theme parks. Many other tourist destinations have their own flagships, such as Blackpool Pleasure Beach in England, Legoland Billund in Denmark, PortAventura in Salou, Spain, or the Prater in Vienna, Austria, one of the longest-standing theme parks in the world. From an academic, analytical viewpoint, theme parks are particularly interesting for two reasons: firstly, the way they offer seemingly thrilling, adventurous experiences (such as rollercoasters) which are entirely staged and artificial; and secondly, the way they are carefully designed to maximise retail expenditure by visitors.

Rojek, Chris, *Ways of Escape: Modern Transformations in Leisure and Travel* (Basingstoke: Macmillan, 1993).

Swarbrooke, John, *The Development and Management of Visitor Attractions*, 2nd edn (Oxford: Butterworth-Heinemann, 2002).

Theory

If in common parlance the word 'theory' means opinion or unsubstantiated guess as opposed to facts, in academic language a theory refers to a set of connected statements used as part of a wider explanation to rationally elucidate complex phenomena; it is in that sense that gravitation, evolution or plate tectonics are theories. Tourism management does not have any such grand theory providing an overall inclusive explanation, yet an increasing number of concepts (such as **communitas** and **liminality**) and models (such as the **Butler Sequence**) provide a strong theoretical basis. The fact that tourism management is a multidisciplinary field makes the process of theory-building particularly difficult, because different subjects and disciplines have idiosyncratic approaches to the notion and importance of theory, not to mention different concepts and methodologies. Theoretical underpinning is particularly important for **research** projects in order to ensure that they build upon previous research and that their premises are duly addressed in their abstract context.

T

3S (or Three S)

The phrase '3S tourism' refers to a type of tourism represented by sea, sand and sun: seaside tourism, inactive holidays in a sunny beachside resort. This has come to emblematise **mass tourism** and **sunlust**. For '4S tourism', sex is added (sea, sand, sun and sex) to emphasize the hedonistic component, both metaphorically and literally, though not in the meaning of sex tourism: '4S tourism' rather characterises young people's holidays (typically customers of the holiday company 'Club 1830') where sexual adventures between tourists in the same resort are regarded as an accepted if not expected part of the holiday experience. With its nickname 'Shagalluf', Magalluf on the Balearic Island of Mallorca is an example of 4S tourism.

Timeshare

Timeshare is a particular system of holiday-property ownership whereby people own the unit but only for a certain period of time, for example two weeks a year for five years. Put another way, timeshare owners buy the rights to use the property. Timeshare owners may then stay there or rent it out or exchange it with other timeshare owners to stay in their property instead. Timeshare units are usually in resorts, in the form of studios and apartments, although the system has also been extended to other types of accommodation such as campsites and yachts. Timeshare is a growing segment of the hospitality industry; many operators (such as Hilton, Marriott, Disney and Butlins) operate such schemes, whose complexity and specificity changes according to the contracts and arrangements. Timeshare raises some specific issues though, for example about legal considerations and insurance, service quality as well as the professional ethics of timeshare agencies, as some would-be timeshare owners have been victims of scams and frauds, whilst others have been victims of very forceful and convincing sellers. In Britain, the Office of Fair Trading has published a leaflet specifically for people who may have been talked into signing a dubious timeshare contract.

Upchurch, Randall and Lashley, Conrad, *Timeshare Resort Operations: A Guide to Management Practice* (Oxford: Butterworth-Heinemann, 2006).

Tour guides

Tour guides shepherd tourists (for various periods of times, from one hour to several days) and provide them with information about the place they visit, especially its natural and cultural resources. They have an important function in the tourism industry because they may influence the level of satisfaction obtained by tourists, as well as their understanding of the destination and its people. From an academic viewpoint, the last point is particularly significant because tour guides, as **culture**

brokers, have an important role of **interpretation**. Maybe surprisingly, the academic literature on the topic is still quite limited, mainly examining the various roles that tour guides may take on (especially with regard to educating and mentoring tourists) as well as issues pertaining to **professionalism** (etiquette, ethics, training, qualifications such as Blue Badge Guides in the UK).

Cohen, Erik, 'The Tourist Guide: The Origins, Structure and Dynamics of a Role', *Annals of Tourism Research*, 12(1) (1985): 5-29.

Pond, Kathleen L., *The Professional Guide: Dynamics of Tour Guiding* (New York: Van Nostrand Reinhold, 1993).

Tourism

The concept of tourism can be defined in numerous ways, depending upon the perspective one prefers to follow; this is due to the **multi-disciplinarity** that underpins the academic study of tourism, and to the fact that concepts are never set in stone but change over time.

- Tourism is an **industry** providing **services** to travellers, from transportation to accommodation to entertainment and ancillary services such as currency exchange. As such, it is one of the most dynamic sectors of the world economy, employing an estimated 200 million people worldwide in 2003 (source: **World Travel and Tourism Council**). In 2003, tourism receipts represented 30 per cent of all service transactions worldwide (source: **World Tourism Organization**).
- Tourism is a socio-geographical phenomenon expressed through considerable flows of people both within their own countries (**domestic tourism**) and across borders (**international tourism**). In 2004, international tourist arrivals reached an all-time record of 763 million (source: WTO), an increase of 74 million from the previous year, despite concerns linked to the Iraq war, SARS and the weak economy worldwide.
- Tourism is an experience (lived either individually or collectively), driven by a range of motivations and purposes, from leisure to business, from health to a search for **authenticity**). Coming from a psycho-sociological perspective, that approach complements the previous points based on economics, as a healthy reminder that tourism is about people: it may be an industry, but it is a people industry.

In addition, one needs to be aware of some technical definitions of tourism, such as the authoritative one from the **WTO**:

The activities of a person travelling outside his or her usual environment for less than a specified period of time and whose main purpose is other than the exercise of an activity remunerated from the place visited.

Generic academic textbooks about tourism management usually start by reviewing these definitions, and many authors will often provide their own as well.

Cooper, Chris et al., *Tourism: Principles and Practice*, 3rd edn (London: Prentice Hall, 2005).

Page, Stephen J. and Connell, Joanne, *Tourism: A Modern Synthesis*, 2nd edn (London: Thomson, 2006).

World Travel and Tourism Council, www.wttc.org
World Tourism Organisation, www.world-tourism.org

Tourism development

The phrases 'tourism development' and 'development of tourism' have two cognate meanings, depending on the context:

- In relation to the history of tourism, they refer to the way tourism gradually changed over the centuries; it already existed two millennia ago (the Romans had seaside resorts, spa destinations, attractions as well as accommodation facilities), and it evolved through time, with some landmarks such as the **Grand Tour** and Thomas **Cook**'s innovations, until the development of **mass tourism** and **alternative tourism** in the second part of the twentieth century. Tourism is still developing, for example with **e-tourism** and **space tourism**.

- In relation to destinations (be they local, regional or national), tourism development refers to the process whereby a place develops its facilities and **infrastructure** to attract tourists and cater for their needs. The concepts of destination lifecycle (see **Butler Sequence**) and **planning** help underline the complexity of the process, as it involves strategic political and economic decisions taken jointly or separately by managers from the **public sector** and the **private sector**. To be successful and sustainable, tourism development needs to follow a thorough yet flexible strategy.

Ineson, Elizabeth M., *Current Issues in International Tourism Development* (Sunderland: Business Education Publishers, 2005).

Pearce, Douglas G. and Butler, Richard W. (eds), *Contemporary Issues in Tourism Development* (London: Routledge, 1999).

Shackley, Myra, *Atlas of Travel and Tourism Development* (Oxford: Butterworth-Heinemann, 2005).

'Tourism for all'

The concept of 'tourism for all' is linked to issues of **accessibility** and social inclusivity, especially with reference to disabled tourists. **Transportation** (for example wheelchair-accessible trains and planes) is an important issue, yet not the only one. Several charities and voluntary organisations have campaigns and information materials targeting tourism providers who may not always be aware of the specific needs of some disabled tourists; for example in a hotel even the noisiest fire alarm might fail to wake up a hearing-impaired guest, but a vibrating mattress could save their life. Under the common banner of 'tourism for all', these awareness-raising campaigns have three main arguments:

- firstly, a legal argument about the obligation to comply with the **legislation** (such as the Disability Discrimination Act in Great Britain or the Americans with Disabilities Act in the USA);
- secondly, a financial argument about the business opportunities provided for disabled travellers as well as their carers;
- thirdly, a moral argument about respectfully catering for everybody, irrespective of their physical abilities and disabilities.

Tourism for All, www.tourismforall.org.uk

Tourism management

Tourism management refers to both an academic subject and a professional practice. As an academic subject, tourism management is the **multidisciplinary** study of the phenomenon of **tourism** as well as related themes and topics (such as tourists' behaviour or the development of tourist destinations). Tourism management is akin to other academic subjects where management is applied to specific professional contexts, such as hotel management, leisure management and arts management.

As a professional practice, tourism management can have two meanings:

- At a micro-level, it refers to managing tourism organisations, that is having managerial responsibilities in businesses operating in the tourism **industry** (private, public and voluntary sectors alike).
- At a macro-level, it refers to managing the **impacts of tourism**, that is maximising the benefits and minimising the costs of tourism development.

Because of the double nature of tourism management, a key pedagogical issue is the balance of the academic and the professional, or put

T

another way the necessary dialogue, metaphorically speaking, between **theory** and practice.

Beech, John and Chadwick, Simon, *The Business of Tourism Management* (London: Prentice Hall, 2005).

Pender, Lesley and Sharpley, Richard, *The Management of Tourism* (London: Sage, 2005).

Tourism management gurus

Tourism management does not yet have the kind of gurus that more established disciplines have, such as strategic management (Michael Porter or Kenichi Ohmae) or marketing (Philip Kotler or Regis McKenna). In the absence of a formalised canon, one can only identify the names of some scholars whose contribution has already marked tourism studies, if not tourism management:

- scholars whose names are associated with a model or theory they have developed, for example Stanley **Plog's psychographic typology**, Richard **Butler Sequence** of the destination lifecycle;
- scholars whose work is associated with often cited books they have written or edited, for example Valene Smith, Dean MacCannell, John Urry;
- scholars whose work is associated with **theory**-building and consequently with **journals** such as the *Annals of Tourism Research*, such as Jafar Jafari, Erik Cohen and Graham M. S. Dann;
- scholars whose academic textbooks have supported thousands of students and hundreds of tourism lecturers: Richard Sharpley, Stephen J. Page, John Swarbrooke to name a few;
- scholars whose work is associated with one area of expertise they have somehow carved as their academic niche such as Philip Pearce (psychology of tourists), John Walton (social history of tourism), Kevin Markwell (gay tourism).

Tourism platforms

In 2001, Jafar Jafari analysed how the philosophies underpinning tourism analysis have changed since tourism really became an object of intellectualisation 50 years ago. Jafar identified four clusters of perspectives that he called 'platforms', mapping in a neat conceptual chronology how they have gradually emerged:

- An 'advocacy platform' in the 1950s and 1960s, most supportive of tourism as a tool of economic development, corresponding to the development of **mass tourism** in a context of economic liberalism where the public sector was expected to encouraging tourism.

- A 'cautionary platform' in the 1970s with the growing awareness of the harmful impacts of tourism.
- An 'adaptancy platform' in the 1980s with the recognition of the need for different practices, hence the articulations of concepts such as **alternative tourism** and **sustainable tourism.**
- A 'knowledge-based platform' in the 1990s that moved away from a focus on tourism impacts to a more integrated and **interdisciplinary** approach where **planning** and **decision-making** is based on facts and underpinned by theory.

As the first years of the twenty-first century have been marked by several tourism-related catastrophes (9/11 terror attacks in America in 2001, SARS (Severe Acute Respiratory Syndrome) outbreaks in 2003, the Boxing Day Tsunami in 2004), a new platform can already be identified; it may be called 'public platform' because of the global public reactions to the above-mentioned catastrophes.

Jafari, Jafar, 'The Scientification of Tourism', in Valene L. Smith and Maryann Brent, (eds), *Hosts and Guests Revisited: Tourism Issues of the 21st Century* (New York: Cognizant, 2001).

Tourism Satellite Account (TSA)

A Tourism Satellite Account (TSA) is a sophisticated accounting system ('satellite' means that this account is dependent on the wider national accounting framework). TSAs fulfil two major roles:

- At an international level, they enable more reliable comparisons between countries through a common frame of reference, based on harmonised statistical approaches and definitions. (The United Nations Statistical Commission, the **World Tourism Organization** and the Organisation for Economic Cooperation and Development have validated the TSA methodology and recommend its use.)
- At a national level, it makes it possible to quantify the economic impact of tourism, by using and cross-referencing data from other national organisations such as central banks, national statistical offices, ministries of finance, etc.

Concretely, a TSA looks like a simple set of tables about tourists' consumption and related indicators, but the methodology to construct the data is very complex and it is a lengthy process. The system was developed in Canada in the 1980s; an increasing number of countries

T

have already adopted it, such as France, Mexico, New Zealand, Norway, Sweden and the USA. The UK is in the process of piloting and finalising its system. TSAs have a lot of potential that is not fully been used yet: they can be of help in **planning**, **forecasting** and **policy**-making, they have implications for other sectors such as trade policies, they can even be adapted, developed and implemented at sub-national and regional level.

Tourism system

A system is a method of conceptualising interrelated elements, stressing how their relationships are essential to understanding a complex phenomenon. Most approaches to tourism focus on one aspect only, for example transportation issues, the marketing of tourism products or the impacts of tourism at the destination. It is useful nonetheless to have an overall view, hence the importance of models of tourism systems. Several representations may be found in the academic literature; for example, Neil Leiper in the 1990s proposed a simple integrated model placing tourism in a holistic framework (see Figure 7).

Figure 7   The tourism system (adapted from Leiper 1995)

This shows how tourists flow from a generating region via a transit region to their destination; at the three stages, tourists interact with tourism providers. It is possible to complement Leiper's model by mapping how three types of factors influence the tourism system: personal factors (about the tourists themselves, that is the demand), industry factors (from the supply side) and environmental factors (external to the tourism, yet affecting tourists, the tourism industry as well as the overall system) (see Table 5).

Table 5 Examples of factors affecting the tourism system

	Origin	Transit	Destination
Personal factors (**demand**)	**Motivations** for travel, **purpose** of the trip	Personal preferences (criteria: speed, price, etc.)	Choices of **entertainment** and activities
Industry factors (**supply**)	**Marketing mix**	**Transport, logistics**	Local tourism providers: availability of attractions, accommodation
External factors (context)	Legal and economic factors: paid holidays entitlements	Environmental issues: pollution	Socio-economic factors: local development

Leiper, Neil, *Tourism Management* (Melbourne: RMIT Press, 1995).

Tourist

The **World Tourism Organization** (WTO) defines a tourist as:

A person travelling outside his or her usual environment for less than a specified period of time and whose main purpose of travel is other than the exercise of an activity remunerated from the place visited.

This technical definition is the one used by most governments for the compilation of national tourism statistics; as recommended by the WTO, the maximum 'specified period of time' from that definition is generally one year, and a minimum length is usually 24 hours away from home, which differentiates tourists from **excursionists**. Two other related technical terms are stayover and stopover:

- A *stayover* is a tourist who spends at least one night in the destination region. Most tourists are stayovers, although some forms of travelling (such as cruises or touring holidays) are ambiguous.
- A *stopover* is a traveller in transit to another destination; in **international tourism**, stopovers are not normally counted as tourists because they do not clear customs, but their situation in terms of domestic tourism is very vague, which partly explains why it is difficult to measure **domestic tourism** precisely.

T

Contrary to a common misconception, a tourist is not necessarily a holidaymaker, that is someone travelling for sightseeing or recreational purposes: **business tourism** and **visiting friends and relatives** are included in the concept of tourist.

Tourist board

Tourist boards are **public sector** organisations; in most countries, they exist at both national and regional level. At local level, tourist boards often take the form of councils or departments attached to local author-ities. At national level, they are usually referred to as '**national tourism organisations**' (**NTOs**), for example Maison de la France is the French NTO. If in theory the two main functions of a tourist board are to promote tourism and to facilitate and encourage tourism development, in practice tourist boards will articulate their visions and missions differ-ently, emphasising some aspects according to their own contexts. These differences of approaches can be illustrated by the following two exam-ples: in 2006 the Welsh tourist board defined its role as 'to provide lead-ership and strategic direction to the tourism industry in Wales', whereas the tourist board responsible for the south-west of England defined its as 'to stimulate and manage the development of tourism to bring economic, social and environmental benefits to the people who live and work in the region and to provide a rewarding and enjoyable experience for visitors'. As such organisations are funded by taxpayers' money, accountability is an important issue. Tourist boards may be linked in different ways to other development agencies, especially at a regional level; as originating from governments and political decisions, tourist boards are subject to changes in their funding and structure, for example in 2003 the two regional tourist boards Southern Tourist Board and South East England Tourist Board merged to form the new Tourism South East.

Elliott, James, *Tourism: Politics and Public Sector Management* (London: Routledge, 1997).

Tourist experience

The phrase 'tourist experience' is very often encountered in the litera-ture about tourism and tourism management. What tourists are offered (what they purchase and expect) is an experience. As a psychological concept, an experience can be defined as the inner state of the individ-ual that gets moved through involvement or exposure to an event. Tourists can go through a wide range of **liminal** experiences, from seeing unfamiliar sceneries (see tourist **gaze** about the importance of the visual) to feeling the adrenaline rush of bungee-jumping (see **extreme tourism**). Each separate component of a holiday may be seen as an experience (transport, activities, food, interactions with other people, etc.), but tourism as a whole can be presented as an experience. This holistic view is important for travel agents and tour operators as what they sell is actually the promise of a liminal experience away from the **alienation** of modern life. Because of their inherent subjectivity, experiences are difficult to study and measure, yet the concept is widely used, especially in academic **journals**.

Ryan, Chris (ed.), *The Tourist Experience: A New Introduction*, 2nd edn (London: Thomson, 2002).

Tourist information centres (TICs)

Tourist information centres (TICs) have several roles and functions:

- They provide information on local tourism; for that purpose, they stock a range of leaflets and related material promoting local attractions and events. They can also provide guidance about local transport and locally relevant issues of interest or importance for tourists.
- They provide services such as hotel booking ('book-a-bed-ahead' scheme).
- They may be involved in **interpretation** through professional tours they organise, or through the historical buildings in which they are sometimes located.
- They may be involved in the promotion and marketing of the local area, in partnership with regional or national tourism authorities.

TICs have improved enormously over the past decade as local authorities have realised the advantages of running such establishments. Following pressures from national tourism authorities, for example in terms of **benchmarking**, TICs have also become more professional organisations, employing trained, salaried staff instead of relying on volunteers. TICs have relatively high running costs, which is why they may have a small commercial dimension (selling souvenirs and local delicacies) to help cover part of their expenses. Local authorities do not have a statutory duty to provide tourism services; local authorities that would like to offer TIC services but are unable to do so because of costs can make use of technological developments such as tourist information points (TIPs). TIPs are booths allowing tourists to access information and print maps of the destination area, and in more sophisticated cases to make hotel reservations through the Internet. In the UK, TICs have

T

traditionally been part of the public sector, but privatisation or part-privatisation are alternatives.

Tour operator

A tour operator is a commercial enterprise involved in the planning, pre-arranging and distribution/selling of holidays to the public. The holidays sold can be either packaged or now, increasingly, tailor made so as to suit travellers' requirements. Tour operators buy the individual elements required to create package holidays in bulk, and then combine them before selling to the public either directly or through a travel agent. The European market is currently dominated by mass-market vertically integrated tour companies, the largest of which is TUI. Apart from these mass-market operators, small niche players still offer customers dedicated package holidays that concentrate on one specific concept, for example golf, sailing or outdoor pursuit holidays. However, as tour operators look at new markets to help build and maintain revenue, these smaller companies are being acquired by the larger vertically integrated groups. This strategy of buying small niche operators is currently followed by First Choice Holiday Group who has purchased a number of specialist companies including Trek America and Exodus Holidays

Yales, Pat, *The Business of Tour Operations* (Harlow: Longman, 1995).

Transit region

The transit region is the zone that links a tourist from the generating (origin) area to their final destination. When in transit, a tourist may be able to complete their journey via one single method of transport (for example a domestic holiday by car) or they will require a mix of modes (such as coach and air) to reach their chosen destination. For **long-haul** journeys, many tourists will need to stopover while waiting for a flight connection (which gives a margin of uncertainty to national tourism statistics as these stopover tourists might or might not be counted as tourists). Whilst some passengers are happy to transit and therefore reach their final destination more quickly, it is also possible for passengers to stayover when transiting between flights. A number of carriers such as Singapore Airlines, Cathay Pacific and Emirates Airlines have created new markets for their respective hubs based on passengers staying over for one or two days. Many transit regions are increasingly trying to market themselves as destinations worth visiting, for example the city of Cherbourg in Normandy is investing in many tourism facilities in order to capture some of the British visitors arriving by ferry on their way to other parts of France.

Transport

Transport (also referred to as transportation) relates to the movement of people and goods from one destination to another. A basic condition of travelling, the development of transport is what enables people to be tourists. Transport is required to reach a destination, but it may also be part of the **tourist experience** itself (cruising being the archetypal example). Tourist transportation can be broken down into land based (car, coach, caravan or train), water based (ferries and cruising) and air (scheduled and charter services). For transport to function, the following four features are required:

- the way, that is the route over which the vehicle operates (this may be man-made such as rail or motorway or natural as in an air or seaway);
- the median/terminal, that is the method for joining and leaving a particular form of transport. (It may also be an interchange point to change from one form of transport to another);
- the unit of carriage/vehicle (also referred to as the mode of travel, this is the area in which the customer is transported);
- the unit of traction, that is the power that drives the vehicle (virtually all commercial transport vehicles today are either powered by diesel or electricity).

Many specialised books and scholars focus on transport as an important element of tourism.

Page, Stephen, *Transport and Tourism Global Perspectives*, 2nd edn (Harlow: Prentice Hall, 2005
Pender, Lesley, *Travel Trade and Transport – An Introduction* (London: Continuum, 2001).

Travel agent

A travel agent is a retailer, offering for sale to consumers products and services created by tour operators, cruise lines and, to a lesser extent today, tickets for airline, train and ferry operators. The agent gains a commission for selling the services of a principal which is normally a percentage of the sale price. Travel agencies may also, on request, design independent package tours to suit individuals' needs. Agents have, however, begun to struggle for the following reasons:

- Commission levels have been capped, fallen or in some instances

T

scrapped completely as airlines in particular look to reduce costs.

- Competition from the Internet (see **e-tourism**) and **tour operators** looking to retail through direct-sell methods have all placed financial pressure on the remaining agencies. This has led to the closure of most independent travel agents with most high streets in the UK now left to multiple agents.
- Tour operators are looking to sell their products through their vertically integrated 'multiple' travel agents, placing further pressure on the independent agents.

Buhalis, Dimitrios and Laws, Eric (eds), *Tourism Distribution Channels: Practices, Issues and Transformations* (London: Continuum Publishing, 2001).

Travel career

The phrase 'travel career' refers to the fact that individuals' primary **motivations** to travel are likely to evolve over time, as they get older, develop new tastes or because of changing role/situation in the **family lifecycle**. To reflect that, Australian Tourism Professor Philip Pearce coined the phrase 'tourism career', with a ladder-like model that builds upon **Maslow's hierarchy of needs**, the leisure needs being relaxation/bodily needs, stimulation, relationship, self-esteem and ultimately fulfilment. Pearce's model is a good example of the way psychology contributes to the study of tourism as a **multidisciplinary** project.

Pearce, Philip L., *Tourist Behaviour: Themes and Conceptual Issues* (Clevedon, Bristol: Channel Views, 2005).

Travel propensity

Travel propensity helps measure the effective tourism **demand** within a population (such as a country, region or town).

- To calculate the *gross travel propensity*, one simply divides the total number of trips by the population size. When expressed as a percentage, the gross travel propensity rate may exceed 100 per cent when many individuals take more than one trip per year; this is the case for the Netherlands where the travel propensity is around 104 per cent.
- Instead of the gross travel propensity rate, it is possible to calculate a *net travel propensity rate*, dividing the population taking at least one trip by the total population.
- By dividing the gross travel propensity by the net travel propensity, one obtains the *travel frequency*, that is the average number of trips

taken by people who are effectively travelling during a certain period.

Travel writing

Also called travel literature, travel writing refers to the texts written by travellers who purposefully record their impressions. Travel writing has a very old tradition, dating back at least to the fifth century BC, when the Greek author Herodotus heavily drew on his extensive journeys, from Egypt to Italy, to document and write his *Histories*. Other famous historical accounts of travel writing include:

- the Chinese Zhang Qian in Central Asia (second century BC);
- the Italian Marco Polo and, a few decades later, the Moroccan Ibn Battuta both on the 'Silk Road' to China (both thirteenth century);
- the German Johann Wolfgang von Goethe in Italy (late eighteenth century);
- the French Gérard de Nerval in Egypt and the Levant (nineteenth century);
- the Scotsman Robert Louis Stevenson in France and America (nineteenth century).

Travel writing has become increasingly popular, with contemporary authors such as Paul Theroux, Bill Bryson and Daniel Kalder amongst many others. It is a literary genre with different approaches and sub-genres (for example with foci on adventure, exploration or conquest) and different forms (for example diaries or travelogues). Professional travel writers are the authors of travel guides.

George, Don (ed.), *Lonely Planet Guide to Travel Writing* (London: Lonely Planet Publications, 2005).

Speake, Jennifer (ed.), *Literature of Travel and Exploration: An Encyclopedia* (London: Routledge, 2003).

Journeys: The International Journal of Travel & Travel Writing

Trends

Trends are anticipated changes, as identified through **forecasting.** In tourism management, trends are about the future of tourism; they result from the combination of **pressures** on the industry as well as changes in the population (demographic changes as well as socio-cultural and economic ones). Trends last, as opposed to fashions which may just reflect short-term interests (such as the Beckham tours which were popular in Japan just after the 2002 FIFA World Cup). Currents trends include the multiplication of short city breaks within Europe as well as the ongoing development of **special interest tourism** and **gay and lesbian tourism**. If extrapolations help predict the continuation of current trends, some other areas are far less certain, for example with regard to **space tourism** or tourism in culturally rich yet politically unstable regions such as the Middle East.

Lockwood, Andrew and Medlik, Slavoj (eds), *Tourism and Hospitality in the 21st Century* (Oxford: Butterworth-Heinemann, 2001).

UNESCO

UNESCO (United Nations Educational, Scientific and Cultural Organization) is a specialised agency of the United Nations. Based in Paris, it was established in 1945. Some of the programmes and activities of UNESCO are of direct relevance to decision-makers in tourism who need to know about them, especially:

- with regard to **heritage**: UNESCO is responsible for the famous World Heritage List that includes popular tourist destinations such as the Acropolis in Athens, the Tower of London and the Red Square in Moscow;
- with regard to **cultural tourism**: UNESCO is carrying out several projects worldwide about cultural tourism, for example one entitled 'Preserving the Khmer Smile' aimed at making Cambodia 'the alternative South-East Asian destination' and another about tourism in the Baltic countries Latvia, Estonia and Lithuania.

Besides, some of the working themes of UNESCO such as sustainable development are pertinent for tourism developers, as they correspond to global concerns that are also present on the agenda of the World Tourism Organisation.

UNESCO, www.unesco.org

Urbanisation

Urbanisation is the process whereby urban areas spread and expand; this is derogatorily called 'urban sprawl'. In developed countries, this has two types of consequences for the tourism industry:

- From the **demand** side, urban centres are concentrated sources of potential customers. When economically possible, **travel propensity** will be high, especially for trips motivated by a desire to escape from urban **alienation**.
- From the **supply** side, urban centres offer not only a range of urban recreational infrastructures and activities (shopping, famous build-

ings, cinemas, operas, music events) but also a particular atmosphere which is a **pull factor** of **urban tourism**.

Dear, Michael J., *The Postmodern Urban Condition* (Oxford: Blackwell, 2000).
Flint, Corrin and Flint, David, *Urbanisation: Changing Environments*, 2nd edn (London: Collins Educational).

Urban tourism

Urban tourism is one of the most highly developed forms of tourism. Whilst the concept itself may be easy to understand (towns and cities as tourist destinations), urban tourism is not a new phenomenon (people have always travelled to towns and cities), but it was only in the 1980s that the concept entered the tourism research agenda. There is now an increasing number of publications on different aspects of urban tourism, including **trends** in demand for urban attractions and the supply of tourist facilities, the built heritage, visitor management, the **impacts** of urban tourism, **policy** issues for town-planners as well as **marketing** and **branding**. Even concepts that might rather seem associated with tourism development in natural areas (such as **carrying capacity** and **sustainable development**) have also proved relevant for the **multi-disciplinary** study of urban tourism. Both **public sector** and **private sector** tourism managers need to understand the importance of urban tourism worldwide: not only does it represent huge business opportunities (from local historic attractions to conference centres), but it also underpins many regeneration schemes (for example with large-scale events such as the **Olympic Games**).

Law, Chris, *Urban Tourism* (London: Thomson, 2002).
Page, Stephen J. and Hall, Michael C., *Managing Urban Tourism* (London: Prentice Hall/Pearson Education, 2002).
Selby, Martin, *Understanding Urban Tourism: Image, Culture and Experience* (New York: I. B. Tauris, 2004).

U

Variability

In tourism, the word 'variability' is used in two ways:

- In a *generic* sense, it may refer to all the elements that are subject to fluctuations, from exchange rate to the weather.
- In a *precise* sense, it refers to one of the four characteristics of **services** (with **intangibility**, **inseparability** and **perishability**). The **tourist experience** is made up of a succession of service encounters; even when they involve the same routinised operations and transactions, they may differ, especially because of differences in human elements such as mood or expectations. For example, a day guide in the rainforest may greet and treat her group in exactly the same fashion on two successive occasions, yet visitors' experience may vary because on the second day the group does not gel in the same way. Variability affects the tourism product and tourism marketeers need to be aware that they can never guarantee consistency.

Variables

Although the term is mainly used in computer science and mathematics, tourism management makes use of variables in **research** projects or in business activities such as **market segmentation** and **forecasting**. Variables represent the features that are changeable. **Qualitative research** may make reference to variables, but they are more commonly encountered in **quantitative research**, as statistics use different types of variables (nominal, ordinal, internal or rational) corresponding to univariate levels of measurement that can then be associated and correlated (bi/multivariate analysis, inferential statistics).

Finn, Mick, Elliott-White, Martin and Walton, Mike, *Tourism and Leisure Research Methods: Data Collection, Analysis and Interpretation* (London: Longman, 2000).
Saunders, Mark et al., *Research Methods for Business Students*, 4th edn (London: Prentice Hall, 2006).

Vertical integration

As opposed to **horizontal integration**, vertical integration refers to one organisation purchasing another one, which is situated at another stage of the production process (for example a tour operator acquiring a charter airline or a travel agent). The logic behind **supply chain management** explains how the use of vertically integrated operations is based on control and quality of the product. Vertically integrated groups have the advantage of dictating exactly what in-house suppliers will offer to the customer; they can also brand each element in order to reflect the name of the parent company, as illustrated by the 'World of TUI' image that is used on all TUI-owned operations worldwide. Fostering economies of scale and further ensuring brand **loyalty** are reasons associated with organisations becoming vertically integrated. Companies also gain an increased bargaining power, which is helpful when negotiating contracts with other suppliers. By buying the whole production chain, vertically integrated companies can also avoid uncertainty based on one level of the chain not performing or breaking the contract. The amount of transactions between levels is also reduced as all accounting is handled internally, which in turn makes for not just efficient but also leaner organisations. See Table 6 for some examples of vertically integrated companies in the tourism industry.

Table 6   Examples of vertically integrated companies in the tourism industry

Organisation	Thomson – World of TUI	MyTravel	First Choice
Main tour operator brand	Thomson	Airtours	First Choice
Airline	Thomsonfly	MyTravel Airways	First Choice Airways
Travel agent	Thomson holiday shops	Going Places	First Choice travel shops and warehouses
Other interests	Cruise ships and low-cost airline		Joint-venture cruise ship with Royal Caribbean
Ownership (in Sept 2006)	TUI (listed on the German Stock Exchange)	UK plc (listed on the UK Stock Exchange)	UK plc (listed on the UK Stock Exchange)

V

Virtual tourism

Virtual tourism is about exploring parts of the world without having to travel. It may sound paradoxical if not meaningless, yet the concept is useful literally and metaphorically.

- Literally, in an age of virtual reality (where 'virtual' refers to computer interactions and simulations), virtual tourism is mainly done using the Internet, although travel literature (such as travel guides and travelogues) and television (television channels, live or recorded documentaries) may also have a role to play. Virtual tourism can be a prelude to travelling, for example to help choose a destination, or a full experience in itself, especially through high quality digitisation, to visit online museums or dream about space tourism.
- Metaphorically, virtual tourism provides a framework to help understand the tourist experience offered by theme parks such as Disney Parks. In such prefabricated illusionistic settings, the distinction between the real and the represented is blurred in a postmodern way, and visitors are taken through **pseudo-events** technologically programmed and created purely for commercial reasons.

Visiting friends and relatives (VFR)

Travel motivation based on the desire to visit friends and relatives is usually abbreviated as VFR. Based on the technical criterion for defining **tourism** (being away from one's home environment for over 24 hours), VFR is a form of tourism, even if many people visiting friends and relatives for a couple of days would not regard themselves as tourists (this highlights a discrepancy between conceptual and perceptual approaches to tourism: with regard to tourism statistics, one does not have to feel like a tourist in order to be counted as one). Domestic VFR tourism is particularly difficult to measure, especially as it may not involve commercial transportation; on the other hand, international VFR tourism tends to be of high value to the transportation sector. In either case, VFR tourism is arguably of little significance to the hospitality industry as accommodation tends to be with friends or relatives, where most meals are also taken. VFR tourism can nonetheless be economically beneficial for local attractions and local entertainment (as guests may be taken out to local sites or events) as well as shopping/retailing.

'The VFR Market', *Journal of Tourism Studies*, 6(1) (1995), special issue.

Voluntary Sector

Like the **public sector**, the voluntary sector is defined as non-commercial (because profit-making is not the aim, hence the phrases 'non-profit organisation' and 'not-for-profit organisations') but, unlike public sector organisations, voluntary sector organisations are not funded by taxpayers' money: they rely instead on donations, legacies and revenue raised from their commercial operations. The term 'voluntary' refers to the fact that some of the staff are volunteers (it is estimated that in the UK 3 million people give some of their time to voluntary sector organisations as unpaid volunteers). The phrase 'third sector' is sometimes used as a (flawed) synonym (as it also includes trade unions and universities). In tourism, at a local and regional level, the voluntary sector covers a wide range of projects, from **heritage** conservation to leisure-oriented schemes via pressure-groups of **stakeholders**; at a national and international level, it is possible to distinguish between:

- charities and organisations whose remit is tourism or a closely related theme (such as heritage), for example Tourism Concern and in the UK the National Trust;
- charities and organisations that are not tourism-specific but may address tourism as part of their agenda, for example ECPAT (End Child Prostitution, Child Pornography and Trafficking of Children for Sexual Purposes), Greenpeace or Friends of the Earth.

Anheier, Helmut K., *Nonprofit Organizations: Theory, Management, Policy* (London: Routledge, 2003).

Kendall, Jeremy, *The Voluntary Sector: Comparative Perspectives in the UK* (London: Routledge, 2003).

V

Wanderlust

Borrowed from the German language (where it now sounds rather old-fashioned), wanderlust refers both to the love of travel and to the urge to travel. It describes an allocentric form of tourism motivated by a desire to explore, discover and experience, as opposed to the psycho-centric, single-resort vacation tourism typical of **mass tourism** and **sunlust**. Wanderlust is also the name of a glossy British travel magazine whose articles on active holidays off the beaten track in uncommon locations illustrate well the concept of wanderlust, for example 'Philippines: Dive, paddle and hike around Palawan, the archipelago's wild frontier' in issue 81 (August 2006), and 'Seychelles conservation: Escape the luxury resorts to discover an island where turtles outnumber people' in issue 80 (June 2006).

Wanderlust magazine, www.wanderlust.co.uk

Wildland tourism

Wildlands are areas where fauna and flora exist free of human interference. Examples include both areas that are controlled and managed (such as national parks) and areas that are usually inaccessible and inhospitable (such as remote desert areas or parts of the Australian bush). Because of the unspoiled natural environment of 'the great outdoors', these places appeal to some tourists who seek to experience the wilderness and solitude. These allocentric tourists' wildland recreation activities (such as hiking, climbing and basic camping) are unobtrusive and tend to have a very low impact on the environment, yet there is a real danger that the increasing number of wildland ecotourists beyond the **carrying capacity** will negatively affect wildlands. Canada and New Zealand are two countries where wildland recreation is an important contemporary issue for researchers, tourism managers and policy-makers. Publications such as the *Journal of Sustainable Tourism* provide many case studies on the topic.

Higham, James, 'Sustaining the Physical and Social Dimensions of Wilderness Tourism: The Perceptual Approach to Wilderness Management in New Zealand', *Journal of Sustainable Tourism*, 6(1) (1998): 26–51.

World Tourism Day

Since 1980, 27 September has been World Tourism Day, an initiative from the **World Tourism Organization** to celebrate tourism and to raise awareness of its benefits and impacts worldwide. The date of 27 September was chosen to commemorate the day in 1970 when the Statutes of the WTO were formally adopted. Every year World Tourism Day has a different theme, for example in 1983 'Travel and Holidays are a Right but also a Responsibility for All', in 1999 'Tourism: Preserving World Heritage for the New Millennium' and in 2004 'Sport and Tourism: Two Living Forces for Mutual Understanding, Culture and the Development of Societies'. On World Tourism Day, celebrations take place especially in the country that formally hosts the day (Qatar in 2005, Portugal in 2006, Sri Lanka in 2007).

> World Tourism Organisation page on World Tourism Day, www.world-tourism.org/wtd/eng/menu.html

World Tourism Organization (WTO)

A specialised agency of the United Nations (like the International Monetary Fund and the World Health Organization), the World Tourism Organization (WTO) is the leading international organisation in the field of tourism. It was officially created in 1975 with a First General Assembly held in Madrid after a long process of development that had started as early as 1925 with the International Congress of Official Tourist Traffic Associations which became the International Union of Official Travel Organisations (IUOTO) in 1947. An important date was 27 September 1970 when the IUOTO's Extraordinary General Assembly adopted the Statutes of World Tourism Organisation (the date of 27 September was later chosen as World Tourism Day). The WTO headquarters are in Madrid. In 2006, the WTO has representatives from 150 countries (as full members) as well as over than 300 affiliate members (from a wide range of organisations such as Air France, the Egyptian Tourist Authority and the University of Queensland, Australia). The WTO plays an important role in the international promotion of **sustainable tourism**, and also in the promotion of education, technology transfers and international cooperation. It aims to encourage a responsible form of tourism that maximises the economic, socio-cultural and environmental benefits of tourism. Its Global Code of Ethics for Tourism, published in 2001, is a key document in that respect (see Appendix, pp. 213–23). The WTO also provides most reliable **statistics** and market intelligence about tourism worldwide; it is regarded as the definitive source of such statistics, and most of its research findings are freely available online.

> World Tourism Organisation, www.world-tourism.org

World Trade Organization (WTO)

Based in Geneva, Switzerland, and created in 1995, the World Trade Organization deals with the rules of trade between nations at a global or near-global level. At its heart are agreements, negotiated and signed by most of the world's trading nations and ratified in their parliaments. These agreements are legal texts that cover a range of activities, including services, hence the relevance of some of the work of the World Trade Organization for tourism. The aims of the World Trade Organization are to liberalise trade and to promote free trade, which arguably is often more in the interests of richer countries; this is akin to the problematics of tourism in developing countries, whose local communities do not always benefit. The political agenda of the World Trade Organization and related issues of liberalisation cannot be ignored by tourism. The **World Tourism Organization** has observer status in the World Trade Organization on issues regarding trade in tourism services, and has established a strategy of 'liberalisation with a human face' linked to its Global Ethics in Tourism. The World Trade Organization and the World Tourism Organization have the same abbreviation (WTO), so care is needed when reading about liberalisation in tourism and WTO policies and declarations. In more recent publications, this ambiguity has been avoided by using the abbreviation WTO-OMT (for tourism: OMT stands for Organisation Mondiale du Tourisme) and WTO-OMC (for trade: OMC stands for Organisation Mondiale du Commerce); for the WTO-OMT the abbreviation UNWTO is also used as the World Tourism Organization has now become a specialised agency of the United Nations.

World Trade Organization, www.wto.org

World Travel and Tourism Council (WTTC)

Whereas the **World Tourism Organization**, as an agency of the United Nations, counts amongst its members representatives from sovereign countries (that is the public sector), the World Travel and Tourism Council (WTTC) represents the **private sector**. Based in London, it mainly campaigns and lobbies on behalf of the tourism industry. The WTTC defines itself as 'the forum for global business leaders comprising the presidents, chairs and CEOs of 100 of the world's foremost companies'. Because of its commercial focus, it has previously concentrated on raising awareness of the economic benefits of tourism as the world's main generator of wealth and jobs, yet it now also takes into account local needs and **sustainability**. In 2003, the WTTC published an important document called 'Blueprint for New Tourism' where it established three priorities to optimise tourism development:

W

1 Governments must recognise travel and tourism as a top priority.
2 Business must balance economics with people, culture and environment.
3 All parties must share the pursuit of long-term growth and prosperity.

The 'Blueprint for New Tourism' is available from the WTTC website; besides the WTTC strategy itself, it contains useful **statistics** such as **forecasts** of tourism employment and tourism demand worldwide.

World Travel and Tourism Council, www.wttc.org

Xenophobia

Etymologically coming from the Greek *xenos* (foreigner) and *phobos* (fear), the concept of xenophobia refers to an irrational fear or contempt of strangers. This complex phenomenon is not only psychological: it also has cultural and political dimensions that may heavily impact on the **host–guest** relationship. Linked to **ethnocentrism** and racism, it may describe some psychocentric tourists' view of the locals, though it is usually conceptualised as affecting locals' feelings towards foreign visitors. Xenophobia is difficult to measure, yet some models (such as Doxey's **irridex**) provide a framework to understand different levels of xenophobic antagonism and to relate them to wider issues of tourism development. Several factors may contribute to xenophobia in tourist settings: the degree of cultural difference, the number of tourists visiting and the quality of their interactions with locals, previous negative experiences and stereotyping, **demonstration effects** as well as the possibilities and limits of intercultural communication.

Yield management

Also called 'revenue management', yield management is a management tool aimed at maximising revenue. Yield management is about understanding **consumer behaviour** in order to anticipate demand and set prices accordingly. Many sectors (such as the telecoms, railways operators and stadiums (for sports events pricing)) now use yield management, but the system was actually developed in commercial aviation in the 1970s. In tourism, it is not only common in the airline industry, but also in accommodation. The underpinning principle is that prices and fares vary depending on the fixed capacity available and on the anticipated demand. Yield management is based on price discrimination, which explains why different customers may be paying a different price for the same hotel room or the same flight. Sophisticated computer yield management systems are used to set pricing, as it involves complex statistical calculations as well as information management. **Low cost carriers** have made the system well known to the public with special eye-catching offers (with a few seats available for £1 plus airport taxes) which seem to be entirely customer-friendly, whereas the aim of yield management is actually to maximise revenue; yield management has proved to be very effective, although some detractors argue that it is difficult to assess the efficiency of the system precisely.

Ingold, Anthony et al. (ed.), *Yield Management: Strategies for the Service Industries*, 2nd edn (London: Thomson, 2001).

Zz

Zoning

Zoning is a system used to help identify and protect areas of fragility; it exists in two forms: spatial zoning and temporal zoning. Through zoning, authorities are able to allow tourists to interact within areas designated as being robust enough to handle such strains, whilst protecting sensitive areas which would be destroyed by tourist intervention. In the United Kingdom, the use of zoning can be illustrated through the existence of Areas of Outstanding Natural Beauty (AONBs) as well as the national parks. Another example of zoning is the Great Barrier Reef Marine Park in Australia: the 1975 Great Barrier Reef Marine Park Act set a policy of zoning, differentiating between types of zones: some where tourists are allowed, others where some tourist activities are allowed and others which are restricted, as well as areas where all human activity, including research, is totally banned. Linked to the concept of **carrying capacity**, zoning is generally seen as a good method to ensure **sustainable development** and balancing interests such as environmental protection and economic integration.

Great Barrier Reef Marine Park Authority, www.gbrmpa.gov.au
UK Department for Environment, Food and Rural Affairs, www.defra.gov.uk

Numbers

3S

See Three S.

4Ps

See Marketing mix.

Appendix:
Global Code of Ethics for Tourism[1]

Adopted by resolution A/RES/406(XIII) at the thirteenth WYTO General assembly (Santiago, Chile, 27 September – 1 October 1999)

Preamble

We, Members of the World Tourism, Organization (WTO), representatives of the world tourism industry, delegates of States, territories, enterprises, institutions and bodies that are gathered for the General Assembly at Santiago, Chile on this first day of October 1999,

Reasserting the aims set out in Article 3 of the Statutes of the World Tourism Organization, and aware of the 'decisive and central' role of this Organization, as recognized by the General Assembly of the United Nations, in promoting and developing tourism with a view to contributing to economic development, international understanding, peace, prosperity and universal respect for, and observance of, human rights and fundamental freedoms for all without distinction as to race, sex, language or religion,

Firmly believing that, through the direct, spontaneous and non-mediatized contacts it engenders between men and women of different cultures and lifestyles, tourism represents a vital force for peace and a factor of friendship and understanding among the peoples of the world,

In keeping with the rationale of reconciling environmental protection, economic development and the fight against poverty in a sustainable manner, as formulated by the United Nations in 1992 at the 'Earth Summit' of Rio de Janeiro and expressed in Agenda 21, adopted on that occasion,

Taking into account the swift and continued growth, both past and foreseeable, of the tourism activity, whether for leisure, business,

[1] United Nations World Tourism Organization (2001) – http://www.world-tourism.org/code_ethics/eng/brochure.htm. Reproduced by courtesy of the United Nations World Tourism Organization.

culture, religious or health purposes, and its powerful effects, both positive and negative, on the environment, the economy and the society of both generating and receiving countries, on local communities and indigenous peoples, as well as on international relations and trade,

Aiming to promote responsible, sustainable and universally accessible tourism in the framework of the right of all persons to use their free time for leisure pursuits or travel with respect for the choices of society of all peoples,

But convinced that the world tourism industry as a whole has much to gain by operating in an environment that favours the market economy, private enterprise and free trade and that serves to optimize its beneficial effects on the creation of wealth and employment,

Also firmly convinced that, provided a number of principles and a certain number of rules are observed, responsible and sustainable tourism is by no means incompatible with the growing liberalization of the conditions governing trade in services and under whose aegis the enterprises of this sector operate and that it is possible to reconcile in this sector economy and ecology, environment and development, openness to international trade and protection of social and cultural identities,

Considering that, with such an approach, all the stakeholders in tourism development – national, regional and local administrations, enterprises, business associations, workers in the sector, non-governmental organizations and bodies of all kinds belonging to the tourism industry, as well as host communities, the media and the tourists themselves, have different albeit interdependent responsibilities in the individual and societal development of tourism and that the formulation of their individual rights and duties will contribute to meeting this aim,

Committed, in keeping with the aims pursued by the World Tourism Organization itself since adopting resolution 364(XII) at its General Assembly of 1997 (Istanbul), to promote a genuine partnership between the public and private stakeholders in tourism development, and wishing to see a partnership and cooperation of the same kind extend, in an open and balanced way, to the relations between generating and receiving countries and their respective tourism industries,

Following up on the Manila Declarations of 1980 on World Tourism and of 1997 on the Social Impact of Tourism, as well as on the Tourism

Bill of Rights and the Tourist Code adopted at Sofia in 1985 under the aegis of WTO,

But believing that these instruments should be complemented by a set of interdependent principles for their interpretation and application on which the stakeholders in tourism development should model their conduct at the dawn of the twenty-first century,

Using, for the purposes of this instrument, the definitions and classifications applicable to travel, and especially the concepts of 'visitor', 'tourist' and 'tourism', as adopted by the Ottawa International Conference, held from 24 to 28 June 1991 and approved, in 1993, by the United Nations Statistical Commission at its twenty-seventh session,

Referring in particular to the following instruments:

- Universal Declaration of Human Rights of 10 December 1948;
- International Covenant on Economic, Social and Cultural Rights of 16 December 1966;
- International Covenant on Civil and Political Rights of 16 December 1966;
- Warsaw Convention on Air Transport of 12 October 1929;
- Chicago Convention on International Civil Aviation of 7 December 1944, and the Tokyo, The Hague and Montreal Conventions in relation thereto;
- Convention on Customs Facilities for Tourism of 4 July 1954 and related Protocol;
- Convention concerning the Protection of the World Cultural and Natural Heritage of 23 November 1972;
- Manila Declaration on World Tourism of 10 October 1980;
- Resolution of the Sixth General Assembly of WTO (Sofia) adopting the Tourism Bill of Rights and Tourist Code of 26 September 1985;
- Convention on the Rights of the Child of 20 November 1989;
- Resolution of the Ninth General Assembly of WTO (Buenos Aires) concerning in particular travel facilitation and the safety and security of tourists of 4 October 1991;
- Rio Declaration on the Environment and Development of 13 June 1992;
- General Agreement on Trade in Services of 15 April 1994;
- Convention on Biodiversity of 6 January 1995;
- Resolution of the Eleventh General Assembly of WTO (Cairo) on the prevention of organized sex tourism of 22 October 1995;

- Stockholm Declaration of 28 August 1996 against the Commercial Sexual Exploitation of Children;
- Manila Declaration on the Social Impact of Tourism of 22 May 1997;
- Conventions and recommendations adopted by the International Labour Organization in the area of collective conventions, prohibition of forced labour and child labour, defence of the rights of indigenous peoples, and equal treatment and non-discrimination in the work place;

affirm the right to tourism and the freedom of tourist movements,

state our wish to promote an equitable, responsible and sustainable world tourism order, whose benefits will be shared by all sectors of society in the context of an open and liberalized international economy, and

solemnly adopt to these ends the principles of the *Global Code of Ethics for Tourism*.

Article 1

Tourism's contribution to mutual understanding and respect between peoples and societies

1 The understanding and promotion of the ethical values common to humanity, with an attitude of tolerance and respect for the diversity of religious, philosophical and moral beliefs, are both the foundation and the consequence of responsible tourism; stakeholders in tourism development and tourists themselves should observe the social and cultural traditions and practices of all peoples, including those of minorities and indigenous peoples and to recognize their worth;

2 Tourism activities should be conducted in harmony with the attributes and traditions of the host regions and countries and in respect for their laws, practices and customs;

3 The host communities, on the one hand, and local professionals, an the other, should acquaint themselves with and respect the tourists who visit them and find out about their lifestyles, tastes and expectations; the education and training imparted to professionals contribute to a hospitable, welcome;

4 It is the task of the public authorities to provide protection for tourists and visitors and their belongings; they must pay particular attention to the safety of foreign tourists owing to the particular vulnerability they may have; they should facilitate the introduction

of specific means of information, prevention, security, insurance and assistance consistent with their needs; any attacks, assaults, kidnappings or threats against tourists or workers in the tourism industry, as well as the wilful destruction of tourism facilities or of elements of cultural or natural heritage should be severely condemned and punished in accordance with their respective national laws;

5 When travelling, tourists and visitors should not commit any criminal act or any act considered criminal by the laws of the country visited and abstain from any conduct felt to be offensive or injurious by the local populations, or likely to damage the local environment; they should refrain from all trafficking in illicit drugs, arms, antiques, protected species and products and substances that are dangerous or prohibited by national regulations;

6 Tourists and visitors have the responsibility to acquaint themselves, even before their departure, with the characteristics of the countries they are preparing to visit; they must be aware of the health and security risks inherent in any travel outside their usual environment and behave in such a way as to minimize those risks;

Article 2

Tourism as a vehicle for individual and collective fulfilment

1 Tourism, the activity most frequently associated with rest and relaxation, sport and access to culture and nature, should be planned and practised as a privileged means of individual and collective fulfilment; when practised with a sufficiently open mind, it is an irreplaceable factor of self-education, mutual tolerance and for learning about the legitimate differences between peoples and cultures and their diversity;

2 Tourism activities should respect the equality of men and women; they should promote human rights and, more particularly, the individual rights of the most vulnerable groups, notably children, the elderly, the handicapped, ethnic minorities and indigenous peoples;

3 The exploitation of human beings in any form, particularly sexual, especially when applied to children, conflicts with the fundamental aims of tourism and is the negation of tourism; as such, in accordance with international law, it should be energetically combatted with the cooperation of all the States concerned and penalized without concession by the national legislation of both the countries visited and the countries of the perpetrators of these acts, even when they are carried out abroad;

4 Travel for purposes of religion, health, education and cultural or linguistic exchanges are particularly beneficial forms of tourism, which deserve encouragement;

5 The introduction into curricula of education about the value of tourist exchanges, their economic, social and cultural benefits, and also their risks, should be encouraged;

Article 3

Tourism, a factor of sustainable development

1 All the stakeholders in tourism development should safeguard the natural environment with a view to achieving sound, continuous and sustainable economic growth geared to satisfying equitably the needs and aspirations of present and future generations;

2 All forms of tourism development that are conducive to saving rare and precious resources, in particular water and energy, as well as avoiding so far as possible waste production, should be given priority and encouraged by national, regional and local public authorities;

3 The staggering in time and space of tourist and visitor flows, particularly those resulting from paid leave and school holidays, and a more even distribution of holidays should be sought so as to reduce the pressure of tourism activity on the environment and enhance its beneficial impact on the tourism industry and the local economy;

4 Tourism infrastructure should be designed and tourism activities programmed in such a way as to protect the natural heritage composed of ecosystems and biodiversity and to preserved endangered species of wildlife; the stakeholders in tourism development, and especially professionals, should agree to the imposition of limitations or constraints on their activities when these are exercised in particularly sensitive areas: desert, polar or high mountain regions, coastal areas, tropical forests or wetlands, propitious to the creation of nature reserves or protected areas;

5 Nature tourism and ecotourism are recognized as being particularly conducive to enriching and enhancing the standing of tourism, provided they respect the natural heritage and local populations and are in keeping with the carrying capacity of the sites;

Article 4

Tourism, a user of the cultural heritage of mankind and a contributor to its enhancement

1 Tourism resources belong to the common heritage of mankind; the communities in whose territories they are situated have particular rights and obligations to them;

2 Tourism policies and activities should be conducted with respect for the artistic, archaeological and cultural heritage, which they should protect and pass on to future generations; particular care should be devoted to preserving and upgrading monuments, shrines and museums as well as archaeological and historic sites which must be widely open to tourist visits; encouragement should be given to public access to privately-owned cultural property and monuments, with respect for the rights of their owners, as well as to religious buildings, without prejudice to normal needs of worship;

3 Financial resources derived from visits to cultural sites and monuments should, at least in part, be used for the upkeep, safeguard, development and embellishment of this heritage;

4 Tourism activity should be planned in such a way as to allow traditional cultural products, crafts and folklore to survive and flourish, rather than causing them to degenerate and become standardized;

Article 5

Tourism, a beneficial activity for host countries and communities

1 Local populations should be associated with tourism activities and share equitably in the economic, social and cultural benefits they generate, and particularly in the creation of direct and indirect jobs resulting from them;

2 Tourism policies should be applied in such a way as to help to raise the standard of living of the populations of the regions visited and meet their needs; the planning and architectural approach to and operation of tourism resorts and accommodation should aim to integrate them, to the extent possible in the local economic and social fabric; where skills are equal, priority should be given to local manpower;

3 Special attention should be paid to the specific problems of coastal areas and island territories and to vulnerable rural or mountain regions, for which tourism often represents a rare opportunity for development in the face of the decline of traditional economic activities;

4 Tourism professionals, particularly investors, governed by the regulations laid down by the public authorities, should carry out studies

of the impact of their development projects on the environment and natural surroundings; they should also deliver, with the greatest transparency and objectivity, information on their future programmes and their foreseeable repercussions and foster dialogue on their contents with the populations concerned;

Article 6

Obligations of stakeholders in tourism development

1 Tourism professionals have an obligation to provide tourists with objective and honest information on their places of destination and on the conditions of travel, hospitality and stays; they should ensure that the contractual clauses proposed to their customers are readily understandable as to the nature, price and quality of the services they commit themselves to providing and the financial compensation payable by them in the event of a unilateral breach of contract on their part;

2 Tourism professionals, insofar as it depends on them, should show concern, in cooperation with the public authorities, for the security and safety, accident prevention, health protection and food safety of those who seek their services; likewise, they should ensure the existence of suitable systems of insurance and assistance; they should accept the reporting obligations prescribed by national regulations and pay fair compensation in the event of failure to observe their contractual obligations;

3 Tourism professionals, so far as this depends on them, should contribute to the cultural and spiritual fulfilment of tourists and allow them, during their travels, to practise their religions;

4 The public authorities of the generating States and the host countries, in cooperation with the professionals concerned and their associations, should ensure that the necessary mechanisms are in place for the repatriation of tourists in the event of the bankruptcy of the enterprise that organized their travel;

5 Governments have the right – and the duty – specially in a crisis, to inform their nationals of the difficult circumstances, or even the dangers they may encounter during their travels abroad; it is their responsibility however to issue such information without prejudicing in an unjustified or exaggerated manner the tourism industry of the host countries and the interests of their own operators; the contents of travel advisories should therefore be discussed beforehand with the authorities of the host countries and the professionals concerned; recommendations formulated should be strictly

proportionate to the gravity of the situations encountered and confined to the geographical areas where the insecurity has arisen; such advisories should be qualified or cancelled as soon as a return to normality permits;

6 The press, and particularly the specialized travel press and the other media, including modern means of electronic communication, should issue honest and balanced information on events and situations that could influence the flow of tourists; they should also provide accurate and reliable information to the consumers of tourism services; the new communication and electronic commerce technologies should also be developed and used for this purpose; as is the case for the media, they should not in any way promote sex tourism;

Article 7

Right to tourism

1 The prospect of direct and personal access to the discovery and enjoyment of the planet's resources constitutes a right equally open to all the world's inhabitants; the increasingly extensive participation in national and international tourism should be regarded as one of the best possible expressions of the sustained growth of free time, and obstacles should not be placed in its way;

2 The universal right to tourism must be regarded as the corollary of the right to rest and leisure, including reasonable limitation of working hours and periodic holidays with pay, guaranteed by Article 24 of the Universal Declaration of Human Rights and Article 7.d of the International Covenant on Economic, Social and Cultural Rights;

3 Social tourism, and in particular associative tourism, which facilitates widespread access to leisure, travel and holidays, should be developed with the support of the public authorities;

4 Family, youth, student and senior tourism and tourism for people with disabilities, should be encouraged and facilitated;

Article 8

Liberty of tourist movements

1 Tourists and visitors should benefit, in compliance with international law and national legislation, from the liberty to move within their countries and from one State to another, in accordance with Article 13 of the Universal Declaration of Human Rights; they should have access to places of transit and stay and to tourism and

cultural sites without being subject to excessive formalities or discrimination;

2 Tourists and visitors should have access to all available forms of communication, internal or external; they should benefit from prompt and easy access to local administrative, legal and health services; they should be free to contact the consular representatives of their countries of origin in compliance with the diplomatic conventions in force;

3 Tourists and visitors should benefit from the same rights as the citizens of the country visited concerning the confidentiality of the personal data and information concerning them, especially when these are stored electronically;

4 Administrative procedures relating to border crossings whether they fall within the competence of States or result from international agreements, such as visas or health and customs formalities, should be adapted, so far as possible, so as to facilitate to the maximum freedom of travel and widespread access to international tourism; agreements between groups of countries to harmonize and simplify these procedures should be encouraged; specific taxes and levies penalizing the tourism industry and undermining its competitiveness should be gradually phased out or corrected;

5 So far as the economic situation of the countries from which they come permits, travellers should have access to allowances of convertible currencies needed for their travels;

Article 9

Rights of the workers and entrepreneurs in the tourism industry

1 The fundamental rights of salaried and self-employed workers in the tourism industry and related activities, should be guaranteed under the supervision of the national and local administrations, both of their States of origin and of the host countries with particular care, given the specific constraints linked in particular to the seasonality of their activity, the global dimension of their industry and the flexibility often required of them by the nature of their work;

2 Salaried and self-employed workers in the tourism industry and related activities have the right and the duty to acquire appropriate initial and continuous training; they should be given adequate social protection: job insecurity should be limited so far as possible; and a specific status, with particular regard to their social welfare, should be offered to seasonal workers in the sector;

3 Any natural or legal person, provided he, she or it has the necessary

abilities and skills, should be entitled to develop a professional activity in the field of tourism under existing national laws; entrepreneurs and investors – especially in the area of small and medium-sized enterprises – should be entitled to free access to the tourism sector with a minimum of legal or administrative restrictions;

4 Exchanges of experience offered to executives and workers, whether salaried or not, from different countries, contributes to foster the development of the world tourism industry; these movements should be facilitated so far as possible in compliance with the applicable national laws and international conventions;

5 As an irreplaceable factor of solidarity in the development and dynamic growth of international exchanges, multinational enterprises of the tourism industry should not exploit the dominant positions they sometimes occupy; they should avoid becoming the vehicles of cultural and social models artificially imposed on the host communities; in exchange for their freedom to invest and trade which should be fully recognized, they should involve themselves in local development, avoiding, by the excessive repatriation of their profits or their induced imports, a reduction of their contribution to the economies in which they are established;

6 Partnership and the establishment of balanced relations between enterprises of generating and receiving countries contribute to the sustainable development of tourism and an equitable distribution of the benefits of its growth;

Article 10

Implementation of the principles of the Global Code of Ethics for Tourism

1 The public and private stakeholders in tourism development should cooperate in the implementation of these principles and monitor their effective application;

2 The stakeholders in tourism development should recognize the role of international institutions, among which the World Tourism Organization ranks first, and non-governmental organizations with competence in the field of tourism promotion and development, the protection of human rights, the environment or health, with due respect for the general principles of international law;

3 The same stakeholders should demonstrate their intention to refer any disputes concerning the application or interpretation of the Global Code of Ethics for Tourism for conciliation to an impartial third body known as the World Committee on Tourism Ethics.

Index

Note: page numbers in **bold** type indicate definitions of key concepts.